T0346520

PRAISE FOR *WARFIGHTER*

"Colonel Jesse L. Johnson was a hero to me when I worked for him as a young airborne lieutenant, and he remains a hero to me and countless others some forty-five years later. His incredible courage on multiple battlefields, his inspirational leadership, his sacrifice over many decades, and his genuine love for soldiers and soldiering make his story a timeless one, as relevant and inspiring today as it was at each juncture along the way—including when I was privileged to serve under him." —**General David Petraeus**, US Army (Ret.); Fmr. Commander, International Security Assistance Force; Fmr. Commander, US Central Command; Fmr. Director of the CIA

"It is imperative that all Americans read Colonel Johnson's story. At a time when fiction, fantasy, and facade too often displace actual accomplishments, courage, and character, we should recognize the authentic heroes among us. I served with Colonel Johnson for more than four decades, in both peace and war, and there is no doubt that he is the real deal. Jesse Johnson's life's journey transcends decades of American conflict, our own national development, and societal transformation. His life is a history lesson in and of itself. I am proud to know Jesse Johnson as a brother in arms and as a friend." —**General Peter J. Schoomaker**, US Army (Ret.); Fmr. Commander in Chief, US Special Operations Command; Fmr. Chief of Staff, US Army

"Colonel Johnson is a warrior's warrior. For over forty years from Vietnam to Iraq, from the 1st Cavalry Division to the Delta Force, Johnson was there standing tall and doing his duty. *Warfighter* recounts his stories from start to finish and is a real page turner. Compelling work." —**Joseph L. Galloway**, coauthor of *We Were Soldiers Once . . . and Young*

"A gut-punch of a memoir. Part thriller bouncing from the jungles of Southeast Asia to the sands of the Persian Gulf, part gripping history of America's wars—overt and covert—since Vietnam, this timeless story of duty, honor, and sacrifice is a testament to the power of the American soldier and a reminder of the debt owed to those who serve at the tip of the spear. In the finest tradition of war memoirs, *Warfighter* depicts with razor-sharp clarity the horrors and heroism of combat through the eyes of those who experienced it." —**David McCloskey**, Former CIA officer and critically acclaimed author of *Damascus Station*

"My late husband, General H. Norman Schwarzkopf, always displayed the utmost respect for Colonel Jesse L. Johnson, as both a fellow Vietnam veteran and as his special operations commander during Operations Desert Shield and Desert Storm. It is no surprise to me that in his own book, *It Doesn't Take Hero*, he referred to Colonel Johnson as 'an unsung hero' of the Gulf War. *Warfighter* superbly depicts the personal and professional bond that developed between them as two veterans dedicated to fighting for their country while protecting the brave young soldiers under their command." —**Brenda Schwarzkopf**

WARFIGHTER

WARFIGHTER

THE STORY OF
AN AMERICAN
FIGHTING MAN

Colonel Jesse L. Johnson
with Alex Holstein

LYONS
PRESS

Guilford, Connecticut

An imprint of Globe Pequot, the trade division of
The Rowman & Littlefield Publishing Group, Inc.
4501 Forbes Boulevard, Suite 200, Lanham, Maryland 20706
www.rowman.com

Distributed by NATIONAL BOOK NETWORK

British Library Cataloguing in Publication Information Available

Library of Congress Cataloging-in-Publication Data

Names: Johnson, Jesse L. (Jesse Loftis), author.
Title: Warfighter : the story of an American fighting man / Colonel Jesse L. Johnson
    with Alex Holstein.
Other titles: Story of an American fighting man
Description: Guilford : Lyons Press, 2022. | Includes index.
Identifiers: LCCN 2021057394 (print) | LCCN 2021057395 (ebook) | ISBN
    9781493065561 (cloth) | ISBN 9781493065578 (ebook)
Subjects: LCSH: United States. Army—Biography. | United States. Army—Non-
    commissioned officers—Biography. | United States. Army. Delta Force—Biography.
    | Iraq War, 2003–2011—Personal narratives, American. | Operation Eagle Claw,
    Iran, 1980. | Vietnam War, 1961–1975—Personal narratives, American.
Classification: LCC E181.J66 J83 2022 (print) | LCC E181.J66 (ebook) | DDC
    355.0092—dc23/eng/20211123
LC record available at https://lccn.loc.gov/2021057394
LC ebook record available at https://lccn.loc.gov/2021057395

♾™ The paper used in this publication meets the minimum requirements of
American National Standard for Information Sciences—Permanence of Paper
for Printed Library Materials, ANSI/NISO Z39.48-1992.

Then I heard the voice of the Lord saying,
"Whom shall I send? And who will go for us?"
And I said, "Here am I. Send me!"

—Isaiah 6:8

CONTENTS

CONTENTS

PART III: THE CALLING

PART IV: INTO THE STORM

ACKNOWLEDGMENTS

We are so grateful for the opportunity to thank the many people without whose support and encouragement this book would have been impossible. Literary agent extraordinaire and dear friend, the indefatigable Tim Hays, who proved a steadfast warfighter in his own right, navigating the harsh terrain of the publishing world to accomplish the all-too-difficult mission of landing us a deal (unscathed). Gene Brissie, Melissa McClellan, and the amazing team at Lyons Press: for giving this book a great home, and for all your marvelous work and fantastic editorial guidance. Our early readers, supporters, and endorsers: General David Petraeus; General Peter Schoomaker; and the late, great Joe Galloway—warriors and heroes one and all. Former CIA officer and critically acclaimed author David McCloskey, for his brilliant literary counsel and unwavering support that proved invaluable throughout the writing process. Mrs. Brenda Schwarzkopf, one of the nicest and smartest people on the planet, who could not have been more generous with her time and fascinating insights about her legendary late husband, General H. Norman Schwarzkopf. The students and staff at UCLA's Journal on World Affairs, and especially Taylor Fairless and Zachary Durkee, for all their early efforts, and for hosting us in a wonderfully instructive Zoom forum on the history of modern warfare with the great Joe Galloway. Former Delta operator and all-around amazing human being Robert Brooks, who was there from the beginning, read every page as it was written, and made sure that the Zoom app always worked right—we could never have done it without you. Former rifle company commander Captain Charlie Hardin took the time to revisit his courageous service and experiences in Vietnam—thank you for all that you did on behalf of our nation and this book. And finally, the heroic Naval Intelligence and FBI Joint Terrorism Task Force veteran Mike Williams, who first proposed the idea of a memoir and then somehow magically managed to gather all the key players together and convince us to make it happen. Thank you, Mike, for being there from the very first "hot wash" at "the safe house," for staying in-it-to-win-it for the long-haul, and for all the great friendship (and outstanding historical notes) along the way.

COLONEL JOHNSON

There should be a special place in heaven for the families of our military personnel. I am forever grateful for the love and support of my three wonderful daughters: Tambra, Felicia and Shannon. The term "military brat" could not be more misleading for the way you so gracefully endured the rigorous hardships of life in the Army—and believe me, you were all as much in it as I was. You are real "troopers," and I am proud beyond words to be your father. To my late brother, Daily Odean Johnson, who still to this day remains my idol. It was his shining example and eternal light that imbued me with the moral strength and character to keep me and those under my command alive through the darkest moments on the battlefield. Still miss him every day. To the late Lieutenant Colonel Tony Herbert, who walked it like he talked it, never wavered in the worst of war, and saved so many lives through his own courageous and inspirational leadership, both on and off the battlefield. To fellow paratrooper and veteran Thomas McWilliams—a great soldier, friend, and hero in his own right—for all the wonderful camaraderie through the decades. I am forever indebted to all those I ever served with—in Vietnam, in Delta Force, in the Gulf War, and beyond—the names in this book, those engraved on that sacred black wall in our nation's capital and so many other memorials a long time coming but never too late, and those who shall remain nameless. Warfighters one and all. I hope my story properly honors you and your service—all that you mean to our country, the American people, and to me—so that your sacrifice will never be forgotten. And I hope our leaders will take heed before they ever again send our young people to shed blood on some faraway battlefield without clear cause or purpose. To my co-author and writer, Alex Holstein: thank you for all your tenacious perseverance, and for rising to the occasion and then some in using your superb literary talent to turn my life-story into "a real page-turner." It's been a fun ride, partner. Excited for all the more to come. And finally, to "My Special Angel," Judith Carol Johnson, the rock who held the line on the homefront and still keeps our family going through both good and bad—I could never have survived without you; stand in awe of your amazing soldierly strength and courage; and love you truly, madly, and deeply as ever.

ALEX HOLSTEIN

I am eternally grateful for the love and support of my two wonderful children, Sophia and Henry, who with each passing day, make me feel ever prouder to be their father. May your inspirational light shine forever. To their magnificent mom and genius scribe, Katharine Holstein, for the "bloodless coup" that proved the opening salvo and lit my literary fuse, all the fabulous input on this and so much else, and a lifetime of loving encouragement—Professor Tripp has finally left the building! To the Chach and Pierre for all the rootin' tootin' highfalutin hijinks. So many friends and family members have encouraged and supported my writing pursuits through the years, it would be impossible to name them all; but I would be remiss not to mention those who have consistently comprised the loudest end of the cheering section: the brilliant writer/actress Tamsen McDonough—never a "killjoy," darling; producer Mike Steinberg; Cousin of the Century Chris Callahan; graphic art guru Alex Van Wey; the great scribe Eli Campbell; filmic impresario Jaren Hayman; author and talk-shop telephone buddy David McCloskey; the secret agent code-named Dynamo; the dashing and debonair Sir Christopher Ljungquist; the stalwart Dr. Paul Alexander; lifelong counterterrorist, military hero, and creative maestro Mike Williams; and uber-mensch of the millennium Max Wasilko. To Nick Holstein, for your forty years of brotherhood and twenty years of service to our country. To my late mother, who passed away knowing that I had finally done it. And to my late father, who always said I one day would. The amazing Judith Johnson, for showing me that "military wives" can be just as brave as their heroic husbands; graciously welcoming me into your home—especially "the safe house"—and for all you and your family have done, far above and beyond the call of duty, in support of this project. And finally, to my dear friend and personal hero, Colonel Jesse Loftis Johnson: may the telling of your tale stand as a tribute to all of our warfighters—past, present, and future—who risk the ultimate sacrifice to keep our nation safe. Thank you, sir, for granting me the tremendous honor of entrusting me with your incredible, inspirational, and courageous life-story. You've pulled a lot of guys out of the jungle—count me one of them. All the way.

PRINCIPAL PARTICIPANTS

THE UNITED STATES ARMED FORCES

General Colin Powell	Chairman, Joint Chiefs of Staff, Gulf War
General H. Norman Schwarzkopf	Commander in Chief, Coalition Forces, Gulf War
General Carl E. Vuono	Chief of Staff, US Army, Gulf War
General Chuck Horner	Commander, Coalition Air Forces, Gulf War
General Buster Glosson	Deputy to General Horner
General Peter Schoomaker	Commanding Officer, Delta Force, Gulf War; later Army Chief of Staff, Iraq War
General David Petraeus	2nd Lt., US Army, Italy; later four-star general, Director of the CIA
General Carl Stiner	C-in-C, SOCOM, Gulf War
General Wayne Downing	Commander, ARSOC, Gulf War
General John Abrams	Office of the Army Chief of Staff, Gulf War
General David C. Jones	Chairman, Joint Chiefs of Staff, Dozier Affair
General Ann Dunwoody	First woman to attain four-star rank
General Creighton Abrams	Father of John Abrams; Commander, US military forces, Vietnam (1968–1972)

General Andrew Goodpaster	Deputy Commander, US military forces, Vietnam (1968–1969), later SACEUR/NATO
General Elvy Roberts	Brigade Commander, 1st Cavalry Division; later Asst. Div. Commander, 9th Infantry, Vietnam
General William Knowlton	Asst. Div. Commander, 9th Infantry, Vietnam; later superintendent West Point; father-in-law of Gen. Petraeus
Admiral John McCain Jr.	C-in-C, Pacific Command, father of POW/future Senator John McCain III
Vice Admiral Thomas Kinnebrew	European Command, Dozier Affair
Colonel Rod Paschall	Commanding Officer, Delta Force, Dozier Affair
Colonel Norm Moffitt	Commander, SOF-Europe, Dozier Affair
Colonel Chuck Vossen	Defense Attaché, Rome, Dozier Affair
Colonel Charles A. Beckwith	Founder/Commanding Officer, Delta Force
Colonel James "Jim" Kyle	Commander, USAF component, Eagle Claw
Colonel Henry "Hank" Emerson	Commander, 1st Brigade, 9th Infantry, Vietnam
Colonel Harold "Hal" Moore	Commander, 3rd Brigade, 7th Cavalry, Vietnam; author, *We Were Soldiers Once . . . and Young*
Colonel Billy J. Miller	Helicopter Pilot, US Army, Grenada/Vietnam
Lt. Col. Richard Cody	Lead pilot, Task Force Normandy, Gulf War; later four-star general
Lt. Col. Jerry Thompson	5th Special Forces Group (SFG), Gulf War
Lt. Col. "Blank" Frank Toney	3rd SFG, Gulf War
Lt. Col. Carl Savory	Delta senior surgeon, Eagle Claw
Lt. Col. Joe Stringham	Commander, 1st Ranger Battalion, Delta exercise
Lt. Col. James Lindsay	9th Infantry, Vietnam; later four-star general

Lt. Col. Don Schroeder	Commander, 2/39, 9th Infantry, Vietnam
Lt. Col. David Hackworth	Commander, "Hardcore" Battalion (Recondo), 9th Infantry, Vietnam; later famous author/journalist
Lt. Col. Anthony Herbert	Renowned hero and witness to war crimes, Vietnam
Lt. Col. Kenneth D. Mertel	Commander, 8th/1st Cavalry Div., Vietnam
Major Logan Fitch	Commander, B Squadron, Delta Force, Eagle Claw
Major Lewis "Bucky" Burruss	Operator, A Squadron, Delta Force, Eagle Claw
Major John Carney	USAF Combat Controller, Eagle Claw
Major Earl Witcher	Pocahontas hometown hero; three-war veteran
Lt. Commander Michael Williams	Navy intel officer, Gulf War
Captain Wade "Ish" Ishimoto	Delta intel officer, Eagle Claw
Captain Jim Tate	Company Commander, Airbone School
Captain Roy Martin	Commander, Company B, 1/8, 1st Cavalry Div., Vietnam
Captain Stone	Intel officer, 8th Cav, Vietnam
Captain Wilkie	Artillery Fire Control Officer, 8th Cav, Vietnam
1st Lt. Ronald McLean	USMC, Da Nang; stepson of actor Jimmy Stewart
First Sergeant Virgil "Top" Greene	Charlie Co. 2/39, 9th Infantry, US Army, Vietnam
Rubio	Ranger, US Army, Eagle Claw
Widehat	Sergeant, US Army, Vietnam
Cowen	Sergeant, US Army, Vietnam
Derheim	Sergeant, US Army, Vietnam
Williams	Sergeant, US Army, Vietnam
Bey	Sergeant, US Army, Vietnam
Clemmons	Sergeant, US Army, Vietnam
Dolby	Specialist, US Army, Vietnam, recipient Medal of Honor
Romero	Specialist, US Army, Vietnam

Bowman	Private, US Army, Vietnam
Stirpe	Private, US Army, Vietnam
Chavez	Private, US Army, Vietnam
John Steele	Private, US Army, WWII (Mission Boston)

THE UNITED STATES GOVERNMENT

Jimmy Carter	President (1977–1981)
George H.W. Bush	Vice President (1981–1988), President (1989–1993)
Dick Cheney	Secretary of Defense (1989–1993)
Alexander Haig	Secretary of State (1981–1982)
Admiral Stansfield Turner	Director of Central Intelligence (1977–1981)
Sam Nunn	Senator, Armed Services Committee, Gulf War
Lt. Gen. James M. Gavin	US Ambassador, France (1961–1962), fmr. CG, 82nd AB
Maxwell Raab	US Ambassador, Rome (1981–1989)
Peter Bridges	Deputy Chief of Mission, Rome (1981–1984)
Edward "Skip" Gnehm	US Ambassador, Kuwait, Gulf War
"Barry"	CIA chief of station, Saudi Arabia, Gulf War
Major Richard "Dick" Meadows	CIA ground team lead, Tehran, Eagle Claw
"Harold"	CIA Officer, Eagle Claw
"Al"	Iranian CIA asset, Eagle Claw

THE VIPS

Ross Perot	Texas billionaire, military booster
Johnny Bench	Hall of Fame baseball player
Bob Hope	Hollywood star, USO performer
Ann-Margret	Hollywood star, USO performer

Jimmy Stewart — Hollywood star and Brigadier General USAF

Gloria McLean Stewart — Wife of Jimmy Stewart, mother of Lt. Ronald McLean

THE BRITISH

General Sir Michael "Mike" Rose — Commanding Officer, 22nd SAS Regiment (1979–1982)

Colonel Andrew Massey — Operational Commander, UK Special Forces, Gulf War

Sergeant First Class Stu O'Neill — SAA observer, Eagle Claw

THE SAUDIS

King Fahd bin Abdulaziz al-Saud — King of Saudi Arabia, Gulf War

Captain Prince Fahd bin Turki al-Saud — Liaison, Saudi special ops, Gulf War; later lieutenant-general, old friend

THE KUWAITIS

Sheik Jaber al-Ahmad al-Sabah — Emir of Kuwait

Sheik Saad al-Sabah — Crown Prince

General Jaber al-Sabah — Chief, Kuwaiti security service; old friend

Sheik Nawaf al-Sabah — Foreign Minister

Sheik Salem al-Sabah — Interior Minister

Sheik Fahd al-Ahmed — Resistance fighter, expert marksman

FAMILY & FRIENDS

Daily Johnson — My father

Lorene Hattie Petitt Johnson — My mother

Daily Odean "Daily O" Johnson — My big bro

Loyce Johnson — My sister

Mona Johnson — My sister

Betty Johnson	My sister
Judith Johnson	My wife
Tambra, Felicia, Shannon	Our daughters
"Aunt" Ann Pitman	Former Civil War–era slave, family friend
Greeny Pitman	Her son, family friend
"Uncle" Bill White	Former Civil War–era slave, family friend
"Aunt" Josie White	His wife, former Civil War–era slave, family friend

OTHERS

Hosni Mubarak	President of Egypt (1981–2011)
Ehud Barak	Israeli commando; later prime minister
Colonel Ulrich Wegener	Founder/commander, German GSG-9

PROLOGUE

My Enemy

October 15, 1968
Brigade S-3 Air
1st Brigade, 9th Infantry Division
En Route to Fire Base Moore
Somewhere over the Mekong Delta
Republic of Vietnam
11:54 a.m.

I held the man's bloodless gaze.

Dull fade in his eyes—I knew he was finished.

Still breathing.

Not for long.

I could tell by the way his chin spasmed. Off each gasp of air. As though to the broken rhythm of his heartbeat. Something about that bothered me. I don't know why. I'd seen plenty of people go that way. My own men. This one was different.

Dusting off the pickup zone, our chopper shaved the treetops, AK rounds plinking the fuselage—parting shots from his comrades nestled deep in the sprawling jungle below. And there the dying man was, on the cabin floor, laid out at my tired feet; this captain of the NVA, the North Vietnamese Army; his left side shot up pretty bad. Blood coated his skin like dark honey. It was pouring out of him now. I held his gaze fast.

Colonel Geraci, my commanding officer (CO), was on the battalion net, calling ahead to make sure there'd be a medic on the pad ahead of our arrival. Not that it would do any good. I thought about how I had been making it through this war, waking up every morning and telling myself that if I could just make it till noon, I'd be good for the rest of the day. I'd make it home.

This guy wasn't gonna make it home.

In a moment, all sound drowned out to a distant echo, and an eerie quiet fell over the cabin, and I realized we were flying with the troop doors slid shut. Normally, we flew wide open both sides, all this brutal wind kicking up, door-gunners ripping bursts off their M-60s or miniguns; the thud of rotor blades, people shouting, radio static—the wild cacophony of warfare. Maybe it was just me, ears tuning out all that background noise; but somehow the silence seemed to crash over me like thunder.

The dying man never made a sound. Never so much as grunted. Never let his eyes leave my own. Face soaked in pain. I wondered what kind of pain it was, what his mind was holding onto just then. Regret. People. Those he'd be missing, worrying about in his last minutes of life. Wife. Children. The war he'd given them all up for.

Slow and shaky-like, his arm rose toward me. Bloodied fingertips brushed against my wrist, trembling in their thirst for human contact. I hesitated. Then his hand took harbor in my own—and I tightened my grip around it, holding it there. In that moment, I was not giving comfort to the enemy; he was no longer the enemy, and I was no longer his. The war between us was over for all time.

I was deep into my second tour in Vietnam—and I had received several of our nation's highest decorations for taking the fight to the enemy and killing them. God knows how many of that man's brethren I had slain. I had shot them, called down artillery and air strikes on their positions, obliterated them right off the face of the earth. For that last silent moment, I held this dying man's hand because he was a fellow soldier, fighting for his country, and now laying down his life for it. I held his hand until his last breath left him; and then I let him go gently—and placed his arm back across his body and slid my palm over his eyes and closed them.

I looked at my watch.

It was five past twelve.

I

AIRMOBILE

1

GUNG-HO NCO

September 21, 1965
1st Bn (Airborne), 8th Cavalry
1st Cavalry Division (Airmobile)
Camp Radcliff—II Corps
An Khe
Central Highlands
Republic of Vietnam

The first time I got shot at was at An Khe.

That was my first night in Vietnam.

First night of my first tour.

First time in combat—if you could call it that: *combat*.

This was more like a taste test. Baby steps. First time and all. The heavy contact was just around the corner.

Kind of a weird relief, though: getting shot at.

We'd been expecting it from the moment we hit the beach down at Qui Nhon, finally put our boots on the ground in Vietnam—that tornado of bullets. By then, the enemy had gone through periods of killing almost a full battalion of South Vietnamese per week. In a war of attrition, they were already way ahead. Just one of the big things that set this war apart from all those before it. This wasn't even your standard North vs. South type of deal—like Korea, or our own Civil War. The South Vietnamese weren't holding any line because there was no line to hold. We would be fighting an enemy that was already dug in all around us, a shadow occupation force that had us completely encircled from within and without—the so-called National Liberation Front, better known as the Viet Cong. "Charlie," we called him—or *her*. (Plenty of women in their ranks.) For the uninitiated, "Charlie" came from the initialism V-C, which in the NATO phonetic alphabet was Victor-Charlie. Or just plain ol' Charlie. Their pals in the NVA, we called "regulars," seeing as they were the "regular" North Vietnamese Army—but most of the time we referred to them as Charlie, too. Charlie-North and Charlie-South. Charlie all around. Even if we couldn't see him—or her.

What we had walked into was the Southeast Asian version of the Alamo. We were surrounded. Hadn't even hit the battlefield and already getting shot at. This was the real deal. So if there was one thing that became crystal clear to us at that baptism of machine-gun fire raining down from all those shadows on the mountain above us, it was that Charlie, North and South, meant business. This was war. Still, you could say—laying down fire on us that first night, right down onto our brand-new base—they were doing us a favor. Keeping us sharp, riding that razor's edge. And if there was one thing they would soon discover about us, it was this: we meant business, too.

The cavalry had arrived.

In that moment, I was ready—or about as ready as any man could be, anyway. Fear was just another mortal enemy I had learned to conquer. Jumping out of airplanes kinda teaches you how to do that—real fast. I was a gung-ho NCO, eager to kick ass for my country. I was a "Jumping Mustang," a paratrooper in the legendary 1st Cavalry Division, spearheading a whole new type of warfare—*airmobile*: riding helicopters instead of horses into battle to attack the enemy at a time and place of our choosing. But it wasn't the choppers themselves that would bring fear to our friends from the North. That's something a lot of historians and Hollywood movies get wrong. (And, boy, have they gotten a lot wrong about Vietnam.) It was what those choppers were delivering to the battlefield—*us*. American soldiers. The best-led, best-trained, best-equipped fighting force in the history of warfare.

H-HOUR: ONE ORANGE SODA AND A HUNDRED PUSH-UPS

Most Americans had spent the last couple of months going to barbecues and ball games, doing all that good, kick-back summer stuff. We'd spent them training under the hot southern sun at Fort Benning, Georgia, getting all amped up and wired tight for this moment—the first deployment of a full sixteen-thousand-strong division of the United States Army to Vietnam. We had trained hard.

Day in, day out, round-the-clock. Rifle drills on the range to make us one with our brand-new M-16s. Full-blast physical training and Iron Man–style runs to get us in shape for the harsh terrain and diabolical swelter of the jungle. Live-fire artillery exercises. Escape and evasion. Land navigation, maneuver warfare, tactical engagement—you name it.

And we jumped—which was more fun than anything else. At least it was for the diehard airborne NCOs like myself who'd been brought in from the 82nd and 101st to train and qualify-up as many of the "straight-leg" non-jumpers as we could.

Last thirty days we'd spent at sea—from the Savannah River to the Atlantic Ocean, through the Panama Canal and straight across the Pacific—four thousand of America's toughest soldiers packed like sardines aboard the *USNS Geiger.* This was no pleasure cruise. We PT'ed every day—most days, twice a day. No room to run, so we made up for it with intense calisthenics: hundreds of push-ups, sit-ups, jumping jacks. We shot a lot, too—zeroed our rifles off the fantail.

On the dawn of our arrival, we geared up and climbed down rope ladders over the side of the ship, packing ourselves onto our landing craft, World War II–era LSTs. It felt like our very own D-Day. Some of the older vets who'd been there—NCOs and officers—remarked on that, the creeping sense of déjà vu. We had a lot of those guys with us. A lot of World War II guys, a lot of Korean War guys, even guys who'd gone into Lebanon back in '58 when we intervened to delay a civil war with which I would become personally familiar many years later. Our brigade commander, Colonel Elvy Roberts, a future three-star general, had jumped into Normandy and Holland with the 101st Airborne, "the Screaming Eagles," and fought at Bastogne. Seeing the ease of motion in those men, their cool professionalism, after already experiencing the worst of war—and now coming back for more—helped flat-line the nerves of some of us first-timers.

Steaming away from our mother ship, I reminded myself that I had learned from the best: the very men who'd liberated Europe, kicked the North Koreans and Chicoms back across the 38th Parallel. I'd served with them in two of the most legendary airborne divisions in the world—the 82nd and the 101st. Spent three years in Germany carrying out exercises alongside the 10th Special Forces Group in preparation for a Soviet invasion. Now, I wanted to serve my country on the battlefield. I remembered the radio broadcasts and old newsreels of my childhood, the Allied landings: *these* guys—locked, loaded, and ready to take on the world. I thought of my father-in-law, Thomas Clayton Story, who'd landed in the sixth wave at Omaha Beach—where the only cover from the hailstorm of machine-gun fire were the heaps of dead American soldiers. Even in death, they shielded their own, soaking the sand and the sea red with their blood. My father-in-law told himself that if he could just make it till noon, he'd make it the rest of the day. And before I deployed, that's what he told me, sitting at his kitchen table:

Just make it till noon, Jess, and you'll be OK. . . .

Now, as we bobbed and chugged through the whispering surf, I killed any urge to check my watch. We were deep into H-Hour, but it was still early morning. No idea what kind of welcome awaited us. Our arrival had neither the prior secrecy nor subsequent fanfare of the D-Day landings. There would be no surprise radio broadcasts to *"interrupt this program with a special bulletin. . . ."* In announcing our imminent arrival, President Johnson might as well have taken out a full-page ad in the *New York Times*. America already had plenty of boots on the ground: the Special Forces at various forward-deployed fire bases, "advising" the South Vietnamese; the Marines at Da Nang Air Base, there to protect US aircraft from guerrilla attack, a security mission that rapidly expanded into preemptive search-and-destroy ops beyond their perimeter; and the "Sky Soldiers" of the 173rd Airborne out of Okinawa, who would suffer some of the heaviest casualties of the war. We knew our enemies were ready and waiting to greet us, though the time and place of that reception were still unknown. They were everywhere. Invisible, but right smack dab in front of us, lying in wait beyond the faded ribbons of mist shifting over the emerald waters and typhoon-sculpted coastline and lush rolling hills of Qui Nhon.

Unable to see beyond the front-loading ramp of the landing craft as it cut through the water, I listened for the sounds of the beach. This was it: the final leg of our journey, to a destination that had drawn us a whole world away from the lives and loved ones that we might never encounter again—at least not in this life. Loaded down like a pack mule, armed to the teeth with my weapons and ammunition, wearing my steel pot helmet and combat boots and fatigues, I wondered if we were about to receive the same "warm welcome" that my father-in-law got at Normandy: burp gun bunkers and mortar fire. His landing craft hadn't even made it to shore—and he and the others had to bail out over the sides and swim through a boiling hellfire the rest of the way. Many drowned under the weight of their own gear, metal rain pelting them to death.

Our craft did make it, without any bullets plinking the hull; as the ramp came down, I prepared myself for instant and deliberate violence. Tightening my grip on my M-16, I chewed at the unlit stub of the cigar in my mouth and tightened my gaze, scanning for the enemy. And I realized there were no machine guns or mortars or bunkers or cyclones of lead awaiting us. As we spilled out of the craft, no red carpet of blood or blanket of bodies met our feet. The closest thing to an army we encountered was a battalion of little kids that amounted to nothing more than an aggressive sales force. Coming at us, all of them holding out make-shift hawker trays twice their size, pushing product like the stadium vendors at a ball game—orange soda. "Fanta, Fanta! Cheap, cheap!"

Then my ears caught a transistor radio playing somewhere, all tinny and full of static, Radio Saigon. And I could have sworn I heard the faint echoes of Bobby Helms singing "My Special Angel." Right then, I thought of my sweet Judith—that was our song. Maybe I was just imagining it, my mind playing tricks on me. (Or playing tricks on me now, all these years later, as I try to remember.) But I was only thinking of her: Judith, my high school sweetheart. The one true love of my life. Back home in Arkansas, chasing after our four-year-old daughter, Tammy, while pregnant with our next; bright-eyed and full of faith, she'd kissed me goodbye, as I went off to war. I held that memory now like treasure, and never felt so far away from home.

The fact was I wanted Vietnam. I had requested it. I was still with the "Screaming Eagles" of the 101st when a staff sergeant buddy of mine found out that the 1st Cavalry Division was looking to load up on NCOs for its newly formed Airborne Brigade. We went to our lieutenant colonel, who'd already been to Vietnam as an adviser and married a Vietnamese woman. He got on the horn to Division: "I got these two young guys here who are just dying to go to combat." (Now there's an interesting turn of phrase.) "So I'm gonna give you their names, and you just get 'em out there."

To give my best in battle was not just a job—it was my duty. To protect my country, my family—my wife, my daughter, my unborn child. My brother-soldiers. More than anyone, Judith knew that going in. She'd be the first to tell you as much, too. My country needed me—that's all there was to it. I didn't care about politics; the biggest political lesson this war would teach me was just how *apolitical* Mr. Kalashnikov's infamous AK-47 assault rifle was on the battlefield. It couldn't have cared less who it was killing. Or who used it to do that killing. War only discriminated between the living and the dead.

"Sergeant Johnson! Drop and gimme a hundred!"

Aw, shit.

The distinctive bark belonged to our battalion commander, Lieutenant Colonel Mertel, who'd done two tours in Korea commanding a rifle company. As we all sat waiting on that beach under the dragon-tongued Far Eastern sun, I'd made the terrible mistake of taking off my helmet and replacing it with my Ranger patrol cap to shade my eyes—and I guess Mertel, now an aviator guy, saw this as the perfect opportunity to lay down the law on a battalion of badass paratroopers who might otherwise take it upon themselves to do the same. In case Charlie decided to shell us, after all. Personally, I didn't think the helmets would do us much good anyway—or our flak jackets for that matter. I knew a lieutenant who caught a bullet that went straight through his helmet, missing his head completely—barely tousled his hair. But who cared what I thought?

I dropped onto the sand.

In the end, my big beach landing came down to two things: one orange soda and a hundred push-ups.

Not exactly *The Longest Day*.

I hit the beach and knocked out my PT, but not fast enough to beat the thud of the choppers flying in from one of our carriers. CH-54 Tarhes. Heavy-lift choppers. Big insectile suckers. Our ride up-country for the long year ahead. Looked like a cross between a potter wasp and a tower crane—that could swallow a Huey whole. The Huey would be our main saddle into battle—what we called "slicks"—but with four thousand of us coming in off the *Geiger* that day, we needed something a little more substantial to move us out. Actually, we wouldn't even be flying on the choppers themselves, but in these giant transport pods attached to their bellies. Yet another first in a day full of them.

As we mounted up and moved out, I took one last long look around at that beach: those little kids hawking sodas, the chaste Vietnamese out for a morning stroll in their loose baggy pants, long-sleeved shirts, and conical straw hats; the white sand and the lush green vegetation; this gorgeous slice of paradise perched on the edge of hell.

Filing onto the chopper pod, equipment weighing us all down, we waddled like penguins. Somehow, I still felt kind of naked: this being one of the few times I'd be flying without a chute strapped to my back. Everyone loaded up and locked down tight, the big heavy-lift helicopter rose slowly into the sky, its thunderous whine and seismic clatter obliterating all other noise and whipping up a sandstorm off the beach that sent those little kids with their hawker trays scurrying for cover. I squeezed my eyes shut and clenched my jaw, trying to get my war-face back on; instead, my thoughts trailed into the past.

REMEMBRANCE

Very first time I ever flew in an airplane, I jumped out of it.

That was at Bragg. At Jump School. On my first tour with the 82nd. First tour in the Army, too. I flew eight times total before ever landing—and that was only because bad weather scrubbed our jump. It wasn't till I joined the Army that I ever set foot on an airplane. Air travel wasn't so common back then—unless you were rich.

I grew up poor. Dirt-poor.

I was hardly the first soldier to ever say that—sure as hell won't be the last. That's something I would come to realize in Vietnam—more than anyone else, it was the poor who defended our nation. The wealthy could afford opinions; it was the poor who held the line.

I volunteered for the military. Not that it made any difference. For all the attention given to the antiwar side of Vietnam—burning draft cards and all that—the conscripts who fought with and under me had as much courage and love of country as anyone else. Most of 'em, anyway. They came from places like Mountain View, Missouri; Blackfoot, Idaho; Winslow, Arizona; Woodlynne, New Jersey; the Bronx, New York. They came from trailer parks and ghettos, the rust belt and the rez. I came from Pocahontas, Arkansas, a small rural town of about five thousand in the foothills of the Ozark Mountains. It was the kind of place that had an icehouse and a cotton gin and a weekly farm auction, and where the postman knew the houses by knowing the families that lived in them, because there were no addresses. The kind of place where the members of the local Veterans of Foreign Wars (VFW) had special uniforms to perform honor guard and rifle party duties at military funerals. And where there was a monument to just about every American war of the last 150 years—and plenty of hometown heroes who fought in them.

Ever since I was a little boy during World War II, sitting at my father's side by the radio every night, listening to Gabriel Heatter bring us *"today's good news"* (good news even when it was bad news) from Europe and the Pacific, I'd aspired to live up to that heroic history, serve my country, and even, if necessary, make the ultimate sacrifice. We didn't have electricity, so our radio ran on one of those big old dry cell "B" batteries that would go dead about every few months or so, and took just as long to replace. Otherwise, if we wanted to hear what was going on in the world, it meant walking two miles to our neighbors' house. I remember being over there with my whole family—mother, father, my three older sisters, and big brother—when President Truman announced the defeat of Nazi Germany, and then later the Japanese surrender. I'll never forget all the hootin' and hollerin', the calls of "Praise the Lord" and the pats on the back, and the hugs and laughter and tears of joy. My father clapped his big, sturdy workingman's hands together and cracked open a beer to celebrate. The end of the war meant loved ones coming home. I had sixteen cousins who served, and they all made it through. Only one got wounded, serving in Patton's tank corps; but a lot of those guys got hit. Hence Patton's nickname: "Old Blood and Guts"—their blood, his guts. Or so the legend goes.

Growing up, I read a lot about all those famous heroes—Patton, Bradley, MacArthur, Eisenhower. I devoured every book I could find about the war and the people that won it. Men like General James M. Gavin, the legendary "Jumping Jim," who wrote the playbook on parachute infantry tactics, and led "Mission Boston"—the 82nd Airborne's jump behind enemy lines five hours before the landings at Normandy to take the critical town of Sainte-Mère-Église.

Reading those tales of courage by the light of a coal oil lamp, never in a million years—or even when I myself first served with the 82nd—would I have ever dreamed of meeting the man himself. But that's exactly what happened in 1962, when my commanding officer, Captain Tony Herbert—himself a maverick war hero who first gained notoriety serving in Korea—selected me to travel to Normandy to carry the colors at the celebration marking the seventeenth anniversary of D-Day. By then ambassador to France, General Gavin was the keynote speaker. A lot of the guys in my outfit at that time, the 505th, had jumped into Normandy under his command; and as we drove around, a few of them would point out where they'd landed—or should I say, where they guessed they'd landed, having jumped at night under heavy fire. Some of 'em would rib each other: *Oh yeah, right, you remember the exact spot where you came down. Sure.* The only guy who knew exactly where he came down that night was John Steele, the paratrooper who got caught up hanging by his chute from the church spire in the town's main square—as so famously portrayed by Red Buttons in the movie *The Longest Day.* As we paraded into the main ceremony, what an incredible honor it was for me, on that solemn occasion, to hoist Old Glory proudly before us and then, during a service at that very same church in Sainte-Mère-Église, sit with Ambassador Gavin and the real John Steele—my own silver jump wings upon my chest. And on that first scrap of land that these two men had liberated all those years ago. The history of the moment hit me like a flash of heat lightning, shining through the veil between past and present—but it was action, not remembrance, that I always craved most.

One time when I was about ten, I heard the grown-ups talking about parachute jumps, so I got it into my head to try one. My aunt lived in a house built against the side of a hill that ran pretty high, maybe ten feet—though it seemed a lot higher to a little boy. Out on the back-porch, I spotted a bunch of umbrellas; took one and opened it up. Then I went to the edge of the porch, leaped off—and made the very important discovery that an umbrella is not a parachute. The Army would have never counted that as a jump, but I still count it as my first "malfunction."

By the time I was a teenager, I knew that I was destined to join the United States Army and become a paratrooper. More than anything, I wanted to jump into the cold black sky in the dead of night and land behind enemy lines and kill bad guys.

Still, the greatest hero of my life—then and now—had no war stories to speak of because he was never once in combat. My big brother, Daily Odean. "Daily O," we called him. I can still see him striding through the front door, his first time back home as a newly minted lieutenant in the 11th Airborne Division. Might as well have been yesterday. Sharp as a blade in his brand-new uniform, with all those neatly sewn patches and shiny pins, silver wings fixed to his chest, and with the way he bloused his pants over those glass-shined jump-boots, a tradition that began in World War II—"devils in baggy pants," the Germans called them. Pretty tough. You could have ripped him right out of a recruitment poster. With his easy movie-star grin, Daily O could have been a matinee idol—and he inspired the best in everyone around him. Just knowing he was there made me feel secure (even the few times he'd knocked my ass in the dirt).

Fact was, I idolized Daily O. A natural-born leader, he walked it like he talked it—and led from the front, and always by example. Wearing that uniform was one way. Hitting the books was another. My father blessed us with his work ethic, but Daily O owned the soapbox on academics, always preaching the virtues of a higher education. He often hitchhiked to and from high school or stayed at my aunt's house, which was much closer to town, so he'd have more time to study. After two years at Southern Baptist College, he left to join the military; though he was always adamant that he would one day go back to school to finish his degree. Color-blindness kept him out of the Air Force; so he went into the Army instead, passing through Officer Candidate School (OCS), then earning his wings at Jump School. From there, he landed at the 11th at Fort Campbell, Kentucky, where he became a platoon leader in Company F of the 511th Airborne Infantry. Fort Campbell was only a couple of hundred miles from our home, so a pretty easy drive. By then, Daily O had a secondhand 1947 Plymouth Special Deluxe convertible, and would come home on weekends. One time he was going back for a few days before taking leave and he asked me to tag along. Dream come true, he didn't have to ask twice. And to top it off, I got to ride shotgun.

When we stopped at a diner along the way, I saw how people reacted to my big brother's uniform, the way complete strangers came over to our booth to shake his hand and wish him well, his coffee cup never more than a few sips empty. The war in Korea was raging; everyone glued to the bulletins on the radio, wondering if President Truman might unleash MacArthur across the

38th Parallel or drop the "Big One" on the Chinese like we did Japan. One guy spotted Daily O's airborne patch and jump wings and gave him a big ol' pat on the back, then turned to me and said: "You're too short to be a paratrooper."

Boy, did I want to kick that guy's ass—but I just nodded and smiled.

We spent the rest of the drive listening to the radio. Not the war news, but Red Foley on the country music station, singing from the Grand Ole Opry.

As we arrived at Fort Campbell, I was blown away. The sounds of men singing military cadences as they ran in formation, the crack of rifle fire in the air, the MPs at the gate saluting my brother as they waved us onto base, all left me stunned. Meeting the soldiers of Daily O's platoon, some of the best in the United States Army, I was star struck. Some of those men were fresh from the heaviest fighting in Korea. I'd spent a big chunk of my life playing imaginary soldier; now I was hanging out with the real deal. They showed me their chutes, how to gear up for a jump—the works. It was as if the pages of all those books I'd been reading the past few years had fluttered into life and invited me to step inside.

I even got to watch TV for the first time—and in the officers' day room, no less. The place was all decked out in battle flags and campaign streamers, a giant unit patch painted on the wall. It was a thrill to watch the one channel available—even when it showed just a test pattern. But the greatest thrill of all was witnessing the camaraderie among the men of that crack airborne outfit. I was envious of Daily O—but proud, too. Men who had seen the worst of combat accepted him as one of their own, even though he had not yet fired a single shot in battle. Knowing what I know now, the soldier that I am and have been, and having seen the respect he commanded—not just from his fellow officers, but the NCOs and the sergeants whose gung-ho grit could mean all the difference under enemy fire—Daily O had the stuff of a four-star general. No doubt about it, he would have been one of this nation's greatest warriors.

A hero. Plain and simple.

But it didn't turn out that way.

THE TIES THAT BIND

As a boy growing up in the rural south, I did all the things you might expect: hunting, fishing, working the cotton fields and doing manual labor. In a one-room schoolhouse that doubled as our church, I learned to read and write and do arithmetic. My first and only swimming lesson came when my brother threw me into the deepest part of a mountain creek. The sink-or-swim technique. Most of my friends learned the same way, and not one of us drowned. I taught myself to drive. I just jumped behind the wheel of my daddy's truck and drove off. I was eight years old. Same age that I got my first horse. And my first shotgun. The horse, I broke on my own—though I got thrown off enough. By the time I reported for duty at the 1st Cavalry, I'd be more than a little glad that they'd traded up their horses for helicopters. The shotgun was for hunting rabbit and any other critters I might come across. I spent a lot of time alone in the woods, learning how to track and shoot and survive—skills that would come in handy down the road. Probably saved my life.

My family lived on a small cotton farm that was pretty much like any other in this neck of the woods: set about three miles deep off a two-lane track of dirt that turned to mud in the winter time—until they decided to lay down some gravel so they could call it a highway. Our house had a kitchen, two bedrooms, a living room, and a tin roof that sounded like a snare drum under the rain. There was an outhouse, a smoke shed, and a storm cellar for tornadoes. We kept a couple of cows, a few chickens, and always had a big fat hog or two running around. Short of the sky falling down, we could get by just fine, and even then we'd probably be all right.

My family's roots in Arkansas stretched back to before the Civil War, which was pretty much the gold standard for ancestral legacies in that part of the world. My father owned the local sawmill, and he was a good, strong family man who believed in the value of hard work and love of country. For a while, he tried raising cotton using horses and mules to work his plow because we didn't own a tractor; but then the boll weevils came and wiped out our crop, so that ended that. The sawmill produced railroad ties and lumber, which were in high demand back then, the country being on a boom of construction in the wake of depression and war.

My mother was a deeply religious woman dedicated to her Baptist faith and a love of God and each other that she instilled in each one of us. I used to go with her to pick blackberries and other wild fruit like pawpaws and persimmons and hickory nuts. Of her five children, I was the youngest, my sister Loyce being the eldest, and between us Daily O and my two other sisters, Mona and Betty. As the little guy of the lot, I had the unenviable chore of collecting wood for the King heater stove in the living room that was our only source of heat. It was a tough gig; especially on Saturdays, when we needed extra kindling to warm the water in the washtub that we pulled into the kitchen for our weekly baths. All that gathering and chopping, and the constant heavy lifting I did at the sawmill, definitely honed my endurance for hard labor and harsh terrain. My mother was also a fine cook, especially for baking pies and cakes. Sometimes on special occasions, my father would slaughter a hog and cut up the hams and shoulders and other parts, salting all the meat before hanging it in the smokehouse. We would use just about every part of that hog, including the brains. Some of the older country folk would even eat the testicles, but my father drew the line there. "We ain't that hard up for food," he liked to say.

(I guess there was a pun intended in there somewhere that I'm only catching now in retrospect.)

My father was a generous man who liked to bring people home for dinner. Anyone, really. Friends, neighbors, the guys who worked for him at the sawmill, even hitchhikers. Didn't matter the color of their skin either—they sat at the table with the rest of us. Back then, the South was going through an ugly upheaval—Jim Crow and the century-old festering wounds of Reconstruction. People in our town kind of just went with the flow of things. I'm not saying Pocahontas was some kind of oasis of tolerance in a sea of prejudice; Pocahontas wasn't Mayberry, USA, and our local sheriff wasn't Andy Griffith. There was no Mayberry, except for on the TV, and we didn't have one of those. What I mean is, for the most part, folks around there didn't carry hatred in their hearts. I never saw any signs that said: WHITES ONLY—at least, not where I lived. We never had shootings, lynchings, murders, the way you did in Alabama and Mississippi. But we did have racial prejudice—*absolutely*. Our schools were segregated—that's the sad truth. And it would remain a source of deep shame for me, especially when I first served in the Army and the Little Rock Nine were making national news—those nine black kids who simply wanted to go to the same high school as all the white kids. Some of the guys would ask me: "Where you from again, Jesse? Arkansas, right?" and I'd just kind of nod. And if it was a black soldier, already knowing the answer when he asked the question anyway, he might smile and say something like: "Oh yeah, that's right—the Badlands. . . ."

Badlands, huh?

Try Vietnam.

Plenty of black soldiers would die there, too. None of it sits well. On the battlefield, I never saw color—only honor. And if there was one saving grace to lift my patriotic spirits on this matter, it was serving in the legendary "Bastogne Bulldogs" of the 101st Airborne's 327th Infantry Regiment—the same unit that Ike had sent down to Little Rock to escort those kids to class. In fact, I would also serve in the same battalion—the just as legendary 1/506th—that JFK later sent to protect James Meredith when he became the first and only black student at Ole Miss. Some people questioned the use of federal troops on domestic soil, thought it was overkill—why all the muscle? Let me tell you why: by backing all those brave kids with the same "Band of Brothers" that had jumped into Normandy and held out against the Waffen SS at the Battle of the Bulge, both

Ike and Kennedy were sending a message: Our nation will not tolerate intoler-
ance, and we will protect those who can't protect themselves. For me, that's a
fundamental component of the all-enduring American warrior creed, and the
truest reflection of what our country represents—ensuring freedom in the face of
tyranny, even on our own soil. Both the 82nd and the 101st, and so many other
units and branches of our armed forces, have delivered that message loud and
clear to oppressed and oppressor alike the world over.

Soon, I would be delivering that same message under the thick jungle canopy
of the Suoi Ca Valley and the flat mud-caked paddies of the Mekong Delta. But
I had no idea just how garbled it would become in the static-filtered chaos of
Vietnam.

For better or for worse, my backwoods childhood represented a much sim-
pler time.

In our town, we were all equal—and equally poor. My father employed as
many blacks as whites and paid everyone the same wage for the same work,
which wasn't much; but it was honest and fair. Down the road apiece from us
lived the Whites, "Uncle Bill" and "Aunt Josie"—who were actually a black
couple. They could remember being sold a time or two as slave children and
vividly recalled the day the South surrendered. Over feasts of cola-glazed ham
and buttermilk fried chicken and collard greens and hushpuppies, how the
Whites relished recounting to us and several of our neighbors the moment of
their emancipation. Greeny Pitman, who had a natural gift for repairing pitcher
pumps, was also a regular at our dinner table. He was the son of Ann Pitman.
"Aunt Ann," as everyone called her, was somewhat of a local celebrity. Over a
century in age, she was already a teenager by the time Abraham Lincoln took the
oath of office and an adult when that same president issued the Emancipation
Proclamation, which called for her freedom. When my wife, Judith, was a little
girl, she and some of the other children would sit at Aunt Ann's feet, warming
themselves by the King heater stove, and listen to her tales of sitting up on a
balcony watching for advancing Yankee soldiers so she could warn her own-
ers—the Pitmans, whose name she'd taken as her own, because like every child
of slavery, she'd been born without one. Imagine that: coming into the world
with no family name of your own—a child of slavery. Bought and sold. There we
were, smack-dab on the cusp of the big-three auto boom and the golden age of
television—though we didn't even own a TV—and the ghosts of the Civil War
were still very much alive and well and wandering among us.

I met Judith in a cotton field. We were maybe five or six years old.

Our fathers needed our fast little hands, though I think we got up to more mischief than cotton picking. One time, I convinced Judith and a friend of mine, J.D., to sneak off to this old nearby church that was kind of spooky. After I dared them to go in first, I locked them inside—just for a bit, but it scared them half to death. Then we went to J.D.'s house, and it was my turn: as we were all horsing around upstairs, I ran into a room and fell straight through the floor, landing on my butt in the middle of the kitchen. I wasn't hurt, but it sure frightened the hell out of me. Judith came down to check that I was OK. As we walked home along the dirt road at the edge of the cotton field under a salmon-pink sunset, I begged her not to tell anyone about my fall. "OK, Loftis"—the middle name everyone called me back then. "OK, Loftis," she said. "I won't tell anyone."

And she never did.

As we got older, our sense of mischief faded out in favor of the harvest, even after my father gave up the cotton business. Our high school ran on a split term so students would be out in the fall and free to work the fields all day. We did it to help out at home and buy our own clothes and maybe have a little left over to go see Roy Rogers or Lash LaRue at the Saturday night picture show. Pretty much all the kids picked cotton. It killed our summers, what with having to make up the classroom time and all, but at least we could afford a decent pair of shoes.

Judith and I dated off and on throughout high school, nothing too serious. We were the same age, but I'd skipped ahead a couple grades thanks to an eidetic memory that allowed me to get straight A's without studying. During the summer, all the kids would gather at the local swimming hole and from time to time I'd see Judith there, and we'd sit by the waterside and talk under a big weeping willow along the bank's green edge. Ours was a warm and gentle courtship; friends first, sweet on each other—but all the time in the world before us. Besides, Judith's parents were pretty strict, which made it hard to date; we'd meet up when we could, at the local café or drugstore or movies.

And I was grateful for her company; my family was going through a rough time at home. Dad had always been an early-to-bed, early-to-rise kind of guy; then one day, he just couldn't rise no more. His health had been failing for some time: in and out of the hospital, his doctors never could quite figure out exactly what was wrong. He'd be sick to his stomach one day, hit with chest pains the next. Daily O's unit had been called up to Korea, but then the cease-fire went into effect and they got stood down; so he left the service and stepped up as the man of the house. At one point, it looked like Dad was on the mend; but one morning I heard my mother screaming and I ran into the bedroom. I saw him collapsed on the floor and I tried to hoist him up, saying, "Daddy, Daddy, please wake up!" Then he died in my arms. I was sixteen years old. We never did find out what killed him.

Soon after graduating high school, I enlisted in the US Army.

A lot of people have asked me why I was so taken with the Army from the get-go. Well, I didn't grow up around boats, so I had no interest in the Navy or Marine Corps. The Air Force never even blipped on my radar screen: I wanted to jump out of airplanes, not fly them. The Army just always seemed like a natural fit—what with my backwoods upbringing and all. As to the Airborne—well, I reckon I've got General Gavin and all those Mission Boston and Easy Company boys to thank for that.

And Daily O.

He tried to talk me out of it: "You got your whole life ahead of you," he said, as he drove me to the bus station at Walnut Ridge. "What you want to jump out of airplanes for? You should be going to college." Daily O was just finishing up his degree at Arkansas State, Jonesboro, having gone back to school, as promised. "I know you're just doing it 'cause I was a paratrooper, so now you want to be one, too. It ain't all flags and glory and medals, you know. You want to get through this, you need to keep your nose clean, your ears sharp, and your mouth shut—ya hear?"

Saying nothing, I gave a crisp nod and hopped out of the car with my duffel bag.

Then Daily O called out: "Hey, you take care of yourself now." He said it like he was real serious, almost worried; but then he hit me with that easy grin, and said, "I mean it."

Never dreamed that would be the last time I would see that smile. Hear that voice.

Several months into my first tour with the 82nd at Fort Bragg, my First Sergeant called me into his office. First Sergeants are a breed unto themselves, not well known for beating around the bush. As a young private, he was the last person on earth—short of an enemy soldier—whose attention you wanted to catch. When I presented myself in his office, he asked me how many days leave I had. I told him maybe ten at the most. I had no idea where this was going.

Then he looked me in the eye and said: "Your brother was killed last night in a car wreck."

I was thunderstruck; no idea what to say or do or think, the world spinning. The way he just came out and told me like that; it was like getting clobbered with a baseball bat or something. Years later, I'd learn (on too many occasions) that brevity was the best and only way to deliver the worst news—the loss of a loved one—to the next of kin.

Right away, the Army gave me emergency leave. Going home to look after the family meant helping my mother and seeing to things at the sawmill. It was a common theme I would encounter two decades later among my special operations brethren: the young son who, in the wake of some tragedy, had to step up and look after their loved ones—brothers, sisters, widowed mothers.

We buried Daily O next to Dad, the turned-over earth still fresh over the old man's gravesite. Devastated but strong, my mother would outlive her husband by forty years. Still in a state of shock at my brother's funeral, I couldn't believe he was gone. Dad died young, but Daily O—he'd only just earned his college degree, had his whole life ahead of him. I don't think I've ever shed more tears for anyone—before or since—and I'd seen my fair share of death by then, and would encounter even more later.

In that moment, I knew what my big brother would have told me.

Stand at attention, eyes straight ahead.

Be a man.

Life goes on.

Around that time, Judith and I started seeing a lot more of each other.

My cousin loaned me his car, and we used to go on long drives and just talk, holding hands against the hum of the road. It took my mind off all the loss behind me and shifted my focus to what lay ahead. Soon I began to feel like she did—that we could spend the rest of our lives together. Us against the whole world.

We got married in May 1959, and a short time later I returned to the Army. As I left, Judith gave me her scarf, and I promised that I would wear it when I jumped. My sergeants frowned on that sort of thing, but I told 'em it reminded me of my girl—and, well, I guess they got over it.

And right now, staring out the window of the chopper-pod, my gaze lingering over the dark and dangerous jungle below, I wished I still had that scarf. I couldn't remember where I'd last seen it, but I could sure remember where I last saw Judith: standing on the pier with little Tammy in her arms, unborn baby slumbering in her belly, waving me goodbye under the groan of the *Geiger*'s horn. Then we set sail from Savannah on the long voyage to Qui Nhon.

2

HAPPY VALLEY BLUES

December 18, 1965
Operation Scalping Mustang
Over Landing Zone (LZ) Tonto
Suoi Ca Valley
Central Highlands
Republic of Vietnam

"Pop the smoke!"

Colonel Mertel's voice was deep and cool when he gave the order, rising in a sharp tenor above the chopper's rotor blades, not to signal alarm in the midst of danger—though there was plenty of that: this was one hot LZ.

"We're taking fire," shouted the pilot.

Bullets plinked the fuselage. The Huey bucked and shuddered. We circled low and fast. As the door-gunner opened up, I heard the brassy, chain-rattling ring of the belt-fed M60 hosing down the tree line. Then the crew chief pulled the pin on a smoke grenade, tossed it out the door. A yellow cloud billowed over the landing zone like mustard gas. The marker would tell the follow-on choppers where to set down and deploy the rest of our troops on the ground.

Gray fog hung low and heavy in the sky like wet cement, threatening a hard jungle rain. Poor visibility meant no fighter cover from our Navy and Air Force friends—none of the high-explosive bombs or napalm that could incinerate the enemy en masse and make even Charlie think twice about pressing any attack. Coming into the massive LZ, we had three rifle companies, almost three hundred men, in an armada of choppers, landing in successive waves. C Company was already on the ground, deploying from their choppers.

Below us, through the thick haze of smoke, I watched the enemy scattering in an eerie slow motion, slipping in and out of sight along the faded edge of the tree line. VC in their black pajamas, a trio of them—ammo-carrier, loader, and shooter—were setting up a crew-served heavy machine gun. Judging from its woodpecker-like report, I guessed it was an old, World War II–era Japanese Type 59. Right then, it was letting loose on a squad of C Company soldiers caught out in the open as they leaped off their chopper and charged the tree line.

"Troops in contact!" I shouted. "We got wounded on the ground!"

Leading the others, I saw one of our guys crumple under fire from that gun.

"Put us down," Mertel shouted to the pilot. He wanted in there fast. I remembered what he told us during one of our briefings as we sailed over on the *Geiger*: "We will never leave anyone behind." Even the dead. Then one of the commanders responded that he would explain to his men that, if at all possible, we would get their bodies out. Mertel cut him right off: "No, not *if at all possible*—it *will* be possible. We will never leave anyone behind—period."

Now, more rounds peppered our bird, chewing up the tail rotor assembly. The chopper convulsed and the nose dropped hard, the engine making a funny whine. Alarm klaxons buzzed and whirred, a nauseating chorus. Mayhem. The pilot and copilot were fighting the controls. On board, there were eight more of us: me; the crew chief; the door-gunner; two RTO's (radio telephone operators, the guys who carry the battalion and brigade net comms packs); our S-2 (intel officer); the artillery liaison officer; and our battalion commander, Colonel Mertel. If they blew this bird up, Charlie would be decapitating the entire op.

"Brace yourselves," the pilot hollered. Not that there was much to brace yourself against, or even hold on to, in the tight confines of the cabin with its open side doors. I wasn't even belted in. "We're going in hard!"

I knew what that meant—crash.

BAPTISM BY "FRIENDLY FIRE" AT THE GOLF COURSE

An Khe
September 21

Less than an hour after arriving at Camp Radcliff, our base at An Khe, I saw the locals drive a nine-inch nail through a woman's tongue. Still only half built, as far as frontline bases went, Radcliff was as big as they come—the biggest helicopter base in the world, home to over 435 choppers of all shapes and sizes: lift-ships, gunships, those flying cranes, and of course Hueys. Throw sixteen hundred other vehicles into the mix and what you had was a transport hub that rivaled the world's busiest airports. The chopper pad alone was so vast we called it "the Golf Course." And we're not talking miniature golf. The lady in question (the one with the nail in her tongue) was one of the many locals we had hired to help us clear and burn brush from the rest of the base. All around us, the rough, green mountain country encroached: heavily forested, deep jagged ravines carved into the rocky terrain—a tough hump for even the toughest among us, and perfect cover for an enemy whose strategy relied on slipping in and out across the Cambodian border, where we couldn't follow them. The woman had passed out from the intense heat of the bonfires and sauna-like humidity. The nail was meant to keep her from swallowing her tongue. Medieval, but effective—it worked.

The advance party had dug deep into double-time getting everything ready, but there was still much to do before we were fully up and running. Our arrival represented the first major ramp-up of our engagement in Vietnam following the Gulf of Tonkin incident. It was a massive logistical undertaking that would last many more weeks. We spent that whole first day building up the facilities that would house and service the sixteen thousand men of the 1st Cav. We didn't have any engineers yet, so it was just us with our entrenching tools. For our quarters, we pitched pup tents with fold-up military cots and air mattresses— about as good as it was going to get for the rest of the tour. We put up more tents for the Operations Center, a chapel, the Officer's Club, the Enlisted Club, a first aid station. Big Lister bags for showers that doused you in water so cold, they must have flown it in from the Arctic—good enough to get the mud and gunk off, though. For warm showers, we just stood in the rain. What we called the mess tent was more like a food bank for the cold C-rations that we'd be living off for the next couple of months, at least until we got a proper kitchen set up. Those C-rats were worse than any of that freeze-dried stuff the astronauts ate; most of ours—according to the dates stamped on them—were canned during the Korean War. Fortunately, as soon as we landed, we had a big pile of mail waiting for us, and Judith had sent a care package with a couple of homemade chocolate cakes packed in real popcorn, which we ate, too. I shared what I had with my buddies, and there wasn't a crumb or kernel left when we were done.

We bought our lumber from the locals, and I saw this young captain with a big pile that didn't quite look right. He said it was red oak. Now, that captain seemed smart enough—I mean, he was a West Pointer and all—but he struck me as somewhat of a city boy; and having grown up working in a sawmill, I knew a thing or two about lumber. *That's not red oak, sir. That's elm.* Still, he insisted: the locals had assured him—it was solid red oak. So we used it to put up one of our facilities—a communications hut, I think, or something like that—and sure enough, a few days later, the soft wood bowed and the whole thing collapsed. It just reaffirmed my commitment that if I ever became an officer, I'd make damn sure to listen to my NCOs, especially the ones who grew up hunting, fishing, tracking—and working in sawmills. It also told me that maybe we should be a little more careful about how much we trusted our new neighbors. In fact, that very first day, we discovered a line of rocks shaped into an arrow that led directly to the commander's hut. One of the locals was playing both sides of the coin, working for us while laying down markers so that Charlie's spotters could zero our key command and control facilities and personnel and rain down artillery or sniper fire on us. (So much for hearts and minds.) That was a much bigger wake-up call than any cold shower I'd take that tour because it was at that moment that I realized just how out in the open and exposed we were, those forbidding hills on all sides concealing who knew what kind of danger. Charlie knew we were here; but just in case he didn't know exactly who we were, the advance party had taken it upon themselves to paint a giant 1st Cavalry shoulder patch insignia—the famous yellow shield with black stripe and horse's head—on a massive slab of concrete along a slope skirting the Golf Course.

Here we are, Charlie. Take your best shot.

He did. Just after dark.

From the shrouded peaks of Hon Cong Mountain, those first rounds cracked open the night air, kicking up the dirt at our feet—Charlie's way of dusting off the welcome mat. The combat veterans among us who'd seen action in Korea knew the distinctive *brrrrrp!* of a Chicom machine gun and shuddered. We cherries stayed tight among them and watched: until the muscle-memory of past battles sent them all scrambling for cover.

It was almost like being in a movie, everyone diving behind mounds of dirt. Sweeping our shiny brand-new M-16s across the hills, we were shooting blind at an enemy dug in too deep to see. Some of our guys were eager beavers, digging foxholes to make up for the lack of cover. But the wild rounds coming in at us were loose and sporadic, potshots off their Russian-made AKs. Charlie was just testing us out: how we would react. After a thirty-day voyage, a D-Day-style landing on a beach that culminated in one orange soda and a hundred push-ups, a long and bumpy chopper ride, and a day of burning brush and working construction under the hot Southeast Asian sun, we were finally at war—though fighting in the dark. This was our wake-up call. No lights. No generators hooked up. A bad smell in the air: gasoline and gunpowder and burnt flesh.

Then came the barrage of tracer rounds—full-auto gunfire, red streaks slashing up the darkness. We had no idea who was doing all that shooting, but whoever it was, they sure were putting up one hell of a fight—not to mention the most spectacular light show. It lasted all night. Next morning, word spread that it was a bunch of CPAs from the finance corps—the guys who handled our payroll—along with some of the hospital staff. Guess they wanted in on the fight. Trouble was, they weren't shooting at Charlie; they were shooting at each other. Blew through a whole couple of crates of tracer ammo. Good thing not a one of 'em could shoot straight to save their lives—or take someone else's. Lucky no one got hurt. All of us frontline infantry guys got a real kick out of the whole thing—a bunch of medical orderlies and accountants getting their grit on. But I doubt we would have been laughing so hard if there'd been casualties.

Someone called it "friendly fire."

I would soon learn there was no such thing.

HOME-FIELD ADVANTAGE

Our first mission was securing "the Green Trace," our perimeter and the outer picket line a couple of miles beyond that—another layer of defense that included observation posts and claymore mines. We had this sort of mascot, a gray mule called Maggie that one of our brother regiments had smuggled over aboard ship. Maggie had free rein of the base. Some nights, we'd detect movement outside the wire and find her out for an evening stroll in the middle of no-man's-land. I heard she finally did trip one of our own claymores, ended up in another battalion's beef stew. But how she made it through even that first night without getting shot is beyond me. Still, all that gunplay—along with all the *incoming* to come over the many nights ahead—drove home to us just how wide open we were.

But then, we didn't come here to just sit around and get shot at—we were to here to hunt down and kill the enemy.

We spent the first few weeks embedded with other units that had already been in country for a while, to get the lay of the land. I went to the 173rd Airborne Brigade at Biên Hòa, just outside Saigon. They were operating in War Zone D, a dense patch of jungle where they'd been deploying Long Range Reconnaissance Patrols (LRRPs) to stab deep into enemy territory and destroy their base camps. That's right: *enemy territory*. This was the heart of South Vietnam—within spitting distance of the capital—but Charlie was all over the place. This was more or less a counterinsurgency, though no one was calling it that—yet.

Known as "the Sky Soldiers," the 173rd was a crack outfit of paratroopers that had been in-country for over five months and involved in some pretty heavy combat. Those guys knew the terrain. Fired up and ready to kick that jungle's ass, I was attached to a squad led by a sergeant with whom I had served in the 101st at Fort Campbell. Soon, I would learn how important it was to maintain an aggressive mindset; both in Vietnam and many years later when I served in special operations, where survival often depended on taking the fight right into the enemy, even when facing a numerically superior force. The NVA was tough, but was in no way our match soldier to soldier. The Viet Cong were ragtag and barely trained at best. But this was their jungle. That was just one of their big advantages: we were fighting on their turf—Charlie owned the playing field.

Right away, we got into some pretty hot contact. We rode into the area of operation on helicopters—offloaded, deployed, moved out toward the enemy position, which we had gleaned in advance through various sources of intelligence. This was my first test on an actual combat operation, and my first fight in the jungle. I had done plenty of real-world-style training; but in training, the enemy wasn't shooting at you with live ammo, and we didn't have any jungles in Germany or Georgia.

We were out for three days, sleeping on the jungle floor and living off C-rations. Movement was slow, methodical, and exhausting. Inch by inch. We'd cover five miles just to make it one. It seemed like that tangled brush was as much our foe as the Viet Cong. In short order, I learned to spot booby traps: tripwire grenades fashioned out of our own discarded C-ration cans and tiger pits lined with punji sticks—sharpened bamboo spikes smeared in human excrement, which Charlie knew would put guys out of action for weeks in the hospital while the docs scraped the wound down to the bone to stave off infection. I learned to scan the triple canopy foliage for signs that it had been trimmed into fire lanes that VC snipers might use to shoot at us from above. And I kept my nose clean to detect the scent of a cooking fire or latrine—both indicators of the heavily camouflaged bunker complexes that Charlie used to ambush us. And it was a pretty sure bet that if we found one, there would be several others nearby. Too often, by the time we spotted a dugout, it was already too late—within ten or twenty yards, Charlie would let loose.

All of this was on top of the merciless terrain itself: thorn bushes and elephant grass that could slice right through flesh; bamboo shoots that shot like steel rods straight up to the sky; vines so thick to step over them, you had to pull your knees up to your chest. We were soaked right through all the time—if not from the waist-deep water or pouring rain, then our own sweat, which drenched our flak jackets as we marched through the stifling humidity. Then there were the armies of insects, leeches, and all kinds of nasty critters I couldn't even name—though not so many snakes. In the years ahead, I would conduct training and combat operations in just about every harsh environment imaginable: arctic, woodland, desert, urban—but by far the harshest was the jungle.

Sure enough, we caught contact as we moved. Engaged a few firefights. We took several casualties. Ten killed. I don't know how many wounded. I don't know how many Viet Cong we killed, either. The numbers didn't matter so much. Not yet anyway.

On search-and-destroy ops back with the 1st Cav, we started pulling regular air assaults, moving out en masse in big chopper armadas. We ran into a lot of booby traps; otherwise, we just hit a lot of dry holes. I'd say our intel was coin-toss-quality at best, as in: fifty-fifty whether Charlie would actually be in a target area (even if they'd been there when headquarters told us so). The North Vietnamese had an invisible foothold in the region, and we were coming at them head-on.

As the battalion staff operations sergeant, I rode with Lieutenant Colonel Mertel in the command chopper. Our main advantages—apart from superior training—lay in our close air support and artillery bombardment capabilities. The NVA and VC knew their best chance at evening up those odds was to engage us as close to our positions as possible because we would probably hesitate to call down air strikes, or "arty," on ourselves. Probably. Didn't always work out that way. For them. Or us.

Our first major campaign centered on the defense of Pleiku, a strategically vital city near the Cambodian border that the North Vietnamese wanted to seize in order to cut South Vietnam in half and establish a key jumping-off point from which to take Saigon. To open their offensive, the NVA deployed two regiments to lay siege to an isolated US Special Forces camp at Plei Me, nestled in the foothills of the Central Highlands. In its defense, the tiny camp only had a twelve-man A-Team from the 5th Special Forces Group on hand to lead a small force of South Vietnamese Special Forces and tough Montagnard tribesmen. Charlie's mission wasn't to overrun the base, but to lure much larger South Vietnamese reinforcements away from the bigger prize, Pleiku, just twenty-five miles to the south. The NVA would ambush and wipe them out en route, leaving both the camp and the town even more vulnerable.

The man sent to lead the rescue of Plei Me was US Army Special Forces Major Charles A. Beckwith. "Chargin' Charlie," as he would become famously known, had spent a year on an exchange program with the British Special Air

Service (SAS) fighting in the jungles of Malaya. Back then, I had no idea who he was, though we did fight and spill blood along some of the same unforgiving soil.

It was our airpower that broke the siege—you better believe it: nearly 700 sorties dropping over 700 tons of high-explosive bombs and napalm on the enemy. By November, Charlie was on the run and trying to regroup to mount a second offensive. General Westmoreland, commander of the Military Assistance Command, Vietnam (MACV)—in other words, the head honcho—ordered in the Air Cav to snap the spines of the NVA and VC forces. They'd just had their asses handed to them and were now hightailing it to the Cambodian border. The North Vietnamese knew how to stretch that home-field advantage. We could only operate inside Vietnam, not Cambodia or Laos. Hanoi played that to the hilt, operating from bases just over the border and running their supply lines through both countries down the Ho Chi Minh Trail.

Several miles east of An Khe, we were in the middle of conducting air assault ops, when we got orders to move to an airfield outside Pleiku, near the famous Mang Yang Pass. It was there that the Viet Minh (precursor to the Viet Cong) had decimated France's Groupement Mobile 100 in one of the last decisive battles of the First Indochina War (1946–1954), leading to the formation of North and South Vietnam. We set up our battalion base camp at the old Catecka Tea Plantation and went straight after the retreating NVA and Viet Cong to where no other force had gone after them before: deep into the heart of their own sanctuary—the Ia Drang Valley.

It was there, at Landing Zone X-Ray, that our brothers in the 7th Cavalry—once under the command of Colonel George A. Custer, now under Colonel Hal Moore of *We Were Soldiers* fame—took the battle right to Charlie. And kicked his teeth down his throat. At a kill ratio of ten to one—despite being outnumbered, though not outgunned. Six consecutive days of round-the-clock B-52 and every other kind of air and artillery strike more than leveled the playing field.

I spent my Thanksgiving at LZ X-Ray, trading up my C-rations until I got one with turkey loaf. Still, it was a somber celebration; November had been a rough month. We lost a lot of guys. Friends. Torn to shreds. We'd engaged the enemy head-on, sometimes hand to hand—whites-of-their-eyes kind of warfare. One morning, as we prepared to load up on the choppers, my buddy, Sergeant Bey—having just finished identifying the bodies of soldiers who'd come back dead the night before—walked up to me and told me to close my eyes. I asked him why. He said so he'd be able to recognize me if I got killed. I'd just as soon die with my eyes wide open—and told him so.

Scalping Mustang
LZ Tonto
December 18
We got wounded on the ground. . . .

"Brace, brace, brace!"

That was the pilot, shouting over a wild din: alarm klaxons and engine noise and machine-gun fire pelting our bird from below. I gripped the metal frame of my seat till my knuckles went full white, slammed my eyes shut, and prayed I didn't get thrown out one of the open troop doors. Descending in a low circle, the pilot straightened out at the last moment before we hit the ground. The term "controlled crash" is misleading. You don't feel the "controlled" part as much as the crash. The impact rattled my spine; and for a split second, I remembered landing on my butt that time I fell through the ceiling at my friend J.D.'s house. Then I snapped back to the present and opened my eyes. We were all still alive. A miracle. Hard rain had softened the ground, but our pilot and copilot were aces who'd flown plenty of combat missions into plenty of hot LZs. They'd brought us down right on the money.

"They don't teach that in flight school," the pilot said, finessing the throttle, a big grin on his face.

"Will she fly?" Colonel Mertel asked.

"We'll see, sir," the pilot told him, still grinning.

Then I heard shooting and spotted the wounded man from C Company, the one who'd been cut down charging toward the tree line. Limping as fast as he could toward our chopper, he'd been hit in the leg and was dragging it behind him like a dead weight; the VC were trying their best to finish him off, a heavy spray of bullets off that Japanese woodpecker gun stalking his broken paces.

I jumped off the chopper and struck out toward him. Grabbing his weapon, our crew chief, Sergeant Jack Clemmons, leaped out after me. Running side by side across the open field, we were about thirty meters from the Huey—halfway to the wounded man—when the VC gun crew let loose on us. Bullets caught Clemmons full in the chest, ripping through his flak jacket. He dropped to the ground. I hit the dirt. Head down—not a scratch on me. Glancing back, I saw Clemmons slumped into the earth, staring at me with his eyes wide open. He wasn't moving. I crawled back to him, felt the faintest pulse in his neck, and started dragging him toward the chopper. The whole time he was looking at me, eyes wide open, but vacant. How that machine gun got him and not me, I will never know. By then, I'd seen a lot of combat, but this was my first time seeing a guy get cut down right beside me.

Our intel officer, Captain Stone, saw what I was doing and climbed down off the Huey. Crawling over to us, he helped me pull Clemmons the rest of the way through the mud and pouring rain. We got him on board and then we crawled back for the wounded C Company man, who was still under heavy fire in the middle of the field. Somehow we managed to get him on the chopper without either of us being hit. And somehow that crippled bird was able to lift off and make it all the way back to An Khe, a forty-five-minute flight. Later, the pilot would tell me that the airframe had taken twenty-three rounds, including one bullet that hit the main combustion chamber, which would normally cause the engine to flame out, and did—just as they were touching down at the Golf Course. The wounded soldier from C Company was expected to make a full recovery. Sergeant Clemmons died en route.

HERE AND THERE

While Captain Stone and I were busy extracting the wounded man from C Company, Colonel Mertel had already hopped off the chopper. With his two radio operators, he took up a position along a high muddy rise where he established our command post. We never operated directly out of our main base at An Khe, always using what today in places like Afghanistan would be called an FOB, or "forward operating base," hunkered down somewhere closer to the LZ or point of contact with the enemy. We called them "fire bases," and ours were more temporary in nature. This was not your typical war where you fought for and held territory, even in a stalemate. This was a war by the numbers: kill more of Charlie than he killed of us. Simple. But not so simple.

Just a month earlier, the audacious success of Colonel Hal Moore's 1/7th Cavalry at LZ X-Ray in the Ia Drang had put it into General Westmoreland's head that we could win this war simply by racking up a high kill count, which suited the statistician-minded Pentagon just fine. It didn't matter who held what hill or LZ or valley or scrap of land and for how long—what mattered was that we mowed down the enemy. As long as we did that, in great numbers, we would prevail in the most violent and deadly game of whack-a-mole in human history.

So when we hit the field, it meant staying out maybe three or five days at a time, and we'd search and destroy, and Charlie would bug out and scatter. Then we'd go back to our fire base or Radcliff, and Charlie would reposition and we'd tango all over again.

Scalping Mustang was no different. Except now we were going into yet another NVA and VC sanctuary—the Suoi Ca Valley. We called it "Happy Valley," but there wasn't a damn thing happy about it.

Once our own chopper was back in the air, Captain Stone and I regrouped with Colonel Mertel at that muddy rise and took over as pathfinders to operate the landing zone, which was about two football fields deep. Our fire base was only thirteen minutes away by chopper, and we were rotating ten or twelve Hueys at a time back and forth between here and there, bringing in the rest of the men from A, B, and C Companies, all while under constant heavy fire and an even heavier downpour—and all while coordinating both artillery support and medical evacuation.

Near our position along the southwestern edge of the LZ, a couple of platoons from B Company had engaged the enemy head-on, and were taking full-auto fire from the tree line. Then I saw a young private stand right up in the melee with his arms flailing, hands swatting every which way. So I ran over to him, throwing a couple of blind shots at the tree line as I went. Then I shouted at that kid with his peach-fuzz chin: "What the hell are you doing?"

"Trying not to get stung, Sergeant!"

"What?"

"All these damn bees, sir!"

"You'll get stung, all right," I hollered. "Those aren't bees, son, those are bullets! Now get your ass down before you get it shot off!"

About five hundred meters from our command post, and well within visual range, stood a large village—just a bunch of hooches with some bigger dwellings scattered among them. We could see the VC in their black pajamas darting in and out of there with their AK and SKS assault rifles, and C Company reported over the radio that they were taking sniper fire from the same location. About an hour into the battle, Colonel Hal Moore arrived by chopper at the LZ and linked up with us at our command post along the muddy rise. After Ia Drang, headquarters had promoted Moore and given him his own brigade, which put him in command of the operation. Right away, he asked Colonel Mertel why he hadn't called down artillery strikes on the village. Mertel informed him that there were several civilians still there being used as human shields. A few seconds later, I got a call over the radio. It was C Company: *We just took a KIA off that sniper.* Moore heard this and turned to Mertel: "Blow that motherfucker off the map."

So that's what we did.

By the time the shells started pouring down with the rain, Colonel Moore was gone.

We hunkered down as best we could, tight against the sodden embankment. The earth rattled beneath us. We were close—what today's Army would call "danger close," within potential range of the kill radius. The shock waves of each barrage pummeled my back and chest, almost knocking the wind right out of me. Then I peeked over the rise and saw a frantic flood of villagers spilling out of their hooches. My gaze slid through the mayhem, landing on one very old woman standing frozen in panic out in the open field. Shells were going off all around her; but she was just looking about herself, no idea which way to go. I lifted up out of the mud and ran into the village. Explosions going off right and left, I scooped her up in my arms. Other soldiers were already doing the same with as many civilians as they could. As I ran with her back toward the rise, the terrified woman started farting in my arms. I could feel it. Over the booming blasts around us, I shouted: "Old lady, if you shit on me, I'll drop your ass right here and now." I don't think she understood a word; probably thought I was trying to comfort her, when all I was really trying to do was save her life without getting crapped on.

We made it back to the embankment and I set her down with the other civilians as our medics began treating the wounded. Chattering away in Vietnamese, maybe she was thanking me or cursing all of us—probably both—but then she seemed to calm down. In a moment, she reached in her pocket and pulled out a small plug of betel nut, which was like the local version of chewing tobacco, and she worked it in her mouth and had herself a good spit. Now and then, I was known to chew tobacco—in between the Winstons that were my choice brand of cigarette—and I happened to have a tin of dip on me and I threw one in. So we just sat there for a long moment, the artillery exploding behind us, chewing and spitting and not saying a word.

More civilians were making their way over, some of them wounded. I saw a little boy, maybe four years old, laid out on a stretcher under the hard rain, and someone said something about him being dead. One of the guys started to pull a poncho over his face, and I told him to stop; the kid looked so innocent lying there. After a moment, his eyes fluttered wide open and we all let out a long breath. Turns out, the poor little thing was just frightened—like all the rest of us. The thing was: as soldiers, we had a fighting chance. In war, civilians are the ones who suffer worse than anyone else. No question about it. Most of the time, we had commanders who tried to keep civilian casualties down—I know I did—but if you had Americans getting killed from a village, you had to take action on that village. Every one of those decisions was a debt you paid later in the dead of night—when you woke up flailing in a cold sweat from a nightmare you couldn't even remember, your wife staring at you with the same frightened look in her eyes. The one known only to those who had seen war.

Next morning, it was a C-ration breakfast: a hunk of beef that was probably recognizable when it was canned back in 1951. It had rained on us all night as we slept on the hard ground, and it was still raining when we woke up. We were all soaked to the bone. Instead of a rooster or alarm clock, we had sporadic small-arms fire and mortar rounds—a regular Vietnam-style wake-up call.

More troops came into the landing zone, including Captain Wilkie, our artillery liaison officer. The Army had all these funny monikers for things. Artillery was "Harassment and Interdiction." Catchy, right? Kind of like calling a tactical nuke strike "Tough Love." That was the official term, anyway. We had our own. In honor of arty's unpredictable accuracy—or lack thereof—we called it "Here and There."

Wilkie went to work right away, calling in strikes on various VC positions, coordinating with his recon sergeant, Sergeant Derheim, and his radioman, Specialist Romero. The rounds whistled through the air overhead, but something sounded a bit off—*too close*. Then a massive boom went off nearby, and I felt a sharp pain in my arm, where a piece of shrapnel bit me. I turned, a steady ringing in my ears that didn't sound terribly loud but drowned out all other noise, and I saw the aftermath—an instant apocalypse. Bodies strewn all over the place, lying twisted in the mud, Sergeant Derheim and Specialist Romero among them. When we put him on the medevac chopper, Captain Wilkie was barely alive. The blast had torn his flak jacket right off him and shrapnel riddled his body, his flesh ripped to shreds. He had been standing between me and the explosion. The kill radius of a US 105-mm high explosive artillery shell is 115 feet. I had been standing ten feet from where it landed. Had Captain Wilkie not been standing between me and the point of impact—had he not borne the brunt of that blast and the shrapnel that came with it—I'd be the one on that medevac, all torn up and bleeding from a thousand cuts.

As soon as Wilkie's chopper dusted off, I went back to the blast area and came upon a big piece of the shell that had landed on us. I picked it up and turned it over, still hot in my hands. The markings were there, exactly where they should be—confirming what I already knew to be true.

When my mother found out I'd be receiving the Purple Heart for my wounded arm, the first thing she wanted to know was what day I got hit on—a Sunday. She replied: "Well, he should have been in church!"

Colonel Mertel ordered me to go get my arm treated, so I grabbed the next chopper back to our fire base. As soon as they were done patching me up at the aid station, I went to find the senior artillery officer. He was sitting in the mess tent with a couple of other officers, already getting his story straight: that the round that killed our guys and wounded Captain Wilkie came from the South Koreans. Their White Horse and Tiger Divisions were operating with us in the area.

"Bullshit," I called out, interrupting them.

"Excuse me, Sergeant?"

From my rucksack, I withdrew the piece of shrapnel from the point of impact and threw it on the table. "Read that, hotshot." I was referring to the markings: M1 HE 105 MM. The Koreans used a much smaller round. That stamp might as well have read: MADE IN THE USA. The man's face went pale. Now, he knew he would have no choice but to report that up the chain—and it would be his ass on the line. I heard later that he was relieved of duty—though that did nothing to bring back the dead.

I thought: *friendly fire.*

Yeah, right.

The mess sergeant caught my anger—and also that my M-16 was fully loaded, its bolt charged. He came over, put his arm around me, and said: "Jesse, what do you say I buy you a cup of coffee?"

Then he took me to the other end of the mess tent and poured a cup from a fresh pot. I remember it was steaming as he prepared it.

"How do you take it?" he asked, with a grin. We didn't have any cream or sugar.

I made no reply.

He handed me the cup of coffee.

I drank it down.

3

FOG OF WAR

Hon Cong Mountain
Outside the Green Trace
Near the An Khe Pass
January 25, 1966
9:31 a.m.

I heard a faint sputtering overhead.

Sounded like a plane; but shaky, a dull groan cutting in and out, the aeronautical version of a coughing fit. Still a ways out, but closing fast on our position.

I came out of the radio tent to take a look.

A thick steel-wool mist hung low and heavy in the sky. Hearing the noise, and me whistling through my teeth to alert them, the others emerged from their own tents to see what the fuss was about. A few of them were looking up with their hands boxed around their faces, like somehow that would magically arm them with X-ray vision to penetrate the cloud cover.

"You see anything yet, Sarge?"

Hell, no.

(But I wasn't about to tell them that.)

All of us had on our flak jackets; the weather had finally cooled enough that we could wear them. One more layer of protection against the elements—and the enemy—though not much of one: these were barely water resistant, let alone bulletproof. And they still made us sweat. They called winter here "the dry season," but only 'cause it rained less. Arkansas winters were bone cold. The only thing bone cold in Vietnam were the mountains. And the battlefield. Even with our rotor blades dusting dirt devils off hot LZs, the humidity this time of year could still give the jungle night sweats.

Coming off Scalping Mustang, we'd spent the Christmas holidays on security duty over at Bien Ho Lake: a gorgeous, jade-and-turquoise-colored volcanic reservoir cradled within a lush, sweeping plateau just a couple of miles outside Pleiku. The locals called it *T'Nung* or *Ia Neung*, the Lake of Tears: the legend being that centuries ago, a massive eruption had wiped out the local village, leaving only the survivors' tears to fill the empty crater left behind. It never ceased to amaze me: *this paradise on the edge of hell.*

Still, what a beautiful setting for Christmas dinner—turkey with all the trimmings—and pretty festive, too, thanks to the division quartermaster, the guys in supply (our scroungers), and the mess cooks. We attended Christmas Eve services in a chapel with a roof sewn from parachute silk and dined on ammunition boxes with tablecloths fashioned out of bed sheets from one of the base hospitals. We even had the top brass fly in to dine with us, a who's who of military legends: Our brigade commander, Colonel Elvy Roberts; First Cav Commanding General Harry Kinnard, who'd also served with the besieged 101st Airborne at Bastogne and advised Brigadier General Anthony McAuliffe to famously answer "Nuts!" to the German ultimatum to surrender in the face of annihilation; and General Harold "Johnny" Johnson, the Army chief of staff himself, who wore a POW ribbon on his uniform, having spent most of World War II as a prisoner of the Japanese, and survived the brutal Bataan Death March. These were men who had witnessed and endured the absolute worst horrors of war—the same horrors we were now witnessing and enduring ourselves. And here they were, on one of our holiest of family holidays—when we would all be most missing home, our loved ones—to break bread with us: the frontline soldiers that they themselves had once been. I shook hands and spoke briefly with each of them. Another tremendous honor. To see these amazing war heroes, some of our highest-ranking and most legendary commanders, sharing Christmas dinner with the troops in our makeshift ammo-dump dining room, well aware of the risk (that the NVA or VC might attack in force at any moment, if only to ruin the holiday, or take out some *boo-coo* brass) was a great lesson in military leadership and genuine patriotism—one that I would carry with me for the rest of my career and pass on, through my own example, as best I could, to those who came up behind me.

This was no vacation, though. As soon as we all finished our last bite of apple pie and ice cream, we were back on duty: running a security cordon with a fifty-mile radius around Pleiku to head off any potential attack. The rest of the time we spent training, brushing up our heliborne assault repertoire: mostly rappelling and parachuting drills—to get us into those places so thick or on a severe enough gradient as to make blowing out a standard LZ impossible. The rappelling part was kind of fun, and would come in handy when I joined Delta Force almost fifteen years later, but also a bit daunting: holding the rope tight for dear life against the seismic *whump-whump-whump* of the hurricane-force rotor-wash and downdraft, hoping to hell you didn't catch a crosswind, as you slid down full speed (*GO-GO-GO!*) 150 feet off the skid of a Huey, with no hitch mechanism—just your hand—to brake your descent into the dense, dark jungle below. And who-knows-what waiting for you down there. *Yeah, that'll wake you up.* Charlie couldn't have cared less that it was all just an exercise; he came locked and loaded with live ammo no matter what.

We had a major who still needed to earn his jump wings, so I set up my own mini-Airborne school, and we did five static line drops off the side of a Huey to qualify him. Of course, Division tried to put the kibosh on the whole thing. After the fact. (Army regs said you had to use an airplane, not a chopper, for jump qualifications.) So I wrote the commander of the Army Airborne School at Fort Benning, Georgia, Colonel Bill Welch, and explained the situation. He responded, "Keep up the good work," and sent along an official diploma and a pair of wings for the major. So much for the regs. (If doing jumps into the jungle or out of a chopper sounded crazy, I'd done five off a barrage balloon when I was in the UK earning my British parachutist badge back before the war. I had already gotten one from the German *fallschirmjäger* after going through their jump-school at Altenstadt—quite a dicey prospect considering the number of World War II vets from both sides assigned to our class, less than twenty years after the war—and I would earn several more badges from airborne units all across the world over the next three decades.)

By mid-January, we were back at the Golf Course, gearing up to hard charge Mr. Victor-Charles head-on, give him some nice New Year's fireworks—a big, blistering bunker-busting B-52 light show. Word soon came down that my battalion, the Jumping Mustangs, had been tapped to carry out a pair of combat drops against the NVA: infiltrate their rear, cut them off, and run right the hell over them—the way they were always trying to do to us. I got all fired up to bring death from above, parachute into battle, the same way my old units, the 82nd and the 101st, had done at Normandy and so many other places whose names only materialized in the pages of history once inked with the blood of our war dead; but then command decided to scrub both missions for who-knows-what reason. Probably because we couldn't find the enemy. Oh well. We were still on jump-status and I still got jump-pay—welcome to the United States Army.

Instead, my unit received orders to hold in reserve and set up a security block between the An Khe Pass and Highway 19. Charlie was playing possum, always one step ahead. Intel would come through on possible locations; but by the time we got there, he'd have already bugged out, split. We'd find cooking pots that were still warm, foxholes, stash huts, munitions caches, and enough rice to feed a regiment. One company found a field hospital built into the trees. Another captured a general's personal toothbrush dabbed with toothpaste, but not the general. It seemed like Charlie's intel was better than ours—at least enough to keep us on the hunt. But we all knew it was only a matter of time before we'd make contact again—and that when we did, it would be heavy. In the meantime, we had to make sure he didn't hit our flanks or activate some local cell to stir up trouble in our own backyard—hence our security mission—as we tried to locate and box in his main force. Our idea of "security" was to kick the enemy's ass before he kicked ours—find him and destroy him. The best way to do that was to intercept his comms. These weren't some slack-ass local-yocal wannabe Viet Cong we were up against; these were the hard-core regulars of the NVA's crack 325th Gold Star Division, one of the six original "Iron and Steel" units of the Viet Minh, who took on the French before us. And won.

We had our work cut out.

I led a small team to set up a radio relay and listening post in the hills outside the Green Trace. Sitting in a radio hut all day monitoring enemy chatter was probably among the most boring of military enterprises—besides cleaning garbage cans, maybe. I hated it. I wasn't a signals guy, and certainly no code breaker—I was a warfighter, and I wanted to be out there fighting the damn war. The only time I was ever happy standing in a radio hut had been on Pearl Harbor Day, just before Scalping Mustang, when Colonel Mertel's voice popped across the battalion net to announce the birth of my daughter, Felicia: "*83-Mike, congratulations, Papa Bear, your wife just had a bouncing baby girl. Mother and daughter are doing just fine. Break out those cigars. Outstanding!*"

Boy was it. Between bursts of static, messages of congratulations filled the airwaves from every GI with ears on the net. If Charlie or the Chicoms—or even the Soviets—were listening, they all knew I had just become a dad for the second time. And I did break out those cigars—the good ones that I'd been saving for the occasion—along with a round of beers for my brother NCOs. But not before I wrote Judith, told her how much I loved her and how thankful I was to her for delivering our healthy newborn baby girl; how happy it made me to welcome Felicia into this world; and how blessed we were that the Lord was keeping us. I wrote so fast my shooting hand went numb. The first photo arrived a couple of weeks later. They became a regular feature with each new letter; each new chocolate cake, packed with a lifetime supply of popcorn. The sting came a short time later: when I looked in that cigar box and saw the few too many left over—the ones I'd been keeping for the guys taken from us too soon, already killed in action. All those brave smiling faces that faded out far too young. And Daily O, grinning from the wheel of his old Plymouth, telling me to be a man. And to watch myself—*ya hear?*—before he faded out, too. That kind of loss, so much of it amid so few bursts of pleasure—it steeled your soul: the more pain you swallowed, buried in the deepest back corner, just so you could keep moving forward. But that darkness never left you, never died even under the light of life's greatest joys.

The sputtering faded.

Then it came back again. Stronger this time. Low and fast.

Almost right on top of us.

"That doesn't sound good," one of the guys said.

When I looked up again, I saw it, the aircraft, an Air Force C-123 transport plane, catching only a glimpse of the fuselage with its US markings, as it rumbled past overhead through a small break in the fog.

"He ain't flying right, Sergeant!"

No, he sure wasn't.

The plane faltered and coughed along its flight path like a wounded bird, yawing funny to the left; the engines howling and dying, and then howling again, as it struggled to gain power and altitude. Then it vanished into the fog once more—thicker now, like a giant smoke ring around the jagged, rough-cut slopes of Hon Cong Mountain—and the sound faded slightly, becoming almost gentle, before turning into a loud scream, the kind like you hear in old movies when a plane goes into a sudden dive. Except this wasn't a movie. After a moment, the screaming stopped, a split second of sudden silence, as we stood there, motionless, staring past the fog toward the mountaintop, as if waiting for a sign. Then came a massive plume of black smoke, rising high and heavy from a steep incline, and the distant crump of an explosion.

I shouted, "Let's go!" and we went. All but the radio team, who stayed behind under my orders to keep ears on those NVA comms. No telling how close Charlie might be to that crash.

We were running full sprint.

Shedding our flak jackets along the way to lose the extra weight.

About a mile or two in, maybe half the distance, we came to a sign, written in both French and Vietnamese, but with a clear graphic warning us of the old minefield left behind from the last war. I was out front. The others followed, each man sparing only enough breath to shout a warning down the line about the danger ahead. No one broke stride. Americans were in harm's way. Our brothers. That's all there was to it. We picked up our pace, dashing across the minefield without a moment's hesitation or—only by the grace of God—any casualties.

The same could not be said of the crash site.

What was left of the plane was a twisted heap of metal, a bent and broken rib cage of charred steel, and a million little pieces scattered over the thick jungle foliage like death confetti. No way anyone could have survived that.

The big cargo jet had plowed through the trees to carve a wingspan-wide clearing, about half a football field deep, into the crash site, spraying a fuel-fed flash fire in its wake. As I emerged from the jungle, the first on scene, I approached the wreckage from the front—which was only apparent because a small fragment of the nose section was still intact. The first thing I saw was two dead bodies splayed across the blood-spattered foliage, thrown from the plane on impact; almost unrecognizable as anything human, the way they were all curled and coiled and knotted up like braided ropes of flesh. Over here was an extra leg that someone had lost; there, a missing arm.

I led the others around the back, and when we reached the tail section, where the cargo ramp had once been, we got a better view inside the main compartment and could see the bodies all lying in a grotesque human heap. Forty-six US servicemen—four Air Force crew and forty-two 1st Cav guys: a mortar platoon from the 2nd of the 7th on their way to Bong Son in advance of our next offensive. A routine flight. Nothing routine about it anymore.

We rushed inside, searching for the smallest sign of life, the faintest pulse, as ammunition and grenades popped off all around us, but thank God none of those mortar rounds. Total chaos. Bodies and parts of bodies everywhere. So much blood. So much death. I flashed on my childhood: sitting by the radio with my family, reports of another crash, another US military transport plane, this one just outside Seoul during the Korean War. Eighteen servicemen killed. Among them, my sister Mona's high school sweetheart and very young husband, Lavel Prater, an Army private, just eighteen years old. I remembered Mona sitting at the funeral, drenched in tears—sobbing, just sobbing, the worst kind of sobbing, but still somehow dignified, dressed all in black, as the chaplain presented her with a crisply folded flag on behalf of a grateful nation. I would never forget the devastation of a young woman's life, ruined in the wake of the loss of a loved one, as the sound of Taps faded beneath her anguish. It was my first military funeral. It would not be my last. So many lives lost in the fog of war. So many young widows and loved ones left behind.

It took two days to pull all the bodies—what was left of them—out of the wreckage. By the time we finished, an Air Force inspection team had determined that the cause was poor weather. As soon as I got back to our relay station, I wrote Judith—to tell her about the crash. I knew she would have seen it already on the six o'clock evening news back home, and this letter would take ten or so days to cycle back to her; but I wanted her to know what happened here, how it really was. (Well, not everything.) I didn't tell her about the body parts, or how these mountains could swallow you whole. Just the powerlessness of the moment, what it was like being the first man on the scene, realizing there was nothing to be done—because, as I wrote to her, in my letter: *They were all dead.*

4

A LONG WAY FROM POCAHONTAS

LZ Cat
On the Cambodian Border
Pleiku Province
South Vietnam
April 7, 1966

I heard a mosquito buzzing in my ear and slapped my own face trying to kill it. Just one slap, but hard enough to snap me awake. For a moment, I didn't know where I was. Lately, I'd been waking up MIA—about ten or fifteen seconds of driftwood in my brain that had me floating someplace else that seemed as near or as distant as the tide. Then my mind would draw a blank on where that someplace was. I'd slept fully clothed with my boots on under my mosquito netting. Not that it did any good. The mosquitoes here weren't like those little Ozark ones off the swamps back home. These were those fat tiger bugs that made you wake up feeling like you just donated blood, except donating blood didn't usually give you malaria. I could feel the bite already. Then I wondered if I'd been dreaming that buzz, because I'd dreamed it before, back home, though never in winter.

Winter here was near dead, the southern monsoon season upon us; wind warming up, gravid with humidity, more rain pouring down like sheets of wet cement with the thunder. I was lucky to have caught maybe two or three hours' sleep at Landing Zone "Cat," our latest jumping-off point for a fresh run of search-and-destroy ops along the Cambodian border. Airmobile had been giving Charlie hell for months, hitting him all over the map: north, south, east, west. We'd been slugging it out everywhere from the Ton Le San River to the "Crow's Foot" of the Kim Son Valley—all across II Corps: Binh Dinh, Kon Tum, and now this latest run out of Pleiku. The gust of momentum off Colonel Moore's "victory" in the Ia Drang had blown us straight into a whirlwind of all-out attrition warfare. We were rapid airlifting entire battalions and artillery batteries deep into one previously denied area after another. At the height of our "winter" campaign, 1st Cav saw almost forty straight days of contact with the enemy. Our whole world seemed set on full automatic. We fought more combat over more days than any American soldier in any prior war in US history—because this was unlike any prior war in US history. We were running so fast, so hard, so often—flying rough-and-ready in our "slicks"—we didn't even have time to code-name the ops. Division would do that in our wake, marking the milestones along our warpath, as McNamara's IBM mainframes tallied those ten-to-one body counts. Matador, Masher, White Wing—the names didn't matter. Not for us. The only names we cared about were those of our fallen, the ones now engraved on that sacred black wall whose silent calls to me ring ever louder as the years pass. It wasn't until much later that we would feel the emotional sting, like that slap to my own face, whirling out of a cloud of darkness to snap us awake. Ambush us. No matter how hot the contact or brief the battle, the violence was always sudden and vicious. And deadly. In war, even a minor scrape could bleed you.

Each battle gave the enemy a better sense of our backbone. Crack regiments of the NVA were testing our mettle. They linked up with local Viet Cong who knew the jungle like I knew the woods back home. Hanoi had sent their toughest to take us on. In every loss, they found victory in their deadly reckoning of our battlefield prowess. They came at us in a tsunami of human waves; banzai-charging our positions to get in as crazy-close as possible, zero-distance combat, if only to make our own artillery and airpower as dangerous to us as it was to them, even if they died doing it. I had learned to respect my enemy because he respected me enough to risk his life to measure mine. The Vietnamese had been fighting foreign occupiers for over three decades. They had taken on the best of the Japanese, the French, and now the big bad Americans—and they had all the woodpecker guns and MAT-49s and even a few Colt .45s and M-16s to prove it. Now they were wielding their precious war trophies against us—along with a rusty-dusty hodgepodge of secondhand Soviet and Chinese-supplied AKs, RPGs, burp guns, and even little knockoff versions of those fearsome Russian rocket batteries with the pretty little name—*katyushas*—that screamed bloody murder so harshly as to scare the bejesus out of the most battle-hardened German troops on the Eastern Front during World War II. They wanted to see what the American soldier could do with our little helicopters and all our glorious war machinery. It was the Chinese "Year of the Horse"—and we were happy to press their luck.

For my actions on Scalping Mustang—pulling that wounded lieutenant off LZ Tonto—the Army had awarded me the Bronze Star, with "V" device, for valor. My first medal. Word had come down from Division: the legendary Major General John Norton, one of the earliest pioneers of heliborne warfare, and the man who would soon be taking over the reins of the entire 1st Cavalry, was gonna come out to personally decorate me, though it would still be another couple of months before the medal ceremony. A long time later, when I was already long retired, someone asked me if I'd ever worried that I might not live long enough to see the day: salute the general, shake hands, get my medal. The thought never occurred to me. We didn't think about it—dying. All we thought about was survival. The truth was we were too busy doing everything we could to keep ourselves and each other alive; with so much contact and combat, we didn't have time to dwell all fancy-free on a chest full of shiny medals—war glory. The risks were far too great to contemplate. I was just lucky to be making it till noon—that's all there was to it—each day, every day. And I intended to keep it that way. Each day, every day. Sure, being decorated was a great honor, but only because of the solemnity of another's sacrifice; even in the safety of retrospect, the pride and pleasure of that moment always dissolved into the sense of despair that would forever pulse through me over the loss of Sergeant Clemmons, the man who fell next to me; gave his own life to save another. Maybe mine, too. I keep that medal in its own shadow box, away from the others; and still to this day, whenever I look at it—and the citation, neatly framed—I don't think about my "actions." I think about Sergeant Clemmons. I think about him jumping out after me from that bullet-riddled chopper to rescue a brother-soldier under intense enemy fire. And I wonder: *Why him?* Why had he been the one to catch those woodpecker slugs and not me? What if the Viet Cong manning that gun had simply flinched a half inch? What if I'd been standing to Sergeant Clemmons's left instead of his right? I'll tell you *what if*: I would have been the one coming home in a flag-draped coffin, my wife the one receiving the next-of-kin notification courtesy of Uncle Sam's Checker Cab company. Those thoughts still send a shudder through me that strikes at my deepest core. But they also strengthened my faith in God. I stayed reading my Bible. And I prayed—*a lot*. I didn't judge my enemy or anyone else—whatever their faith or lack thereof. I just took comfort in my belief that the Lord was there watching over us, forgiving us our many sins, and salving all those wounds that would never heal.

HOMETOWN HERO

Hometown Hero—that's what they were calling me back in Pocahontas. Judith had sent me a press clipping from the local paper. It said that I was one of the most highly decorated to come out of Randolph County (I'd already been put up for a second Bronze Star, this one for meritorious service, in the months since Scalping Mustang), and that the county could take pride in my example as a testament to the latest generation of soldiers fighting in Southeast Asia. *Huh.* Latest generation. A damn fine compliment, yes, maybe, sure—but it also showed just how deep we were into this fight: that this wasn't some one-off quick-hit mission like that Lebanon deal back in '58, or the impending incursion into the Dominican Republic with my old outfit, the 82nd Airborne, or Grenada or Panama later on in the eighties. The press back home were already casting us as the "latest generation" of war-fighter, like all the ones before us. Except this was a whole new era of long-haul warfare—the longest in American history so far (till 9/11 and Afghanistan, that is). And it seemed that the folks back home, for the most part, also understood that we might be here for a while, regardless of what the White House might be telling them—or *not* telling them. Locking us soldiers in for a whole yearlong tour was kind of a dead giveaway—certainly to our wives and children. The clippings were a good morale boost—probably more so back home. A lot of the guys in this outfit had clippings. Especially the old-timers, tough hombres who'd spent their entire adult lives going to hell and back. These were three-war veterans whose hat trick of Combat Infantryman Badges put them in a category with even fewer veterans than had won Congressional Medals of Honor in the same three wars. They didn't need to flash the medals or read their own press—the wear and tear of warfare showed like scar tissue in the blackened lines carved deep into their cold hard faces. You knew just by looking at them, the dark light in their eyes. Their courage hung over them like a welcome burden. These were men with nothing to prove—and yet here they were, ready to go right back at it in whatever hell with whatever enemy Uncle Sam said posed a clear and present danger to the United States of America—even if that danger wasn't so clear and present after all.

We had plenty of guys like that back in Pocahontas—hometown heroes. There was this one I knew growing up, Earl Witcher, biggest one of all, which was saying a lot in a town that had buried so many of its sons as casualties of war—enough to pave a whole walkway in bricks bearing their names. His family lived on the other side of our cotton field. I used to see the man in the flesh from time to time, when he'd come home on leave. Tales of his derring-do colored many of our local conversations: how he—like a few of the other fellas in our outfit—had jumped into Normandy with the 82nd in World War II and fought with the famed 187th Regimental Combat Team in Korea. He was one of the earliest soldiers to earn a green beret—before anyone even knew what that was—and rose to become command sergeant major of the 10th Special Forces Group, the first to deploy to their new overseas base in Bad Tölz, Germany. Out there in the ashen twilight, puffing a cigarette, he would stare off into the distance for hours. And sometimes, he would turn and catch me in his gaze—or, at least, that was how I imagined it back then: this ghost soldier fixing me with that thousand-yard stare in the fading light.

With the clippings had come another photo from Judith. I looked at it all the time: the little patch of black-and-white that held my wife and children, Judith listing slightly doing her best to balance Felicia in a bundle on her hip, four-year-old Tammy clinging to her leg—both getting so big. I looked at it now. The more I stared at them, the more distant they seemed in that monochrome haze. I wished time would freeze just long enough for me to make it back home and find them standing there like that, waiting for me. I wished I could dive into that picture right then, be there with them, bleed color into it from the love in my heart—fill the space that felt so empty without them. I could only drift for so long before forcing myself to snap back into the moment—get my mind right for the dangerous and violent job ahead, if only so I could get back to them alive.

My battalion, the 1st of the 8th, had conducted the very first night air assault of the Vietnam War, taking Landing Zone "Cat," one of several forward LZs we were using as we swept the thick jungle terrain west of Pleiku. We'd spent most of March hopscotching between LZs, mostly within the vicinity of Plei Me and the Ia Drang, where the first decisive battles of the war had gone down back in October and November; running reconnaissance-in-force missions as we sought to cut off Charlie's infiltration routes out of Cambodia—no-man's-land for us—smoke out any of his basecamps in the towering, knife-edged peaks of the Chu Pong Massif; though all we'd been hitting this last little while was a bunch of dry holes, with maybe quick bursts of contact at best. The deeper we penetrated, the more we realized the enemy had not only gone to ground but hightailed it most *ricky-tick* back across that border—their sanctuary: a secure flank and rear all rolled into one, where, no matter how much we hurt them on contact, they could rest, resupply, recuperate, refit, rearm, and come right back at us fresh, locked and fully loaded. We'd even found telephone lines trailing all the way back into Cambodia—talk about reaching out and touching someone. Apart from a few NVA and the usual VC stay-behind elements, Charlie was gone—ghosting us. We knew where the hell he was; we just couldn't go after him, thanks to the White House wanting to fight this thing according to a rule-book that seemed written in invisible ink—made up as they went along—all in favor of some grander political scheme that ruled out a basic military one.

After all the combat of the previous months, things had pretty much ratch-eted down, settled into a lull—at least for the time being. Some of the guys felt like maybe we had 'em on the run—the same wishful thinking as in Washington. Or at least they told themselves that, knowing better, because most of us cer-tainly did: *know better*. Something dark brewing in the air. You could smell it, feel it: burning in and out—like a faulty electrical wire—beneath the humidity.

The less contact we had with our enemy, the calmer our LZ; but the "Cat" command post was abuzz with activity: message-traffic and intercepts coming in nonstop across the various comms nets as we coordinated with Brigade HQ and Division, sizing up the latest intel on our enemy's whereabouts. As an opera-tions sergeant, it was my job to help the brass draw up assault plans that would give us our best shot at busting Charlie right in the chops, which was more like a game of pin the tail on the donkey meets blind man's bluff. Given the green light, we'd have gladly punched right into Cambodia and chased him all the way up the Ho Chi Minh Trail. Get the job done, go home. *Search and Destroy from Saigon to Hanoi!* How 'bout that for a bumper sticker? I was working over a map when one of the younger guys, a specialist, approached me with a slip of paper in his hand. "Message for you, Sergeant—just came in across the battalion net. Someone flying in to meet you, sir. A major."

This perked up some of the ears around the map-table. Most everyone had heard about the whole big deal with General Norton coming to personally deco-rate me with my first Bronze Star. Now, I had some major flying in. It wasn't every day that a senior officer flew in to meet with an enlisted guy. I could just hear the others razzing me about it later over beers: *Jesse's got all the boocoo brass coming in—when's Westie gonna call you up, put LBJ on the line?*

(Yeah, right.)

The young specialist handed me the slip with a curious look.

I hit him back with my best hard-ass glare—the kind that I'd learned from the Black Hats who taught me how to jump out of airplanes with the 82nd at Bragg—and told him to carry on.

He split on the double.

So did I. That slick was due any minute.

I waited on the helipad as it came down, just that major in the pilot's seat, no one else. He was flying solo. I watched him the same way I watched him all those years ago. From a distance. With measured awe. Through a rotor-whipped haze of dust and sunshine. As he stepped off the bird, replacing his helmet with the black Stetson "Cav Hat" popular among the "Troopers" of the 1st Cavalry Division. This mythic legend and hometown hero. The original ghost soldier. Earl Witcher. *Major* Earl Witcher, considering he'd made officer since his days wearing the green beret—now earning his three-war veteran hat trick flying choppers in Vietnam. *Man.*

We saluted, sharply, and shook hands. Then Earl broke out a wide grin, and slapped a big hand on my shoulder, and said: "Come on, Sergeant, let's go find us a place to sit a minute."

It had been over a decade since I'd seen him—my childhood inspiration—but he was the one who seemed more surprised to see me: little "Loftis" Johnson, that quiet kid who used to spy on him across the cotton field, now all grown up into a gung-ho NCO. And here we both were, a couple of good ol' country boys from the same rural badlands, who wanted nothing more than to serve our nation and defend freedom, holding a hometown reunion in a war zone halfway around the world. It was our mothers who'd set the whole thing up—through a flurry of letter writing that could have taught HQ a thing or two about effective written communications and logistics—arranging a little in-country get-together between their two boys. Kinda like a childhood play date, but with grown men and real guns. There was no *playing* army out here.

We found a fallen tree that made for a good bench under a rare patch of shade. We didn't talk much about the war—mostly about home. It was like we were sitting there all over again, on a back porch somewhere—staring at the darker, denser, dewier, pine-smelling Ozark-mountain woodland, the few times the Johnsons and the Witchers got together, me sitting on one end, him on the other, both of us quiet, our two families between us. He talked about his career a bit and gave me some advice, about the Service, navigating the politics, nothing really about combat. Nothing he might have told me maybe ten years ago, back home, before I ever went in—but then I'd already been blooded, with two Bronze Stars and a Purple Heart to show for it, and Major Earl Witcher knew that well enough; though I doubt he knew it was partly due to his own example, his dedication to duty. Maybe. Every now and then he'd stop and set that gaze—that thousand-yard stare—along the tree line, and shake his head, grinning, and he'd say, in his low cowboy drawl, two or three times maybe:

"Boy, that's something—little Loftis Johnson, all the way over here, a real-deal United States soldier. . . ."

There were moments, bursts of pondering, when my head would spin in a tornado of strange disbelief: the two of us meeting in the middle of a jungle ten thousand light-years from home—along the Cambodian border no less—near places whose names we probably would have never known if it hadn't been for the war.

Then, still looking around, he said, "We're sure a long way from Pocahontas, huh?"

When it was time for him to go, I walked him back to the helipad. The LZ was pretty flat and wide open, blown out by artillery and explosives during our initial insert. You could still catch glints of brass where we'd fired our M-16s into the tree line, pouring out of the Hueys. I wondered if some of that lead had ended up in Cambodia. When we reached his Huey, the ghost soldier glanced back at me one last time, eyes still gleaming with surprise; and he nodded once, just slightly so. Then he climbed back aboard the chopper, flipping off his Cav Hat to replace it with his helmet.

It would be over twenty years before I had the honor of speaking to Major Earl Witcher again, but he would be even more surprised when I called him long past this war and shortly before another to invite him to the 35th anniversary of the 10th Special Forces Group. Why the hell would I be calling him about that? he wondered, aware only of his own connection to it. "Because I am currently the commanding officer," I told him. He couldn't believe it—of 10th Group? "Yes, sir, I'm a full-bird colonel now. . . ." I think it was then I heard the phone drop.

Now, I saluted as the slick's rotors wound up with a soft howl. Major Witcher saluted back, sharply again, aviator shades glinting off that serpent-tongued sun. I ducked low and ran off the pad before those blades whirled up that cyclone-force wind that could whip the surrounding earth into a devil-cursed frenzy, thudding the air. Then the chopper took off fast—and the world was so far away again.

5

CRAZY HORSE

The Vinh Thanh Valley
Near "the Oregon Trail"
Binh Dinh Province
South Vietnam
May 27, 1966

The round that cracked past my ear was from a Mosin-Nagant 91/30 bolt-action rifle—most likely with the original mass-produced PU scope still attached to it—the preferred weapon of Soviet snipers on the Eastern Front during World War II. The Sovs had produced about twenty million of them during the war, so they had plenty more where that came from beyond the several cargo vessels' worth that they had already delivered to the North Vietnamese. A gift of solidarity from Uncle Ho's old Communist comrades in the Kremlin. The Mosin's soft-nosed 7.62-mm round issued a distinctive report: more like a whiz and a whap as it struck home, kicking up a cloud of dirt from a mound near my foxhole. Relying on Soviet military doctrine of the same period as the rifle had made Charlie a good sniper; if the mound had been a man, he'd be dead from a chest wound by now. Unusual that this one missed. (Must be a new guy, or maybe scattering us to prepare the way for something bigger.) The bullet fragmented and ricocheted off a tree behind me. That could have been a twofer. The Mosin was effective well beyond the range of our M-16s.

I shouted: "Get down!"

The others hit the dirt, diving into their foxholes.

Those NVA snipers had been raining lead on us all week. This was the other side of Happy Valley, our battalion command post tucked in between a pair of shiny, black dagger-sharp peaks that rose majestically over a deep sliver of a gorge, where the enemy held the high ground. The Mosin issued one more *whip-snap-bang* from the dense, verdant foliage high in the tree line. The round landed nearby again. Closer, this time. The sniper was starting to catch a bead on us, zeroing that stubby little PU scope. I heard a voice of prayer from the foxhole next to mine. I called over: "You OK?" The foxhole belonged to Private First Class Artis Jones out of Chicago. With him was the voice of prayer: Captain Ralph Spear, our battalion chaplain. Over the chaplain's loud, steady-calm incantations, Jones waved back at me, singing: "Amen! Amen!"

(One thing you learn right away in war: there is no such thing as an atheist in a foxhole.)

The Jumping Mustangs were on the homestretch—short-timing it through one long brutally hot summer of warfare. Our last tango with Charlie before the end of our tour, at least those of us who had arrived with the first wave of 1st Cav way back in September. I was an assistant operations sergeant; but by mid-summer, I'd be training up the new guys—our replacements—teaching them how to hunt, stay frosty and survive in the jungle. Over the last several months, my battalion, the 1/8, had earned quite a badass battlefield reputation for itself—not only within the Division, but also among the enemy. We left "death cards" on the bodies of our fallen adversaries, to let Charlie know who'd done the killing. (Yes, something we've all seen in the movies, but we did it first—in real life.) In response, the VC put prices on the heads of two of our battalion's company commanders. Almost a mark of respect.

Search-and-destroy was still the order of the day—the entire war, for that matter. In the tumultuous wake of our winter campaign, Charlie had kept up his favorite "now-you-see-me, now-you-don't" vanishing act: fleeing the valleys, scattering into the jungle, jumping back and forth across the Cambodian border. He'd also proven a quick study, readily adapting to the 1st Cav's new style of airmobile warfare, finding the weakest points to our greatest strength: our ability to instantly leapfrog into his rear at a moment's notice. NVA and VC forces were learning to stick to areas of dense foliage and high, rugged peaks to limit how close in we could get with our slicks, allowing them to pinpoint where we might insert our troops so they could already be there, awaiting our arrival, lying in ambush. With Ho Chi Minh's birthday rolling up, everyone from Westie on down to the freshest-face buck private knew Hanoi would be planning to light off a lot more than just a few bottle rockets to celebrate. Charlie loved a festive firefight.

Once again, a US Special Forces/Montagnard base camp had fallen under threat. The North Vietnamese were sticking to much the same doctrine on which they had cut their teeth against the French as the Viet Minh, and us last October—the Plei Me playbook: harass small remote outposts using diversionary tactics to draw in and trap larger forces, then unleash hell from the jungle. We caught intel early on that our enemies were gearing up to launch a massive offensive in the Vinh Thanh, to include simultaneous raids on the Golf Course, the An Khe Pass, Highway 19, and Happy Valley Road. The base camp was just the match that Charlie was gonna use to light the fuse on the whole damn powder keg. Initial estimates from the Green Berets themselves put the Viet Cong force at platoon strength. That soon turned into a battalion, then two battalions, and before we could blink twice, the entire 2nd Viet Cong Regiment—hard-core guerrillas who'd been rolled into the NVA command structure under the crack 3rd "Yellow Star" Division. They were well trained, disciplined, tough, dedicated. The man who would soon decorate me with my first Bronze Star, General John Norton, had decided to send in units from various 1st Cav regiments—including the 8th—to hunt down and wipe out the VC before they could attack the camp in force, or set up to ambush us as we arrived in relief. On our side, in the thick of it, were several foreign forces, including the local Montagnard tribesmen at the Special Forces camp; several ARVN, or South Vietnamese units; and, of course, the tough South Korean "Rock Tiger" Division: a cruel ruthless bunch whose commander had a real hard-on for kill counts, even bigger than McNamara, but more out of bloodlust than bean counting. By the numbers.

The fighting was fierce, especially for 1st Cav—zero-distance with the enemy, most of the engagements denied air cover due to inclement weather, and beyond the range of our tube artillery. You better believe Charlie knew that, too. Before he sucked us in. This was brutal, on-the-ground, classic infantry combat under the cloak of a modern insurgency, the repeat-cycle warfare to which we'd all grown accustomed—ferocious uphill battles in jungle so thick it seemed almost alive with the enemy, a front full of heroes holding lines that no one could really draw on a map. I was honored to have served alongside so many of them during that campaign, not only witnessing but also drawing inspiration from their actions. Men like Captain Roy Martin, commander of Company B of the 1/8, who'd been a sergeant first class with the 187th Regimental Combat Team in Korea before becoming an officer and one of the finest company commanders I ever came across. Leading from the front during the heaviest fighting, Captain Martin was his usual cool self under fire, as he put his life in harm's way several times to protect the men under him, personally taking out three dug-in-deep enemy bunkers and a trio of snipers who had him triangulated between their fields of fire, actions that earned him the Distinguished Service Cross. Another of those heroes was young Specialist David Dolby, who, on that same night, May 21, took charge in place of his badly wounded platoon leader and repeatedly put himself in the direct line of fire to pull wounded off the battlefield, destroy several machine-gun nests, and call in air strikes and artillery that saved the lives of the rest of his platoon and inflicted heavy casualties on the enemy. For his daring four-hour display of selfless courage that night, standing as an inspiration to us all, Specialist Dolby earned the Congressional Medal of Honor. (And just to show you how tight the ties that bound the brotherhood remained in the decades following Vietnam: Dolby's squad leader that night was a young sergeant by the name of Lonzo Peoples, a good buddy of mine, who almost twenty years later would serve as my command sergeant major when I finally returned to my original outfit, the 82nd Airborne, as a battalion commander.) Dolby would go on to serve four more tours in Vietnam, and thereafter retire as a staff sergeant. About three days after the same engagement, Captain Roy Martin was flying a reconnaissance mission over the battlefield when his Huey came under heavy fire and Martin was hit in the leg. Back at base, I helped lift him off the chopper, his left thigh all tore up with a large gaping hole drenched in blood. Looked like fifty-cal. Makes an ugly mess. Fortunately for Roy, the round caught the meatier portion of the leg. He was close to going into shock when we took him off the aircraft. After months in the hospital, he was able to return to limited duty, but the limp in his step would stay with him for the rest of his life. He never once complained.

1/8 Battalion Command Post
Vinh Thanh Valley
May 27th

I could hear our battalion chaplain still in prayer.

Another round smacked my position.

Despite the chaplain's faithful supplication to the good Lord above, someone had already caught a bullet. He'd make it, but the next guy might not be so lucky. One minute, you're talking to your buddy about Willie Mays hitting his 512th record-breaking homerun, the next, that same buddy suddenly drops flat off a gunshot. Just goes down. In a spray of blood. Or an explosion that makes him disappear—blows him into body parts. Gruesome. The stuff you learn to put behind you in the blink of an eye; but then it comes back to bite you one year, two years, twenty years later, catches your gaze as you hit that horizon with your own thousand-yard stare—sunrise, sunset, dusk, dawn. The dead of night. They call the pauses between our wars—each one after the other—"peacetime." For those who've witnessed the horrors of battle, there is no such thing.

Spying the wood line over the lip of my foxhole, I kept my eyes peeled for any sign of enemy movement, waiting to hear the shrill blast of whistles blowing and bugles blaring—waiting for the sky to rain mortar shells and the jungle to spit tracer rounds over shouts of *"Tiến lên!"* ("Forward!"), Charlie's favorite battle cry whenever he tried to overrun us.

This latest wave of attrition warfare would last through June; both sides trying to out maneuver, out ambush, out snipe each other to run up the scoreboard on the kill count. We didn't even know what this operation was called. I'd only learn the name later in a letter from Judith: *Crazy Horse*—in honor of the legendary Lakota warrior who'd famously fought the cavalry in the Great Sioux War of 1876—as Walter Cronkite had recently informed her on the CBS evening news, right before *The Joey Bishop Show.*

By the time Crazy Horse was all said and done, we'd end up taking down an estimated five hundred enemy KIA—*estimated*—in return for the eighty-three more young Americans whose names we'd all too soon be chiseling into that oblique black wall in our nation's capital. But that was plenty enough to satisfy the Pentagon's bean-counting kill-ratio minimum quota—for whatever algorithm the armchair brass and their Beltway bosses were pencil pushing through their death ledgers that week. (By the numbers.) Plenty enough on the flip side to satisfy General Võ Nguyên Giáp, the commander in chief of the North Vietnamese forces. Giáp was well versed in the kill-ratio calculus, having used it against the French to bleed them to death by a thousand cuts and send them packing back to Paris two years shy of a decade-long war that ended much like ours: with too many casualties abroad and too much political turmoil back home. It was the same MO they'd run when they were the Viet Minh—except now they had a better-equipped, better-trained, better-led national army in the NVA; and a full-fledged, hard-core, dedicated, battle-hardened insurgent force in the Viet Cong. We wanted to go right for the jugular, slice Charlie's throat open with a slew of decisive victories—and the mother lode of B-52 strikes to help get the job done—but Giáp knew better than to show us his jugular. As soon as we started maxing out that kill count, Charlie went to ground, vanished into thin air. Poof. And when our search-and-destroy and their hit-and-run blended yet again into one big game of cat and mouse, we tried to adapt by encircling the valley and putting the same chokehold on them that they'd been trying to put on us. By then, it was too late. We had their main infiltration route covered, what we called "the Oregon Trail," a ten-mile stretch cutting like a hellish slice of heaven between the two valleys—the Suoi Ca and the Vinh Thanh—but we knew there were others. All over the map. We just didn't know where exactly.

"*Incoming!*"

Not the sniper. The artillery I had just called in—155-mm howitzer—to take out the sniper.

Prayer could only do so much.

But our prayers were answered, as heads bowed low in our foxholes, those shells whistled right over us, thumping down danger-close enough to rattle my rib cage as they pounded our own tree line—where our enemy held shadowy refuge—but thank God not us.

On the final night of the operation, as we broke camp to return to An Khe, the Rock Tigers went out hunting one last time. Their commander was furious: he'd wanted at least five hundred enemy KIA—to match us, the Americans. The Tigers were only at 495. The next morning, as I made my way to the helipad to catch the last chopper home, I saw the bodies lined up in a neat row outside his tent: five bullet-riddled corpses, dead Viet Cong, baking under the hot sun, flies buzzing around their bugged-out eyeballs.

I shot a look at the sergeant next to me.

Then I spit a wad of dip and said: "Guess we all made our quotas."

II

SOLDIER-CHARLIE-SIX

6

FALSE FLAG

GUNFIGHTER-FIVE: *Soldier-Charlie-Six, Gunfighter-Five, what's your status?*
SOLDIER-CHARLIE-SIX: *Gunfighter-Five, Charlie-Six, we just took two KIAs.*
GUNFIGHTER-FIVE: (Inaudible . . . static)
SOLDIER-CHARLIE-SIX: *Say again, Gunfighter-Five, you're breaking up. . . .*
GUNFIGHTER-FIVE: *Charlie-Six, you said two KIAs?*
SOLDIER-CHARLIE-SIX: *Affirmative, two KIAs. Looks like a grenade-in-the-can type-deal, sir. Keepsake trap. We need a Dust Off, ASAP.*
GUNFIGHTER-FIVE: *OK, roger that. Gunfighter-Five out.*

Charlie Co., 2/39th
9th Infantry Division
Near Fire Base Moore—III Corps
Long An Province
South Vietnam
May 18, 1968

"Yo, check out this flag!"

The young soldier who spotted the souvenir was a private, barely eighteen, new guy, fresh from the world—a "cherry." The flag that had caught his attention like a shiny rock belonged to the National Liberation Front, the Viet Cong, and had been left draped on prominent display across the front of a nipa palm bush at the far edge of the ghost-town village. Made for a good war trophy. Or something else.

I was a new guy, too, though not as new as the young private.

I looked over and saw him already reaching for the thing.

Another man standing much closer—a PFC six months in-country, half his tour done—saw him, too. He shouted a warning at the new guy, the cherry, and ran to him, but it was too late. The young private tugged down the flag, triggering the tripwire underneath, and the two hand grenades attached to it. The explosion rocked the earth under our feet and killed both men in a blinding flash of light.

⊫══⊐

Mainz, Germany
1961
Day "0"

I first met then-Captain Tony Herbert when I arrived at Lee Barracks to report in for my new assignment to the 505th Airborne Infantry Regiment. Herbert was the commanding officer. A hero of the Korean War, he'd earned four Silver Stars and been wounded several times in action, including three by bayonet, then toured the United States promoting the war effort with Eleanor Roosevelt, who told the young master-sergeant to go get himself the college education that would help him earn a commission as an officer. He would go on to write several books and later grow into somewhat of a controversial figure as Vietnam kicked into overdrive and he blew the whistle on a slew of alleged war crimes. Among all the heroes and legends that I had the honor of serving under or alongside and learning from, throughout my career, it was Herbert's heroic example of leading from the front—both in combat and command—that would inspire me more than any other person and most influence shaping the soldier I would become on the battlefield, and without a doubt ensure my survival.

This was clear right out of the starting gate, as I was handing my packet over to the personnel sergeant that hot August day, and Herbert stepped up out of nowhere to swipe it from the man's hand. He looked at the folder, giving my service record a cursory once-over, then looked at me, the hard workingman's glare of a Pennsylvania coal miner's son imprinted on his face, and he said, "All right, go down to B Company, get your shirt off, and get ready to run."

To the Teufelsstein, "the Devil's Rock," in the majestic Haardt Mountains near our base, the Alpine air crisp and the hot sun beating down on us as we went full blast up the steep rugged trails singing airborne cadences. Herbert out in front, singing the loudest. Then the route flattened out, and in a moment the foliage began to thicken into a dense tangle of jungle vegetation, bamboo shoots sprouting from the earth before my eyes; the oak, beech and pine woodland mutating into the mighty teaks of the Central Highlands, their sad flaccid leaves dripping leeches like black tears over our shirtless bodies. No one seemed to notice, except me, as we kept running. In a moment, the jungle parted like a curtain, spilling our column into a burned-out field of elephant grass that stank of av gas. A sign, in French, warned us of land mines. At the end of the field was the flaming wreckage of an airplane, an Air Force C-123, like the one that would crash out of An Khe. No one stopped. We picked up the pace, singing our airborne cadence, running through the minefield, and then I saw Herbert spin around in a sudden about-face and sprint back toward me yelling "No, wait, look out!" as the Viet Cong appeared in the tree line and I felt my foot hit the small piece of metal that I looked down to see sticking out of the earth, and I heard the brassy ping of the crude firing mechanism, like a Garand rifle ejecting a spent clip, and I knew that I'd just stepped on one of Charlie's mosquito mines. Then the explosion came, and I snapped awake.

Fort Jackson
South Carolina
1968

Waking with a start from a nightmare was not an ideal way to kick off the morning, but it had become a somewhat routine part of my life over the last year or so since returning from the war. Most of the time I couldn't even remember what I had dreamed, just that it was bad. Other than my military duties, my adjustment to life back home had proven much harder than I had imagined. Picking up where I left off with Judith and little Tammy, meeting Felicia for the first time at eight months old, left me feeling overjoyed but also a bit overwhelmed, out of sync: trying to get used to the idea of being surrounded by loved ones, not enemies. Trying to get the jungle out of my head. Mornings were their own kind of minefield. At breakfast, Judith would always make sure to keep the kids hushed up from horsing around too much because loud noises could make me jumpy. No matter how much I distracted myself, the nightmares always put the war back on my mind. Front and center. Echoing in the hollow quiet of the unspoken.

I threw myself into my work. When I first got back, Judith had driven all the way to Memphis to pick me up at the airport. It was the first time I met Felicia, cradled her in my arms, saw her in the full-color flesh that had always been lost in the bottomless distance of all those hazy Kodak portraits that were all I had till now. We spent an enjoyable leave in Arkansas, visiting family, relaxing, then went on to my next posting at Fort Benning, where I was assigned to the Airborne School, arranging to ship all our newly minted paratroopers off to their next assignments. Some of my commanders had been encouraging me to apply for Officer Candidate School (OCS). I had thought about it—my brother Daily O had become an officer through the OCS route—but most OCS graduates had college degrees, and I had only gone to high school. Shortly after I arrived at Benning, I bumped into an old friend of mine, Joe Corino, who had just reported in for duty after earning a "direct commission" as a second lieutenant. Joe and I had served together twice in the 101st and had bumped into each other several times in Vietnam. He told me that a couple of our other NCO pals, Bob Jones and Maxie Myers, had also become officers via the direct commission route. Joe thought that with my war record—two Bronze Stars, a Purple Heart, my rank, my reputation—I'd be a shoo-in for one myself, which would allow me to bypass OCS. I reached out to both my former commanders in Vietnam and my current ones at Benning. All of them to the man encouraged me to go for it and issued sterling letters of recommendation in support of my application. About four months later, I was enjoying a rare day off when I received an urgent phone call from headquarters telling me to get my ass back to my company pronto. Apparently, I had shipped some recent Airborne graduates to the wrong place. As I drove back, I was mortified, racking my brain trying to figure out how I could have possibly screwed the pooch so badly. I went in to see the First Sergeant, who, without another word, escorted me straight in to see the company commander, Captain Jim Tate, both men wearing the kind of tight faces that said I had really messed up. "Now you want to tell me how the hell we're supposed to sort out this total clusterfuck with these troops being sent to the wrong place, Sergeant?" Captain Tate snapped.

Standing at attention before his desk, I started to respond, but before I could even get a word in edgewise or otherwise, he cut me off.

"Or should I say 'Lieutenant?'"

"Sir?"

"*First* Lieutenant, actually. . . ."

Now, I was really confused. "Excuse me, sir?"

Both men broke into a fit of laughter, and as I was still trying to wrap my head around what the hell was going on, Tate came out from behind his desk to shake my hand. "Congratulations, Lieutenant Johnson, your direct commission has been approved. You even skipped a grade. You're an officer now. Just don't go off getting any big ideas about becoming too much of a gentleman—this is the Army, after all. . . ."

Yes, sir.

On June 23, 1967, I received the oath of commission as a First Lieutenant of the United States Army. No more Mr. Gung-Ho NCO. After completing the Infantry Officers Basic Course, I transferred to my next assignment at Fort Jackson, South Carolina. In-processing was a bit of a headache, kinda like being stuck in a traffic jam, or in this case tied up in red tape: Army civil servants are a breed unto themselves, and woe betide any soldier who disrupts their fragile bureaucratic ecosystem. That I had received a direct commission, something half the civil servants had no idea even existed, was confusing enough. Skipping grades in school seemed a lot easier than skipping them in the military. My automatic bump to first lieutenant made me exotic, which required a whole separate pile of paperwork. (I think they had to access some old musty vault deep inside the Pentagon to find the correct forms, or at least that's how they acted.) But I got through it all right, and even got to request my own assignment. I chose 3rd Brigade, knowing that it was the training brigade for troops going to Vietnam. While reviewing my records, the personnel officer, Captain Elizabeth Schriebner, noted that I had served in the 1st Cavalry Division, then pointed out that Jackson's own deputy post commander had also served with 1st Cav—Brigadier General Elvy Roberts.

"Yes ma'am," I replied. "He was my brigade commander."

She asked if I knew him, and I told her that I had met him several times while in-country. She closed my file and said that she would confirm my assignment once she had discussed the matter with the general. I thought that was odd, but who was I to question the wisdom of a captain?

In the meantime, I got my family settled into the base's officer housing, in our case an old hospital that had been converted into spacious apartment units that provided more than enough room and all the necessary amenities—much cheaper than renting or purchasing off base. Convenient, too. Within a few days, I received a call summoning me to General Roberts's office. Anxious about the meeting, I reported to his aide-de-camp a few minutes early. The aide-de-camp ordered me to take a seat, but before I could, General Roberts emerged from his office and ushered me inside. We spoke about our time in-country, reminiscing about various senior NCOs and officers that we both knew who had also served under his command, and Christmas at Bien Ho Lake. Then out of the clear blue sky, he asked: "How would you like to be my aide-de-camp?"

Despite my initial shock, I answered without hesitation: "Yes, sir."

Then he asked: "Why?"

"Well," I replied, "I've just been commissioned, and I believe the best place to learn how to be an effective officer would be right here from you."

That seemed to be the right answer.

"OK," General Roberts said, "we'll try that then."

He rose from his seat, indicating that the interview was over, then called his current aide-de-camp into the room and unceremoniously announced that I would be replacing him.

The young captain was a little taken aback. "Yes sir," he responded, slipping me a bit of the stink eye. "But I would like to request two weeks to break him in."

Roberts said, "You got the rest of the afternoon. He starts tomorrow."

And that was that.

Roberts did indeed turn out to be the perfect mentor for a young officer. He held the distinction of having graduated from West Point with the famous class of January 1943, when the Army decided to commission the top half of the class six months early to get them deployed and bolster the war effort—a lot of heroes in that group. Roberts was one of the original Bastogne Bulldogs; and after the war his fellow Bulldog, General Kinnard, had personally selected him to help innovate the airmobile concept that would form the core nucleus of the revamped 1st Cavalry Division. I was honored to serve as his aide-de-camp for about nine or ten months, before he called me into his office to show me a letter from Major General Julian Ewell, another Bulldog who'd earned the Distinguished Service Cross at Bastogne and had just received orders from General Westmoreland to take command of the 9th Infantry Division in Vietnam. Ewell wanted Roberts as his Assistant Division Commander. General Roberts looked up at me and asked, "You want to go along?"

Right away, staring straight ahead at ease, I answered, "Sign me up, sir."

What the hell—why not? The Army had already told me I was gonna have to go back again anyway. But that wasn't the reason. It was Vietnam. Something about that unreconciled hell that I couldn't quite get my head around. Unfinished business of an unknown origin. Whatever the case, it was my duty. As long as Americans were fighting in a war, shedding blood, sacrificing for our country, I had to be there with them. I wanted to go back.

Judith didn't get a vote. Once again, she would be left home for a whole year not knowing if her husband and the father of her two small children would ever return. Her battle—*her* second tour—would be the next twelve months spending every day pretending not to worry that *this* was the day that some stranger in a uniform would turn up on her doorstep to deliver a next-of-kin notification of my death. The sacrifice of our loved ones in warfare is perhaps as great if not greater than that of the soldiers themselves. We risk death. They risk the aftermath. In that way, they become soldiers, too, fighting on a different front. Judith hated talking about Vietnam, and she sure as hell didn't want to talk about me going back. I remember this one time, shortly before I deployed again, we were at the doctor or dentist for one of the kids, and I sat in the waiting room, where of course the coffee table was stacked with old magazines, including several backdated issues of *Fortune*, which had done a cover story on the Jumping Mustangs back when I was still in-country on my first tour. I searched through the stack, all well thumbed, and sure enough, what do you know, there it was, stuck flat at the bottom, all worse for wear with one of the staples missing and the cover half falling off: the May 1966 issue, a photo of then-Colonel Roberts and the 8th Cav command staff on the cover. I remember hearing about it at the time. When Judith came out, I wanted to show her, but then thought better of it and tossed the issue back down on the table.

South Vietnam
May 1968

I arrived back in Saigon on the heels of the Tet Offensive. On final approach into Tan San Nhut Air Base, the feeling finally struck me—more than just a conscious thought, something deep down, like a tripwire mine in my gut—that I was back in-country, back to war, after less than two years away from it. I guess it hadn't really dawned on me until the pilot came over the cabin PA to announce our landing. I had been sharing a row with two young lieutenants, first-tour guys, and when they saw the look on my face, one of them said: "Damn, if just the landing announcement turns you pale as a ghost, it must be rough down there."

A lot had changed, other than the stifling humidity and the sickly sweet half-ripe/half-rotten odor in the air. The hustle bustle of Saigon—pedicabs, taxis, the insectile buzz of Vespas, the olive-drab jungle fatigues of hundreds of US servicemen, sprinkled among a sea of locals in their traditional *áo dài* tunics and trousers with straw hats—seemed to vibrate with the edgy, smoke-hazed angst of a city that knew it was on the verge of collapse, whether tomorrow or in ten years. Tet had been a military victory for the United States, but an even greater political one for the North Vietnamese. When I arrived on my first tour, 80 percent of the American people supported the war. By the time I came back for round two, with almost a half million more troops in-country, only

50 percent did. Even Walter Cronkite had lost hope, going on air live in front of a television audience of millions to declare the war a "stalemate" and urge peace negotiations as the only solution. As President Johnson said, "If we've lost Walter, we've lost Middle America."

I arrived at 9th Infantry Division headquarters with a service record marked "second tour volunteer." (I never understood why the Army made that distinction—other than to sort out the sane from the insane.) General Roberts had arrived a few days earlier and was already hard at work. He offered me a job in G-3, the Operations Section, a cushy gig that would have kept me at a desk at Division HQ.

"No, thank you, sir," I told him. "I want to command a rifle company."

Desk job? Forget it.

Plenty of people to push pencils.

I went over to the division personnel officer, a major, for my assignment. He wanted to send me to the in-country training program run out of the 9th Infantry's so-called Old Reliable Academy in Saigon for "orientation."

I said, "You really think I need that shit, sir?"

He looked up at me with a *well-pardon-the-hell-out-of-me* kind of look on his face, and replied: "OK, hero, you want to go straight into the suck? You got it. I'm going to send you to 2nd Battalion. In the Plain of Reeds. They've been pinned down plenty out there lately. In fact, just yesterday they lost a company commander. You'll get all the action you can handle and then some—guaranteed."

GUNFIGHTER-FIVE: *Soldier-Charlie-Six, Gunfighter-Five, how copy, over?*
SOLDIER-CHARLIE-SIX: *Gunfighter-Five, comms are good, go ahead. . . .*
GUNFIGHTER-FIVE: *Charlie-Six, dust off en route. Be advised, Big Papa-Two is on board. . . .*

Near Fire Base Moore
May 18th

Well, shit.
   Big Papa-Two . . .
   Knowlton.
   That was his call sign.

Brigadier General William Knowlton, another World War II vet, who'd earned a Silver Star leading a small reconnaissance unit behind German lines to hook up with the Russians, east of the Elbe—going so far as to occupy, with that same small unit, a pretty good-sized city in Czechoslovakia, after securing the surrender of several numerically superior and hostile SS units in the area. When headquarters radioed to inform him that he'd stabbed too deep behind enemy lines, taking territory reserved for the Sovs, Knowlton responded: "You want me to give it back?" He would go on to earn two more Silver Stars in combat, this time in Vietnam, under fire, despite his general's rank—another hero leading from the front—and then return to the United States to take over as superintendent of West Point, where he would become father-in-law to one of its star pupils, a brilliant cadet to whom Knowlton always referred as "Young David," who himself would go on to serve under me during his first assignment at the 509th Airborne Combat Team in Vicenza, Italy. But that was a ways off yet.

Now Knowlton, Big Papa-Two, an assistant division commander of "the Old Reliables," the 9th Infantry Division, was flying out to see firsthand what had happened with this flag trap. I had only been on the job for two days as a rifle company commander when that young private decided to grab the war trophy that killed him, along with the brave soldier who got caught in the blast trying to warn him off. A keepsake trap. Rigged to a grenade-in-a-can. Two actually. Coiled up like a couple of rattlesnakes under a nipa palm bush, pins pulled in advance, striker levers primed inside their cans; until that poor kid started playing capture the flag, and tripped the wire, which yanked both grenades out into the open at the same time, the spoons flying off, and *boom*—double blast.

I got back on the radio: "Affirmative, Gunfighter-Five, Big Papa-Two on board. I can hear the rotor blades. . . ."

(From the moment it took off—we were that close to home, just outside the perimeter.)

"Charlie-Six out," I told the handset, then handed it off to my RTO, the one carrying the battalion net radio, as I looked back across the ghost village, toward the blast site, and shouted, "Hey, get your asses back out of there before you get them blown off." A couple of the guys had strayed too far within the blast radius. I knew that the VC had a nasty habit of rigging secondary tripwires and the like to kill any first responders lured in by the initial blast. (Al-Qaeda and ISIS were hardly the first to run that MO.) I just wished I had been dialed in better with my men to prevent that initial blast in the first place. Pushing pencils? I'd be the one pushing pencils now, already writing a pair of letters less than a week into my tour to notify the next of kin of the loss of their loved ones, trying to find the right words, and then realizing there were no right words.

Knowlton's dust-off flew in fast. As the slick hovered inches above the deck and he hopped off, I ducked under its rotor wash to greet him, get him up to speed. I was pretty shaken up, losing two fine young American soldiers so early in my command—especially like this, over a damn war trophy. With the scene cleared of any secondary booby traps, Knowlton took me aside. Right away, he told me to prepare myself—this was just the beginning. I would suffer more casualties. "You've been here before. You know how violent this place is—how dangerous. All you can do is stand up and keep marching on," he said. "Lead by example. Show the new guys the ropes."

(*Don't go picking up any souvenirs.*)

And accept one very cold hard fact: "There will be more letters."

7

THE RIGHTEOUS SIDE

The Chiêu Hồi Program was a massive Psychological Operations (PSYOPS) campaign to promote defections among the Viet Cong. The term Chiêu Hồi, roughly translated, means "Open Arms." Those VC who defected were known as "Hồi Chánh"—from the phrase "Hồi Chánh Viên," or "members who have returned to the righteous side."

The Plain of Reeds
June 1968

It was the last time any of us would ever walk up on the dikes.

We were trudging the mud of the mighty Mekong Delta, making meticulous haste across the flat open rice paddies, a sprawling patchwork quilt of flooded bronze and emerald-colored wetlands blanketing acres upon acres of grassy, marshy terrain. I was on point—about twenty yards ahead of the rest of Charlie Company. Back on the first tour, in the deep green mountains of the Central Highlands, we always had two guys on point, one with a machete to cut through the jungle, one with an M-16 to kill anyone trying to take out the guy with the machete. Down in the Delta, we didn't need the machete so much, so it was just me out front. I always took point. Most of the time anyway. More than any of my men. I wanted them to see their commander out front—to know that there wasn't anything I would order them to do that I wouldn't do myself. My RTOs were the only ones that hated me for it because if I was out front, they were out front, or at least a few paces behind, keeping the battalion and company net radios within easy reach. "Sir, you're on point again," they'd warn me, as though I'd just wandered ahead by accident. My response was always the same, paired up with a good hard-ass glare: "Yeah, I don't give a shit."

The thing about being up on the dikes, out in the open like that, was the exposure: to the enemy, the elements—the heat and humidity almost as insidious as the Viet Cong. Sure, you could dive down in the paddies, get all muddy-wet crawling through the ankle-deep, leech-infested water, but so could Charlie—and he was usually the one lying in wait for us. Or behind us. We stayed up on the dikes because we could move faster—Point "A" to Point "B"—spread out on several dikes across the floodplain, checking our twelve and six and every dot on the clock in between. The paddies were just the walkways between the strips of jungle where we did most of our fighting; but offered zero-cover or concealment, easy pickings for any sniper or machine gunner hiding in the tree line.

I kept my ears sharp for the dull click of gunmetal. Something about the *Hồi Chánh* we had with us sniffing so far up my six as we walked along the dike. Too close for my comfort. Guy only flipped a few weeks ago. Who's to say he hadn't flipped right back again? Or maybe he never flipped at all. Maybe he was still VC, still "Charlie" rather than "Charlie Company." Maybe. Company commanders had a notoriously short shelf life in Vietnam. By the time I took over Charlie Company, they had so few officers available that the acting commander was a staff sergeant, my predecessor having been medevac'd out the day before after being gravely wounded in action. I had enough to worry about out here that could kill me; I didn't need some damn "ex–Viet Cong" breathing down my neck.

I felt my foot sink as I slogged one more step through the wet mud.

The landscape of the war had changed since my last tour. Back then, up north, operating in the mountains, we had to carve out our landing zones—and get real creative how we did it—blowing open the rough, razor-edged slopes and thick foliage with artillery or air strikes, sometimes straight demolition. That was II Corps, the Central Highlands, much closer to North Vietnam. This was IV Corps, the Plain of Reeds, the southernmost area of operations, the whole place pretty much one big landing zone—flat open rice paddies, muddy dikes, dry riverbeds that could flash flood on a whim, and just enough tropical vegetation to cloak Charlie's movements. Tet had changed things. Charlie was still the same. It was our side that was different. New rules of engagement. Air strikes requiring about a dozen signatures. A lame-duck president personally picking targets from the Oval Office. The truth was, we'd kicked Charlie's ass at Tet. Bled him near dry. Wiped out more than half of his 85,000-strong attack force. Blown his networks. Took prisoner several high-ranking officers. In any other war, that would be a major victory (*technically*). But this wasn't like any other war. That's what Washington and all the journalists who threw up their hands in defeat didn't understand.

Hanoi's "victory" didn't come in their homeland, but in ours—after the fact. The Viet Cong never fired a single shot in the United States but still won an important battle that broke the hearts and minds of the American people— mostly due to the way it was depicted rather than the way it was. It didn't hurt that their benefactors in the Soviet Union had sunk a good chunk of dough into antiwar propaganda campaigns and radical movements in the United States to undermine the war effort, manipulate public opinion. A billion bucks. (In *1960* dollars.) About as much as they splashed out on arms for Charlie. Tet's failure notwithstanding, it proved the VC were still operating with impunity in South Vietnam. They could infiltrate and wreak havoc at will. Whether the missions themselves failed from a tactical perspective was beside the point. They could bleed us. What had started as an open insurgency was rapidly turning into a stealth invasion and occupation by the Communist North. *Search and Destroy from Saigon to Hanoi?* Yeah, maybe two, three years ago. But now? Forget it. Unless we were willing to nuke the North, light off World War III with the Sovs and Chicoms—something President Johnson, in usual vulgar form, had referred to as "rape rather than seduction." It might have seemed like we were on offense, going out and hunting our adversary, but we were the ones with our backs against the wall. And if before we'd been fighting this thing with one hand tied behind our backs, now we were hog-tied. Our rules of engagement were all over the place. Back with the 1st Cav, we could kill anything that posed a threat before it killed us. We made a regular exercise out of the "Mad Minute," spraying a wall of lead from every weapon in our arsenal—machine guns, M-16s, pistols, grenade launchers—for a full sixty seconds to kill or flush out any enemy who might be lurking in the darkness of the jungle. Those days were over. No more Mad Minutes. My first time out with Charlie Company, we touched down in a clean LZ. As soon as we got on the ground, moving out toward a row of nipa palm trees, I whistled for my RTO, got on the battalion net, and called in a Cobra gunship to hit the wood line with rockets, blow the shit out of anyone who might be waiting to ambush us, same tactics we would have used with 1st Cav back on my first tour. Within thirty seconds of the first rocket hitting the area, I received a call from my battalion commander wanting to know the position of the enemy forces firing at us.

"No incoming fire," I responded. "Just softening up the target area, sir."

Wrong answer.

"I don't know how you guys operated in that Horse Cavalry outfit up in II Corps, but down here we don't fire unless fired upon—understood?"

Yeah, understood.

Hell of a way to fight a war.

And the restrictions would only get worse as things dragged on.

I spent Christmas morning that tour calling down air strikes while under intense enemy fire from a tree line that I had just started lighting up with napalm, when the pilot suddenly cut short his run halfway through the dump and begged off. I got on the radio: "What the hell is going on up there?" What was going on—as I found out seconds later when the reply came through from Division—was that the powers-that-be had negotiated a temporary cease-fire to commence at noon sharp. It was 12:01. Someone must have forgotten to give Charlie the memo—he was still shooting at us.

Even with all the official hamstringing and political interference back with 1st Cav, at least then America seemed in it to win it. Now, it looked like Washington was in it simply to prolong the inevitable: a full-scale American withdrawal from Vietnam in the name of what they would eventually brand as "peace with honor"—whatever the hell that meant—worried more about how the war was playing out on television than how it was actually playing out on the battlefield. It had reached the point that President Johnson had become the conductor-in-chief of his own Arc Light orchestra, running a Rolling Thunder symphony with thunderous B-52 bass drums directly out of the Oval Office. If the president and his "Tuesday Cabinet" had wanted so badly to pick targets to bomb, they should have enlisted.

FIRED UPON

As far as shooting first, Charlie was happy to oblige us—as happened on the afternoon of June 23, when I received word that Bravo Company, under the command of Captain Frank Till, a good man and fine soldier, was in danger-close contact with the enemy and about to be overrun. Till himself had been taken out of action with a neck wound. I had direct orders from General Roberts to take in Charlie Company, join the fight, and kick ass. We came in hot about a half dozen football fields away from Bravo Company's position. No longer did we have the luxury of the Golf Course with an armada of choppers and air support at our disposal—these days, you went with whatever airpower you had available, which was never as much as before; in this case, a little more than half as much as I would normally prefer to get all of us safely into the LZ, a swamp of elephant grass and knee-deep water. As soon as the slicks started peeling off, Charlie opened up on us, true to form, from the tree line, pouring a hailstorm of lead on our position, hitting us with everything he had: woodpecker guns, captured M-60s, Chicom RPDs.

The war was all tactical now, no real battle plan. Back with 1st Cav, we spent a lot more time poring over map tables, planning our ops days in advance—all the way up the chain—running everything under code names (even if we didn't always know them till after the fact), a big-picture approach. These days it was all "saddle up and move out" at a moment's notice—rapid reaction in the vein of: *9-1-1, what is your emergency?*

I was the first one off my slick, and barely got one step through the sludgy windswept grass—crouching low in the downwash of the chopper—before a Viet Cong guerrilla popped up and ran at me with his folding spike bayonet extended from under his Chicom assault rifle, shouting a war cry. I didn't even have time to properly aim my CAR-15, so I shot him one-handed off the hip, fast-draw style, put two in his chest. The guy dropped back dead in the flat wet elephant grass.

"Sir, you John Wayne'ed him!" shouted a young private called John Stirpe, nineteen years old out of Rochester, New York, as he leaped off the chopper.

"Spread out low, let's go!" I shouted to the others. Bullets snapped and cracked all around us. Buzzed our helmets. Single shots. Bursts. This was the most vulnerable moment for any infantry company: off-loading from choppers into a hot LZ, stuck out in the open under fire and in a world of chaos. We had come in with our usual complement of eight to ten slicks, arriving behind a pair of gunships that had already softened up the battle space; but the enemy had learned our procedure. They knew exactly when and how to hit us—and our Hueys made nice big juicy targets. We had to get off the landing zone and fast.

I whistled for my RTO, the company net, got on the handset to my platoon leaders, a couple of sergeants and a fresh-faced lieutenant:

"First Platoon, Second Platoon, Third Platoon: fix bayonets and charge the tree line."

The copy-backs came in from each man in quick succession, as called, down the line:

First Platoon: "*Roger that, sir. Fix bayonets and charge the tree line.*"

Second Platoon: "*Copy, Captain. Fix bayonets and charge the tree line.*"

Third Platoon: "*Er, say again, sir, you're coming in weak and distorted.*"

A flurry of AK rounds whipped and snapped past my ear. I shouted deep and loud into the handset, if only to convey a confident tenor of authority. As I had learned from Tony Herbert, a commander only yelled to be heard above the din of battle, and never in a panic. But I needed that lieutenant to move his ass off the LZ before he got himself and all his men killed: "You heard what the fuck I said, Lieutenant! Fix bayonets, get on line, and charge! Now get your ass going! Charlie-Six out."

I understand why the young man was scared; hell, I was scared. But out here, on the battlefield, fear could kill you faster than a bullet, along with everyone else relying on your command. You had to swallow it whole and wire it tight. That was the one lesson of Vietnam that would so well serve me and my fellow operators—some of them also veterans of this war—years later with Delta Force: you have to go all in on the battlefield, no holding back. Fear was as much an enemy as the little bastard trying to put a burst in you off his AK. And I don't care how brave you are, you'd have to be a psychopath to be unafraid. (And I think even the craziest psychopaths would soil their drawers if faced with an enemy as tough and ruthless as the Viet Cong. Or the Taliban. Or ISIS. Or any of the other enemies we've been up against over the last half century.) I had a wife and two children at home that I desperately wanted to see again and spend my future old age going to barbecues and ball games, watching the Super Bowl and the World Series with a cold beer cradled in my lap. But you had to go head-first off the deep end. It was the only way to survive. *Fix bayonets and charge the tree line. . . .*

So we did.

Took out Charlie's machine-gun nests with a blanket barrage of full-auto into the nipa-palm-dotted tree line. Sometimes it felt like you were in a war against the foliage, hosing it down as if trying to light the whole world on fire, just hoping to hit something human as you charged into the fight. A half dozen or so frags on each enemy position. A lot of close-in combat, hand to hand, the thwack of our bayonets thrusting into the flesh of our adversaries. We caught them by surprise; they hadn't expected the charge of the light brigade. We busted through their flank, but paid dearly for it: one killed, several wounded. (It could have been worse, but any day you took a casualty was a bad day, even in the meat grinder of the Mekong Delta. A good buddy of mine, Charlie Hardin, who also commanded a company in the same battalion at that time, said to me many years later: "Company Commanders don't earn medals, Jess—we just make the mistakes that get our men killed." Charlie's shadow box has two Purple Hearts from his time in-country.) By the time we reached Captain Till's location, he was losing blood fast and going into shock. The bullet that caught him had left a nasty hole just above his shoulder, maybe half an inch shy of the jugular. I radioed for a medevac. The one overflying our position happened to have the battalion surgeon on board. They landed and we loaded Frank onto the chopper. Saigon was a short flight away, so they airlifted him directly to the 3rd Field Hospital for immediate treatment. Months later, I spoke to the OR doc who saved Frank's life that day. He told me that if Frank had arrived any later, he'd be dead. The medevac chopper that airlifted him had taken six hits dusting off the LZ. About two years later, while serving as a Black Hat at Benning, I bumped into a warrant officer chopper pilot who told me how he'd flown into a shit-hot LZ in the Delta to pick up a wounded captain. I asked him the date and location of the action, and when he told me, I informed him that I was the one that had called him in. It turned out that he'd received the Distinguished Flying Cross for piloting that medevac with Captain Till. I offered up a smile and told him he owed me a beer for giving him the opportunity to earn a medal. We laughed, then knocked back a couple of cold ones and talked about everything but the war.

The battle lasted the rest of the night, unrelenting. It seemed like Charlie was throwing everything he had at us, trying to make up for the debacle of Tet. In addition to Bravo Company, I took command of a third company whose commander had been killed coming off a chopper to reinforce us. I called in all the air strikes and arty available to dump hell on the enemy all night long, as we set up to encircle him just as he was trying to encircle us; but he still kept coming, fighting tooth and nail to find a gap in our lines, break out, and finally, despite suffering horrendous casualties, escape. We later captured documents confirming that we had been up against a fully reinforced battalion of NVA-controlled Viet Cong, which explained the relentless onslaught and heavy fire that lasted the night. It was clear that Charlie was on the warpath in III and IV Corps, and he didn't plan on heading back north anytime soon—or ever.

For my actions during the battle, the Army awarded me the Silver Star. General Roberts presented it to me personally. Then two days later, on June 25, I earned my second Silver Star clearing an enemy bunker complex that had us pinned down, putting myself in the direct line of fire several times ahead of my men. Charlie loved his bunkers. The VC dug 'em in deep, just back from the tree line, then used tunnels to shoot-and-scoot between them or vanish off the face of the earth. Literally. That's how they had ghosted us up in the Central Highlands, that's how they were ghosting us down in the Delta—that is, when they weren't trying to suck us in and cut us to pieces with overlapping hornet's nests of lead. We were lucky that we took no casualties, other than the one soldier who caught a bit of shrapnel from his own hand grenade because he was still within the blast radius after he tossed it into a VC bunker. We killed several of the enemy, and after the battle we lined up their bodies on the ground. Then I called up our brigade commander, Colonel Henry "Hank" Emerson, an outstanding military commander who would develop innovative quick-reaction-force and encirclement tactics to, in his words, "out-guerilla" the Viet Cong, and years later—as Commanding General of the 2nd Infantry Division in South Korea—go on to mentor a brilliant young battalion commander, Vietnam veteran, and future secretary of state by the name of Colin Powell. We called Emerson "the Gunfighter" for the Patton-like six-shooter he wore on his hip. It was a fitting moniker. The ribbons on his uniform included two Distinguished Service Crosses, five Silver Stars, and two Purple Hearts. When I got him on the horn, I informed him that we had eleven of the enemy with us in the LZ. As usual, the Gunfighter was already overflying the battlefield in his command chopper (later that August, he would end up suffering severe burns in a fiery crash after getting shot down by the Viet Cong). Emerson radioed that he was coming in to pick the eleven VC up for questioning. I told him they were all dead. It took a moment for his response to come through, off a heavy burst of static: *"Good work, Charlie-Six. Gunfighter-Five out."*

I caught my third Silver Star a few weeks later about eleven klicks northeast of Tan An, when we blew out yet another bunker complex that lit us up as we came off a calm floodplain into a narrow patch of jungle where Charlie had set up an ambush. Too close for air support, we stuck it out with our rifles and grenades, blowing out each of the trio of emplacements one at a time with fusillades of full-auto fire—both 5.56 and 7.62—and a blizzard of shrapnel. As the shooting died, one of my sergeants, Chris Cowen, out of Woodlynne, New Jersey, on his first tour, went hard charging ahead of his squad to probe the tree line. I shouted at him to be careful, but it was too late. A lone VC gunner had dug himself deep into the mud of his emplacement and opened up on him from the high ground, catching Cowen in the chest with a short burst off his Chicom machine gun. Cowen was dead before he hit the ground. Another man risked his own life to crawl over and drag him back to safety behind a rice-paddy dike, but there was nothing to be done. That VC gunner was still firing at us, pinning us down along the tree line. I called up our ARVN translator, had him get on the megaphone and try to make a convert out of this guy, get him to *Chiêu Hồi*, come on over to the righteous side. He spit back at us with a heavy burst of lead. Meantime, while all that megaphoning was going on, one of my men, a nineteen-year-old African American PFC out of Virginia—a draftee like Cowen—had managed to use the distraction to slip around the VC gunner's flank. I couldn't decide whether this crazy kid had more balls than brains; but the next thing I know, I'm watching him leap up onto the bunker, pull the pin on a grenade, and toss it between his legs into the narrow shooting slit beneath his feet. He was looking right at me the whole time, a big grin on his face, sticking around just long enough to snap off a sharp salute (because why not add a dash of flair to the fight?). Then, at the exact moment the grenade exploded, blowing out the emplacement, he dove off the bunker, rolling into the foliage. The tragic absurdity of warfare never ceased to amaze me. Nor did the extraordinary courage of even our most reluctant draftees. (I put the kid up for a Silver Star, but I don't remember if he got it.) The blast blew the gunner out of the bunker, but the Chicom machine gun that killed Sergeant Cowen survived without a scratch (a testament to the durability of Soviet-designed small arms). I mounted it on the wall of my office back at our fire base and kept it there for the duration of my command.

My foot made a wet sucking sound as I lifted it from the soft mud.

I started to take my next step, not really paying attention to anything other than the tree line—

"*Dừng lại! Dừng lại!*"

(*Stop!*)

It was the *Hồi Chánh* up my six. I almost turned my rifle on the guy, but then I looked down—and froze. Before me was the tiny, butterfly-shaped firing mechanism of a mosquito mine, protruding like a periscope just a half inch above the surface of the dike. My foot was hovering right over it. That *Hồi Chánh* had just saved my life. I told him I was going to give him a medal for that. I was only half joking; but that night, sure as shit, he showed up with an interpreter to claim his decoration; so I promised him I'd order one and he was happy, though I'm sure he ditched the thing by the time the NVA took Saigon, if he wasn't already dead. Still, I wondered how he'd spotted that mine. Or if he put it out there himself. Maybe back when he was VC. Or even after he'd *Chiêu Hồi*ed. The night before the patrol. You know—so he could "save" me. Anyway, if he didn't put this one out, he certainly put out plenty of others—so he knew what to look for. Either way, I was alive, so who cared? I did order that medal for him, though I don't remember which one. I don't even remember if the guy ever came back to get it. It was fifty years ago, and I was fighting a war. And the guy probably flipped back to the other side by the time it got there, anyway—'cause that's what kind of war it was. One thing I do remember: after that, we didn't walk on the dikes anymore.

A couple of weeks later, we were on patrol again, wading through the rice paddies, the mud, all soaked to the bone in the sunshine, but now with some pain-in-the-ass reporter embedded with us. A TV guy. I didn't much like having reporters along, unless they were *friends of ours* and knew how to handle themselves in the field, when to shut up and stay out of the way: guys I had read, like Neil Sheehan of the *New York Times*, or Joe Galloway of UPI, who would end up as the only civilian of the war to receive the Bronze Star with the "V" device (for his heroism at LZ X-Ray) and go on to coauthor the brilliant *We Were Soldiers* with General Hal Moore. Guys who not only respected and cared about soldiers but also understood what soldiering was all about, especially in this war. We'd just had a guy like that with us by the name of Henri Huet, a damn fine French war photographer for the Associated Press and *Life* magazine, who was half Vietnamese himself and was with us the day Sergeant Cowen died. After we blew out the bunker with the Chicom machine gun that killed him, there was a wounded VC on the ground, the one who'd been manning that gun; and our own machine gunner took one look at him, put his M-60 on him, and let loose a full 150-round belt. I glanced at Huet, saw him making a point of turning his camera away and looking up at the sky like he hadn't seen a damn thing. He never reported on it. Because he understood.

Anyway, this TV guy didn't strike me as one for the elements, humping the mud knee deep and dirty in a rice-paddy swamp that was nice if you liked leech soup—what with that Manhattan manicure and his brand-new leather boots—and it wasn't long before he noticed that he was the only one walking along the dikes. I was up on point when I heard him quietly ask one of the privates, Stirpe, why none of us were up there with him, considering how much easier it was to hike the mud than the marsh. "'Cause," Stirpe told him. "Captain ordered us not to."

"Really?" the newsman replied. "Why?"

I was the one who answered him this time: "Land mines," I shouted back. He froze. "Land mines . . . ?"

"Keep walking," I said. "You'll find out."

There was a pause. I could hear his mind working.

In Vietnam, land mines were a leading cause of American casualties, including a correspondent or two. Everyone knew that, especially the journalists who reported on those casualties. I had a feeling about what was coming next:

"Captain, I think I've seen enough now, sir," the newsman said. "If you'd be so kind as to call me a helicopter, I'd be glad to get out of your hair."

I said, "*My pleasure,*" and whistled for my RTO.

8

JACKPOT

Long An Province
July 17, 1968

"Lieutenant, you better get your fat ass back here!"

That was me—on the radio to my XO. Guy had just left the mailbag with the company payroll under a Huey with its rotors going full blast—a $10,000 tornado of cash. Well, not cash really, MPCs—Military Payment Certificates. Not quite as good as cash but better than an IOU. So, this L-T, my Number 2, this piece of work, what does he do? He leaves the bag untied and half open under an idling chopper—so of course the thing explodes all over the place—then jumps on that same chopper and dusts off before the rest of Charlie Company finds out that he just blew their payday all over a rice paddy.

"You're gonna police up every last bill," I barked at him as soon as the slick set back down at our LZ—all that cash floating in muddy water that might (or might not) be hiding a minefield.

It hadn't taken long for me to discover that being in charge of a rifle company wasn't just about leading combat operations. I had 140 soldiers under my command—both reluctant conscripts and hard-core volunteers—from all over the country and all different walks of life, though all dirt-poor. And it was my job to take care of every single one of 'em while keeping us on mission. All these guys had their own problems and presented a panoply of personal challenges to me as a commander. More than anything, I wished I could have kept every one of them alive and unscathed long enough to make it home to their families safe and sound—but the war had other ideas. I made mistakes like anyone else and took time to learn from them. My first couple of weeks in command were an adjustment period, to say the least. I had five platoons to look after, including a mortar platoon that would often slip my mind, until the staff sergeant in charge of it would call over the company net: "*Sir, you forgot us again. . . .*" (Thank God for kickass-competent NCOs.) General Knowlton had told me to lead by example as much as by command, and I took his advice to heart. But it was hard to tell if it was working—if my example was making an impact, resonating with the men—until one day, a few weeks into my tour, out on patrol, after wading through the rice paddies, I stopped to take off my boots, dry my feet, and put on fresh socks—something I did three or four times a day when out in the field to prevent jungle rot. Then I looked around and realized that, without a word from me, all my men were drying their feet, too, slipping on fresh socks that they had packed in advance without being told to do so. There was Chavez, the young Mexican kid out of Winslow, Arizona, who didn't know how to swim and almost drowned when he got taken in a flash flood brought on by the monsoon, before I dove into the raging waters to pull his ass out. Kid was flailing so hard, I shouted at him: "You keep fighting me, son, I'll drown you myself!" (They gave me a Soldier's Medal for that one.) There was Bowman, the half-hippie oddball wannabe Quaker-pacifist and self-proclaimed "conscientious objector" who refused to fire his weapon on the grounds that it violated the Ten Commandments ("Thou shalt not kill")—until Charlie threw a shot his way, and it suddenly dawned on him that it might be a good idea to shoot back. I smiled at his story. "Oh, so you grab your weapon when it's your ass on the line? That's not very conscientious of you, now is it?"

"On the grounds of self-defense, sir," he said.

(Yeah, right.)

And then there was Widehat, Yaizley Widehat, a full-blooded Native American straight off the rez. Not sure which one. Cheyenne River, I think. Lakota Sioux. Private Widehat would have been Staff Sergeant Widehat by now if he hadn't been busted back in rank so many times for fighting whenever anyone insulted his heritage—which happened quite a bit. A hell of a lot more than it should have anyway. (Who could blame him?) His company commander was so fed up from his last little scrape, he'd decided to have him brought up on charges for a court-martial, send him upriver for a hard stretch at LBJ, Long Binh Jail, a miserable hole of a place just outside Saigon that stood as the main prison for US soldiers serving in Vietnam. That's when I intervened, asked my fellow captain if he wouldn't mind transferring this "hard case" to my company instead of court-martialing him.

"What in the hell for?"

"Because—I want him."

"Widehat?"

"Yeah, Widehat."

He dead-eyed me for a second or two, trying to read my angle, but not really caring either way. What did he need the headache for?

"Fine. You want him, Jess, you got him. He's *all* yours."

When they brought Widehat from the stockade, I sat him down across from me in my office. I didn't want him standing at attention or at ease before me. Not for this. I told him that I asked for him because I knew he was Indian. "I'm Indian, too," I said. "Part anyway. Cherokee. That's why I chose you." The term "stone-faced" was invented for guys like Widehat, but now he looked at me. "You're a great soldier. Think about your ancestors. Honor their warrior legacy. No more wasting your fight on a bunch of morons. This is Vietnam."

From then on, and for the rest of his tour, the only fights Widehat ever got into were against the enemy. Charlie Company was glad to have him. Every sergeant in the battalion knew that it didn't matter what rank the battle-hardened Native American wore on his uniform—if there was anyone who could spirit them out of the jungle and make sure they got home safe and sound, it was *Private* Widehat. He was one hell of a soldier and saved the lives of many men, including a couple or two who'd probably insulted his heritage. I was proud to have him in my company and honored to serve with him.

OPERATION EL MATADOR

OSCAR-36: "*Soldier Charlie Six, Oscar-36, come in, over. . . .*"

I felt it before I saw it. Someone had shouted a warning, but it was too late. Some of my men—the city boys especially, but most everyone anyway—were wary of the local wildlife, warier even than they were of the Viet Cong. That's 'cause some of the local wildlife hated us. More than the Viet Cong did. Water buffalo hated us. They hated the way we smelled, and they could smell us a mile away. Even if they had a ring in their nose. Like the one that charged at me that day. I can understand it—why he was pissed off. Why he hated us. He's out there grazing emerald-green grass, basking under the sun in his little mud puddle of a watering hole, and here we come interrupting his day off from whatever plowing the locals normally had him doing with the *whump-whump-whump* of our choppers and all our noise and combat-ready commotion as we rolled into his personal sanctuary on patrol. But it was one of my grenadiers, a city boy, who set the whole thing off when he saw the big bull—the biggest among the scattered herd—all two tons of him, lift its head from its little grazing patch to glare at us and stomp its foot once with a huff, which sounded more like a quack from a duck.

"He's gonna charge!" the young grenadier shouted.

"He's not gonna charge," I half shouted back, not even looking his way. Not even paying attention as I watched one of my RTOs tune into the battalion net on his radio. That was the moment the grenadier decided to take matters into his own hands—preemptive strike—and brought to bear his M-79 to launch-and-lob a 40-mm grenade into the side of the massive beast, which only pissed it off even more. Now it did charge, running at the first target it could find within range—*sir, look out!*

I looked the wrong way.

Water buffalo—even a big sucker like this one—can run at up to thirty miles per hour. Fortunately, they take about as long as a Volkswagen Beetle (Judith and I had owned one in Germany) to get there. I don't know how fast the thing was going; I just knew that when the contact came—its flat head and broad curved horns dipped low—it hurt. Direct hit. Flipped me up and over in a reverse somersault that sent me tumbling down a steep muddy slope into a creek bed of stagnant water that was so putrid it must have doubled as the local septic tank. (*Olé!*) Broke my damn watch on a sharpened stick of bamboo, snapped the band right off. For a second, I thought I'd fallen into a punji pit. My pack had blown open and my gear had scattered all over the creek. I scooped up my rifle before anything else, made sure the action was clear, scanning the terrain around me. Not for Charlie—that pissed-off water buffalo.

"Charlie-Six, Oscar-36, where the hell are you . . . ?"

Mid-summer had brought us a new battalion commander, Lieutenant Colonel Don Schroeder, call sign "Oscar-36," an outstanding tactician and leader who cared deeply for the welfare of his men.

"Charlie-Six, respond."

Tumbling into the rut, it felt like it went a lot deeper down; but the slope itself sat on a steep incline whose soft wet mud made it difficult to climb without sinking into it. I was having trouble getting back up to the top.

"Charlie-Six, you better get your ass on the radio ASAP."

My RTO called down to me: "Sir, Colonel Schroeder's on the radio. . . ."

"I can hear that, Einstein! Answer the man!"

"Oh right, OK. . . ." He got on the handset: "Er . . . Oscar-36, this is . . . er. . . ."

"Who the hell is this?"

"Er . . . I'm the RTO, sir. . . ."

"I don't talk to RTOs, son. Where's your Six?"

"He's not available right now, sir. . . ."

"Well, where in the damn nation is he? Still in Four-Corps, I hope. . . ."

"I can't reach him, sir."

"Why the hell not?"

"He's busy."

"Busy doing what?"

"He fell in the canal, sir."

"What the hell's he doin' in a canal?"

"Er . . . he's trying to get out. Sir."

"What?"

By now, Schroeder was furious—and so was I, sliding back down in the mud every time I neared the top. That grenadier was due one world-class ass-chewing as soon as I got back topside.

"A water buffalo knocked him in, sir."

"Say again?"

"A water buffalo charged at him and knocked him into the canal, sir."

Now, as I clawed my way back to the top once more, I could hear Schroeder cracking up across the airwaves. *"All right then. . . . Well, please tell Charlie-Six when he's done playing matador, if he could see about getting his company back out to the LZ. Choppers are inbound. . . ."*

Yeah, we could hear them in the near distance.

My RTO was about to acknowledge when Widehat appeared, a silhouette backlit under the sun, and gave me a hand up. I cleared the lip and grabbed the handset.

"Oscar-36, Charlie-Six, roger that. Heading to the LZ."

"Roger, Charlie-Six. Welcome back to the war! Oscar-36 out."

Of course, there was still the matter of that pissed-off water buffalo, now circling back around to finish what it had started, everyone trying to get the hell out of its way as it prepared one last long charge to eject us from its watering hole. It was then a Cobra Gunship appeared over the tree line, spotted the danger below, and let loose a 2.75-inch explosive-tipped rocket that blew the poor rampaging bull into about ten dozen buffalo burgers. The story of my short-lived career as a matador would stick with me for the rest of my service in the United States Army, if only because of the conversation piece that Charlie Company gifted me as a going-away present a few months later, when I finally relinquished command to take on a new assignment—a small brass plaque that would be a permanent fixture on my desk for the rest of my career, engraved with a single word: *Olé!*

"Jackpot!"

My XO. The one who had blown our payday all over the Delta by leaving it under a chopper. My backside was still sore from the water buffalo—hence known as *El Toro*, the name the men had given the poor wild thing on the short hump over to the LZ—taking me out.

"Jackpot!" the lieutenant declared once more, splashing through the rice paddy as he stuffed the last of the sodden bills back into the cash bag.

I glared at him.

"I mean, I got all the money—sir."

All but forty bucks, anyway. That would come out of his own pocket. About a month's pay, all told, for him—what with what he owed the five or seven little kids from the local village that he hired to help out, and they ran a hard bargain.

"Jackpot, huh?" I grunted, still eyeballing him as I spit a big wad of dip.

As the payday chopper lifted off again, another arrived in its place, disgorging a stubby, barrel-chested tank of a man with a steel-pot helmet strapped to his cannonball-shaped skull, a pair of Ray-Ban aviators over his eyes, and a cigar stuck in his mouth. The finishing touch was the M-79 grenade launcher he carried in place of an M-16. Above the "Old Reliables" patch on his left shoulder, he had a Ranger tab, and he wore his sleeves rolled up to the crisp cut of his sergeant stripes—three-up, three-down, with a diamond in the middle. My new First Sergeant—Virgil "Top" Greene—reporting for duty. I knew from the moment I met him, seeing him snap off the sharp salute of a seasoned NCO, that we'd get along just fine. The first thing he told me was how eager he was to get it on with Charlie. I assured him that Charlie would not keep him waiting long.

9

CROSSOVER POINT

Long An Province
July 23, 1968
8:43 p.m.

The chopper dusted off fast from the jungle.

It was night, raining. I was alone.

No comms. Just my rifle.

Charlie had seen my chopper. They were looking for me.

Hard rain now. Plum-black sky. I could hear small-arms fire. Intense. Close-in. It sounded like a thousand Jiffy Pops going off all at once. Charlie had cut off one of my platoons, nineteen guys. I had caught the message traffic on my way back from Saigon, an ops meeting to deal with the ongoing rocket attacks there. As I flew back to Fire Base Moore, Charlie Company had charged into battle without me, answering an urgent call for help from a cavalry squadron that had gone in to conduct a simple recon mission only to run into a much larger enemy force than expected:

CHARLIE THREE-ZERO: *Big River-Eight, Charlie Three-Zero, we are in heavy contact! Unknown number of enemy forces. . . .*

BIG RIVER-EIGHT (Fire Base Moore): *Say again your position, Charlie Three-Zero—*

CHARLIE THREE-ZERO: (Inaudible . . . static . . . gunfire)

My chopper had to land at Moore to refuel. I grabbed up some extra magazines and grenades, then ducked into the radio hut. Doused in the red glow of their transmitters, the comms guys were trying to tune in the battle. It was pouring rain by now. The drumming sound on the roof, the chopper-buzz in the background, loud bursts of dirty air off a weak signal, made it hard to hear. They were catching a lot of static.

"Charlie Three-Zero, Big River-Eight, how copy? Charlie Three-Zero—"

"Big River-Eight, Charlie Three-Zero, we are cut off, in heavy contact—"

As I stared at the transmitters, they roared white noise.

"Come in, Charlie Three-Zero, over."

"How far out are they?" I asked.

The radioman's face was grave as he answered, "About a klick west of the LZ, sir. We're just not sure where exactly." He gestured to the other radio. "Chatter we're picking up, Captain, it sounds like Charlie may have a full battalion out there."

More static.

"I'm goin' after them."

"Sir?"

I started for the door, charging the breech on my CAR-15.

"By yourself, sir?"

"Tell 'em I'm on my way."

"Yes, sir, but . . . how are you gonna find 'em?"

"I'll find 'em," I said, and left.

When I got back to the helipad, my chopper was topped off and ready to go. I hopped on board and slammed the troop door shut against sheets of rain. "Let's go!" We could barely see out the windows. Just me and the pilots. The flight was fifteen minutes. It was a bumpy ride; the sky knocking our bird around like a sparring partner, the pilots fighting the controls the whole way. I think the lightning might have saved us a couple of times, flashing over treetops that had risen into our flight path.

"Where do you want to be put in?"

It was the lead pilot asking me over the chopper's intercom.

I shouted back, "At the point of heaviest contact."

I knew that we'd be able to see it from the sky: a light show of tracer rounds, red and green—the green, Charlie's color, rising up to greet the chopper as we came in. I knew that the heaviest contact—the most tracer fire—would be where my platoon was cut off. We dove in fast. The chopper hung its skids inches off the ground as I leaped down, then lifted away again. I had to move. Not much time. Before my guys got overrun. Bullets cracked within inches of my ear. Flash of lightning. Quiet thunder. I saw movement in the underbrush. An animal, the wind, an enemy soldier. I snapped off two rounds, then moved out. I navigated the darkness by the sound of battle, picking my way through the shadows. My footsteps mapped the terrain. Machine-gun fire and tracer rounds—red and green—guided my way, raking the terrain around me. I could hear the platoon ahead, pinned down along a narrow copse of dead trees. A parachute flare flashed and sizzled against the cloud cover, a diamond-bright starburst that set the night rain on fire. There were gaps at our rear; the enemy scattered under the light. They were right up in our faces but hadn't circled back far enough to get all the way behind us. I used the lull in the fighting to slip through their lines and crossed a dip in the terrain to reach Charlie Company's position behind the blackened trees. As soon as I materialized from the jungle, one of the soldiers spotted me, and I saw the relief wash over his face, as he alerted the others in a loud hush: "Hey look! It's the Six! He came! He's here!"

And so it went on down the line to the rest of the nineteen:

The Six is here!

Then the VC hit us with everything they had. Heavy fire poured down on us from the high ground. They had machine-gun nests set up—emplacements, fields of fire, plus roving infantry. I sent two men farther back to run rear security, engage any scouting parties, and had everyone else spread out and fire up the rise. "Let's go, get on the line!" I shouted. The terrain was pretty wide open, a few scarred trees, lots of undergrowth, ankle-deep mud, the darkness our only cover. And our enemy's cover, too. They were trying to hit us head-on, overrun us. From the sheer volume of fire, I knew that the radioman back at Fire Base Moore hadn't embellished his estimate: Charlie must have been at full battalion strength to be coming at us like this. Charlie only came strong when he felt strong. When he had the muscle.

"We need to break out of this," I shouted to James Williams, the platoon sergeant, and a damn fine one who'd kept these guys alive most of the night without a single casualty, never mind the fusillade of automatic weapons fire.

"They've been trying to dig into our flank, Captain."

Red tracer fire slashed up our position, close enough to feel the heat off the rounds. We ducked low.

"Who's shooting that?"

Red tracers were American. Charlie used green because that was the color produced by the barium salts found in Soviet and Chinese tracer rounds.

"It must be the Sixtieth, sir—Second of the Sixtieth."

Second Battalion/60th Infantry. Under the command of Lieutenant Colonel James J. Lindsay, a recent recipient of the Distinguished Service Cross who would go on to become a four-star general and the first commander in chief of Special Operations Command (SOCOM) under President Reagan.

"They had a company operating somewhere up along our right flank, Captain. On the other side of the creek."

That's where the rounds were coming from, so it must be them. I nodded once and said, "Charlie's splitting the difference."

Firing both ways between our two positions, either side of the creek. They would fire, duck, wait for us or Lindsay's boys to shoot back—more likely to cut each other to pieces with our own red tracers back and forth at each other—then pop up and fire the other way, or fire both ways at once, but always between our own volleys. It was a constant barrage; but also carried a rhythm, which made Charlie's moves predictable, when he would shoot, one way or the other, something we could time, as I explained to the 2/60's commander after I called over the RTO and got on the handset.

"The rest of our guys are east of here," Williams said. Scattered across the rice-paddies on the other side of the creek. I told him what was about to happen and had him pass it down the line. Another flare sailed on its parachute, its ghostly white light flickering over the jungle. We got down real low in the undergrowth, trying to make ourselves as small as possible. The 2/60 opened fire, popping off a light volley to draw out the enemy, then dropped back down. Now it was Charlie's turn. Except this time, when they came up to shoot, instead of waiting it out, we let 'em have it. So did the 2/60. All we had to do was stay down while we shot back, our weapons raised over our heads, firing blind. The VC were the only ones in the cross fire. Red tracers slashed back and forth across the creek, cutting them to pieces, as we let the barrage rip over our heads. When the shooting died, we held still for a long moment, watching for runners, anyone who might come rushing at us looking to go out in a blaze of glory. But most of them—the ones who weren't dead—had broken off and bugged out. Most—but not all. Eight Viet Cong had stayed behind to man the machine-gun emplacements, a trio of makeshift bunkers, that had been raining hell on us. I led the assault that ended their war, charging ahead of the line—fast, close-in, brutal, ugly. Point-blank bullets and bayonets. Nothing you can blink away. Nothing left when we were done. We punched through their lines, then crossed the creek to link up with the 2/60 guys and from there, the rest of our company in the rice paddy fields to our east.

By now, we had heavy fire and incoming rockets hitting us at several positions. That VC battalion was launching a full-court press. I rallied the men and ordered them to set up a defensive line along the outer paddy dikes. We were stretched thin, and I was worried about our flank, but I was sure we could hold out long enough to turn this thing around as we poured in reinforcements. Then Charlie's green tracers started hosing down the LZ where our choppers were landing the troops. I got a radio call: *"I don't know who this is. My Six is dead. I got wounded."* The young lieutenant was frantic. The VC had caught his company coming off the choppers—had them pinned down at the LZ. *"Can you help me?"*

Without hesitation, I replied: "Yes I can."

Then I set off low and fast across our fire-swept flank.

10:53 p.m.
US Estimated Strength: 190
Enemy Estimated Strength: 550–650

Machine-gun rounds raked my path. Along the way, I passed my mortar platoon, already dug in farther down our line, and when I reached the LZ, I brought them up to help us move out the wounded. The young lieutenant had done everything right—by the book—the way he called for help. He just needed reinforcements. Now he had them. My guys started lobbing mortar rounds at the tree line where Charlie's green tracers had given away his position. The thumping rounds laid down good cover from that side as we carried the wounded to the choppers—but then those tracers started slashing up the sky from several pockets along the perimeter, turning the LZ into a hornet's nest of hot lead.

I was on the radio with Colonel Emerson, our brigade commander. What had started as a run-of-the-mill recon mission had blown up into bitter, all-out warfare. We were outnumbered at least three to one, and thanks to the thunderstorm, the only air support available was from the parachute flares that kept sailing over us; and most of those were coming from my mortar platoon. But I had two companies, including mine, from 2nd Battalion—plus Lindsay's boys from the 2/60—now linked up under my command, and I had arty getting geared up to put some firepower down on the enemy.

"Damn stud!" Emerson called out over the radio. *"You got yourself a task force now. Go kick ass."*

Under fire, I moved farther out on the LZ to lay down cover for the guys coming off the choppers. We still had reinforcements coming in and wounded going out. Those choppers were eating a lot of lead. I got on the radio to help guide them in and direct everyone into the fight. That's when I got the call from First Sergeant Greene. A lone slick had gone down southeast of the LZ. A couple of rice paddies over. No radio contact. Greene and I agreed to link up on the way. I rounded up four or five guys to come with me. As we moved out, chattering bursts of machine-gun fire chased us from the LZ. The rounds whizzed and cracked all around us. About halfway across the paddy, I spotted the red beam of Greene's flashlight, winking at me through the darkness.

"Sir, we've got VC all over the place," he said. "Crash site's less than half a click east."

Charlie was all over that, too.

Greene had another four or five soldiers with him. I ordered a couple of the guys to stay behind to cover our egress route and the rest went with us to the crash site. We reached the chopper first, but the VC hit us as soon as we got there. Opening up from an anemic patch of trees on the far side, they pelted and pounded us with machine guns and mortars. Bullets pinged the smashed-up fuselage, some of them ricocheting inside the troop cabin as we helped people off. One of our wounded took another round. Our arty was up and running, and I called down several strikes that landed close enough for the earth-shattering shock waves to blow out the rest of the windows in the cockpit. Several times, I saw First Sergeant Greene put himself in the line of fire ahead of our soldiers to lay down cover with his grenade launcher where the "Here and There" accuracy of our artillery wasn't doing the job. It bought us enough time to get the dead and wounded off the bird, and then get the hell back across our strip of the Delta—but not before I called down one more massive round of arty on the crash site, this one timed to rain down on the chopper just as the Viet Cong, sensing our withdrawal, came out of their hides to rush the wreckage.

The battle was up and down all night. Raging outbursts of violence interspersed with sporadic lulls that came only with the distant crackle of gunfire, the thump of a mortar with no explosion. Ghostly flares. Charlie was using the lulls to adjust their positions. The violence was just cover to probe our defenses, search for gaps in our lines that they could then exploit to mount their main offensive. I was still worried about our flank. I struck out to the far end of our perimeter, circling back across a small patch of nipa palm trees that skirted a barren paddy along its outer edge. I was alone, but I knew they were out there. I could feel them. Their movement on the wind. In the whispers of the jungle. I crouched low, each step gentle in its footing, as I scanned terrain that, even between the lines, read like a no-man's-land. The enemy was everywhere, crawling in every shadow. Three of those shadows turned out to be real: what at first appeared to be the branches of the same tree suddenly transformed into three separate rifles as the shadows floated in slow, deliberate motion through the fog off the Delta marsh—three Viet Cong commandos, a scout team, armed with AKs. I put two bullets into each man's chest in less than three seconds. Their bodies dropped in rapid succession. I kept moving. Another flare lit up the sky,

melting away the thick night gloom in a bright lustrous haze. I crouched low behind a muddy berm, raised my head—and saw them. Scurrying along a higher
embankment that was probably much closer than it appeared in the gauzy light,
it looked as if the trees were dancing in the wind, covered head to toe in nipa
palm fronds, natural camouflage. They were cutting a fast, smooth pace; preparing to attack our flank in force, looking to find a breakout path through our
position and overrun us from the inside out. I never understood why they were
so dead set on punching through our lines that night—why they didn't just fall
back into the jungle, disappear, like they normally did—but there were a lot of
things about this war that I would never understand.

When I got back to my company, the small-arms fire was picking up again.
To distract us from what was about to kick off across our flank. I told my guys to
hose down the dense thatch of foliage across the dikes on that side. Then I got
on the radio and called the mother lode of arty down on top of Charlie's positions. We must have hit a nerve because as soon as our arty came down, they
started firing rockets like crazy at us from their reserve areas, trying to disrupt
our strikes. At one point, they came close—a trio of their sappers that slipped
through our lines, these guys slithering through the mud and listening through
the lulls between explosions to track my voice calling in the artillery strikes that
were blowing their people to shreds. If they could capture a captain—a company commander, no less. . . .

"Oh shit!"

It was Stirpe who cursed as he let rip the long burst from his M-16, burning
off a whole mag of twenty rounds, more than enough to kill the three muddy
sappers. Stirpe who spotted them crawling up within arm's reach of me. And
saved my life. Even if they were just looking to kidnap me, I had enough friends
who'd fallen captive to the VC to know how they treated prisoners. The Geneva
Convention wasn't part of their playbook.

"You OK, sir?"

I gave a cold crisp nod in response, as if unfazed, when in fact I was still in a
state of mild shock. I finished calling in my last adjustment on the arty. Then I
stood from my position—and the rocket hit. All I felt was a small sharp pain in
my chest, and my lungs deflated without me drawing breath. I blacked out for a
sec. Maybe just went dizzy. Then I realized that the blast impact had knocked
me on my ass. Everyone swarmed around me. Still sitting up, I shouted at them
to hold their positions. Loud enough that my throat burned, though I couldn't
hear my own voice. Someone called out "Medic!" and I saw the medic crawl
over. He crawled fast. Then everything went black again. When I came to, the
medic had his knife out and was slicing open my fatigue shirt and I thought:

why the hell is he doing that? Why doesn't he just unbutton it? A couple of other guys were helping him. I heard someone say I was out from blood loss. My RTO was on the radio calling in a medevac. I reached up and grabbed the handset. My RTO had been speaking with Lieutenant Colonel Schroeder, Oscar-36, our battalion commander. *"I'm always getting your RTOs"* he said. Schroeder wanted me out. I said, no sir, not yet. A medevac would give away our position. I told him I would fight until the fighting was done and then come out. When my men were safe.

Schroeder insisted. The RTO had chewed his ear off about my chest wound, how bad it looked. But I was adamant. I would not leave my men.

Overhearing this, the medic said, "Captain, you've got a piece of shrapnel in your chest the size of a dime. As in, bigger than most bullets. Now I can't take it out here, sir. We need to get you to a hospital."

"Just bandage it up and let's go."

I gave the handset back to the RTO.

"Medevac's canceled."

The medic knew better than to argue. He stuffed a big wad of gauze into my wound to stanch the bleeding and wrapped a bandage around my chest, taped it up tight. He did a great job—or at least good enough to keep me in the fight. I had the others help me to my feet, my shirt hanging off me in tatters. Someone said something about the field flooding from the rain. I looked around and saw the water rising in the elephant grass. We were standing in a live marsh. I ordered the men to fill their air mattresses. We would use them to stay afloat in the rice paddy's water, keep our heads just high enough to see the enemy. I knew it was only a matter of time before the tidal wave came. If the Viet Cong weren't here looking for a fight, they would have bugged out as soon as the first load of reinforcements landed. We had held them off this long, but they hadn't come at us full speed yet. I set myself up behind a sodden embankment with a good eye on our forward perimeter. Then I had First Sergeant Greene and Sergeant Williams collect every last claymore mine in our arsenal—twenty-four in total—and wire them up in an arc around the front of my position, with the whole thing rigged to a single plunger that I set up at my lookout point at the top of the embankment, my body half-submerged in the water, floating on an air mattress, like everyone else. We stayed like this for almost nine hours, slicing the shadows with our tracers back and forth for the better (or worse) part of the night. I didn't even want to think about how many leeches I had crawling over me. It was cold, wet and miserable; all of us pruned, bone-numb, caked head to toe in black mud. Many wounded but still in the fight. Ready to hold the line. Even if there was no such thing.

Scanning the distance under the flickering light of a flare, I spotted this odd figure, an inch big at first in the distance, but then drawing into closer focus as he stumbled toward us across the paddy from Charlie's side. He was stumbling because his hands were tied behind his back, and he was wearing a blindfold. As he approached our line, staggering through the mud, I shouted: "Grab him! Then everybody get down and stay there!"

A couple of soldiers joined me as we slithered up from the mud bushfighter-style and dragged him back into the grass with us. Then the VC hit us with their own version of the Mad Minute, burning off every rifle, pistol and grenade launcher in their arsenal. As we returned fire, our interpreter had a go at Mr. Blindfold. It turned out that he was a South Vietnamese POW, an ARVN soldier, that Charlie had sent our way as a decoy to catch us out in the open with their latest barrage. We were lucky. No one got hit. On that volley. Then the rockets, the 107s, started flying again—en masse—explosions booming around our position, and I knew it was coming. I knew they were just softening us up for the big push.

Sergeant Williams crawled up next to me. I could see the worry on his face. "Sir," he said. "What if Charlie snuck sappers in our line to turn those claymores around on us?"

I stared at him a moment and shook my head. "Don't say that again."

There was a moment of quiet.

Strange.

Like the whole world was at peace for just that one moment.

Then the whistles blew behind shouts of "*Tiến lên!*" and a hundred or so AKs opened up on full auto all at once as palm-frond-covered waves of black pajama–clad Viet Cong came rushing at our lines in a Japanese-style banzai-charge. I waited until they were almost on top of us—my guys opening up from the flanks—and then hit the plunger three times: one, two, three. *Boom-boom-boom.* Twenty-four claymores lit off all at once. A big bang. Not quite nuclear; but then claymores rely much less on explosive force than the 700 little steel balls that each contains—and projectile-vomits in a 100-meter forward blast radius when detonated. And twenty-four of 'em—well, that would be 16,800 of those little steel balls. Teeth, hair, blood and eyeballs splattered the marsh. I looked down and saw that the water around me was swirling red with blood. It reminded me of what my father-in-law, Thomas Clayton Story, had told me about hitting Omaha Beach on D-Day, all the blood in the water.

We crawled forward over our positions and pressed the attack. Smoke everywhere. My rifle up on my pack, I was calling in artillery, shooting at shadows across the Delta. The shells howled over us, thumping down in a pattern that sent Charlie's side of the battlefield into a frenzy. They went into full retreat, their whistles screeching in protest. I stood from my position, popping off shots at the dark rushing mass. Dawn broke along the horizon. Colonel Emerson had called in a mechanized battalion whose armored personnel carriers were just arriving on-scene in time for the mop-up. The problem was the volleys of thick red tracer rounds from their fifty-cals, slicing across the rice-paddy from several points along the perimeter, but mostly from behind us. I dropped back down before I got taken out. They were shooting at the retreating Viet Cong, but with my people in the middle of that meat grinder. I got on the radio and shouted at them to cease fire.

A voice responded: "*You guys taking 'friendly fire'?*"

I didn't know who it was, whether he outranked me or not, but I shouted back at him: "There's no such thing as 'friendly fire!' Now *cease*-fucking-fire!"

The fifty cals stopped.

In a moment, Lieutenant Colonel Lindsay called me up: "*Charlie-Six, you mind letting me have my company back now that you're done with them?*"

I laughed. The 2/60.

"Yes sir, you got it."

"*Why, thank you so much, Charlie-Six. . . .*"

I laughed again. Then I looked around, the APCs groaning past us through the sludge, and I wanted to cry. Just for a moment. Until I pulled it back together, found my bearings again.

Biting my lip.

A lot of people died there that night. In the mud.

I went for my cigarettes, but I had lost the pack somewhere.

My bandage had slipped off. It was hanging off my torso, all torn up and tangled with the shreds of my fatigue shirt, soiled with dirt and blood, a gaping hole in my chest. The sliver of shrapnel that had made that hole turned out to be closer in size to a nickel than a dime. That hurt worse than anything, when they pulled it out—the needle they stuck in beforehand, and the digging around they did to make sure none of it had gone into my lung. Worse than when it happened—worse than it hurt as I stood on the battlefield with the shrapnel still in there, all clotted with grime. I keep it in its own shadow box, that nickel-sized piece of shrapnel—along with the Purple Heart that came with it. My second one.

I got on the radio and called in a medevac.

Colonel Emerson offered to pick me up in his command-and-control bird.

"Roger that," I said. "Ready for dust-off, sir. Charlie-Six out."

10

NEXT OF KIN

Pocahontas
November 14, 1952

The radio blared static on a faded signal.

The battery was dying. My father would have to order a new one soon.

Despite the poor signal, we still listened, sitting there. My family and me. We could still hear the news:

We interrupt this program to bring you a special report. Dateline: Washington. November 14th. War news from Korea: The Pentagon reporting the loss today of a United States Air Force transport plane that crashed into a mountain outside Seoul. The plane, a Fairchild Flying Boxcar, was carrying thirty-seven US Army servicemen and seven Air Force crew. The servicemen were returning to Korea following a short leave in Japan. All forty-four on board were lost.

I remember our silence after that. No one broke it.

My sister Mona was sobbing a bit.

Then the static came again, dying with the battery.

A day or two later, I was out playing when my mom called me in for supper. It was almost evening time, but unseasonably warm, and the sun was still out, setting across the cotton field in a molten blaze of orange light. I could feel the air clinging to that final burst of heat, hear the insects chatter and buzz, smell the rich soil—and then all that nature suddenly dispersed under the groan of a yellow taxicab pulling up to our house. Taxis were a rare sight in this neck of the woods. It was a Checker Cab. I thought the driver looked cartoonish in his little yellow cap. His face was grim, and his body language skittish. He had a flimsy in his hand, and he was asking for a Mrs. Mona Prater.

My sister.

When she appeared in the doorway, the cabbie removed his hat and nervously handed her the flimsy. I watched her read it. I watched her face lose all color and her eyes go dead cold. I watched the flimsy slip from her grasp as her legs went wobbly and she let out a low, keening wail. My mother was there, holding my sister as she collapsed in her arms and cried. I was confused. I reached down and picked up the flimsy off the ground:

WESTERN UNION TELEGRAM

THE SECRETARY OF THE ARMY HAS ASKED ME TO EXPRESS HIS DEEP REGRET THAT YOUR HUSBAND PRIVATE FIRST CLASS LAVEL PRATER WAS KILLED IN A PLANE CRASH THAT OCCURRED AT APPROXIMATELY 14:40 HOURS, 14 NOVEMBER, 1952, 20 MILES EAST OF SEOUL, NEAR CHO-OK, KOREA. MORE DETAILS TO FOLLOW IN FURTHER CORRESPONDENCE. PLEASE ACCEPT OUR SINCEREST SYMPATHIES IN YOUR BEREAVEMENT.

Fire Base Moore
August 1968

We were honoring our dead today.

Once again.

We did that a lot—honor our dead.

The memorial service was in the battalion chapel. We all stood at attention as the chaplain offered a sermon about our lost brother, gone too soon from this earth. This soldier was unknown to me—or at least I didn't know him as well as the others. He hadn't been with us very long, a "cherry." That hardly made it easier. Another young man gone—his life snuffed out because of a mistake that I probably made as his company commander. Just like ol' Charlie Hardin liked to say. And as General Knowlton had said: there would be others. Men whose faces I saw that day in the chapel, honoring the dead as we would soon honor them: Stirpe, the brave young private who saved my life, but would soon lose his own to wounds suffered in combat. Oscar-36, Schroeder, our courageous battalion commander, who always had our backs, cared so much about the welfare of his men. His final fight would come the following February, while flying a routine overwatch in Dinh Tuong Province, when he ordered his chopper to land so that he could check out a pair of Vietnamese men standing around a nipa palm patch, and one of them whipped out an AK from behind a bush and unloaded half the mag into his chest. By the time his war ended, in two courageous tours in Vietnam, Don Schroeder had earned a Bronze Star (with "V" Device), a Silver Star, a Distinguished Service Cross, and of course, a Purple Heart, awarded posthumously. I thought he was invincible; one of the most self-less, dynamic and outstanding commanders I ever had the privilege of serving under. In any war. Then he was gone.

We paid our final respects: a pair of the departed's boots stood up with a rifle and bayonet stuck in the ground between them. Everyone thinking that their boots and rifle could be the next ones on display. Including me. For my most recent actions in Long An Province, going in on my own to lead my "task force" and rally them to turn the tide of the battle, I was to receive the Distinguished Service Cross. General Andrew Goodpaster, deputy commander of all US forces in Vietnam, would personally decorate me at a ceremony to take place at the eleventh hour of the eleventh day of the eleventh month, on the fiftieth anniversary of the armistice that ended World War I. (Four years later, when he was Supreme Allied Commander Europe, and I arrived at NATO headquarters in Brussels to serve on his staff, General Goodpaster was able to rattle off the name and rank of every soldier who'd been on the viewing stand that day. He also remembered that I had been the only one of nine recipients to make the ceremony; the rest were either killed or wounded in action, in most cases the same action that earned them the medal.) I was proud and honored to wear that medal. But it made little difference. Being a hero didn't make me any less mortal.

As company commander, it was my duty to write the next of kin of every fallen soldier under my command. It was the greatest sadness of my life, writing those letters. Hands down, the hardest thing I ever had to do—harder than the war itself. Someone died, I wrote. And wrote. I think about nineteen total. That one summer. That's the number that stayed on my mind: *nineteen*. I hated to think about it—the number—just the guys it represented. They weren't just numbers. They were people. They were surfers from California and cowhands from Texas. Black, white, and everything in between. Reluctant conscripts and gung-ho volunteers. First-time "cherries" and three-tour diehards. Every single one a soldier. Every single one so very brave. Every single one an American.

I wrote.

And no one ever wrote back. Not a single relative. (Which was normal. And understandable.) Until Joe Cowen, who'd lost his youngest son, Christopher—Sergeant—Cowen to the Chicom machine gun that now hung on my wall. The same action that earned me my third Silver Star. Mr. Cowen's letter arrived about a month after his son's death. I read it to the guys in Chris's platoon, and there wasn't a dry eye in the room. In it, he thanked me for my condolences in the next-of-kin letter that I had sent his family after his son's death. He said that they were "proud to know" that Chris had died serving with "a fighting outfit" and that they hoped the Lord would watch over us on our long march to "final victory." In the postscript, he requested any photos of Chris that they might want to share, especially anything that showed him with the platoon. And there was an open invitation to any of us who might want to come visit once we made it home. (If we made it home.)

The more I read Mr. Cowen's letter, the more stricken I became with sorrow. Now the big question was whether I should write back. Such matters required delicacy. You had to be careful not to cross any lines, become too emotionally attached. But I talked it over with the guys in Chris's platoon, and in the end, I decided it was the right thing to do. In my response, I told Mr. Cowen that their son was an excellent squad leader and a courageous soldier who cared about his men and put others above himself. Every loss hurt us, but his had hit especially hard. A lot of us had grown close to Chris. Among the photos I sent was a snapshot of me posing with the Chicom machine gun that we'd captured the day he died. I wanted his father to know that we'd gotten the bastard who killed his boy. A few weeks later, Mr. Cowen wrote me back thanking me for the photos. In his letter, he included a clipping of Chris's obituary from the *Philadelphia Inquirer*, a sad but lovely tribute that featured his high school senior portrait. That was the last time I heard from Mr. Cowen. His son Christopher was twenty-one years old when he gave his life for his country.

Staring at that clipping, the photo, I thought of Lavel Prater. I thought of my sister, Mona, and her wailing cries, carrying that death with her for the rest of her life. I knew what came at the retail end of every notification. I knew how it devastated the next of kin. I remembered the Checker Cab, and the poor driver with his little yellow cap, the flimsy in the dirt. That's how they did it then. All the way through my first tour. That's how they notified you. A taxi and a telegram. (Except the time a flood hit Pocahontas and they sent a boat with a preacher out to our neighbors, the Fields, to deliver the news that their son J.M. had been killed on Okinawa.) Now we sent an officer and a chaplain. (Thanks to Julie Moore—Hal Moore's wife—who proved as tough as her husband raising the roof on the Pentagon to force the change. This, of course, as Columbus, Georgia, home of Fort Benning and the 1st Cavalry Division at the time, became known as "Widow City" in the wake of the Ia Drang.)

<hr/>

JUDITH: I was living with the girls in Pocahontas. We had rented a home from our church. It was the pastor's house, but he was living in another residence at the time. With two small children and a home to look after, I was run pretty ragged, but my thoughts—and my deepest fears—never strayed from Jesse and the war. I tried to keep the girls busy—swimming lessons, Bible study, school for Tammy—so that they wouldn't have to think so much about their dad being gone. But I did keep a color portrait of Jess in his military uniform on the wall of our living room, and I made sure they prayed in front of it every day.

My parents lived nearby, and my mother would always stop in on her way home from work at the shoe factory, just in time for me to watch the six o'clock evening news—ABC, NBC, CBS—and catch up on the war. I wrote Jesse every night, as the horrors of Vietnam played out on the TV—"stay tuned for *The Dick Van Dyke Show!*"—fearing that I would see him being loaded onto a chopper with all the other dead and wounded, and the next letter I got from him would be his last. One day, while Tammy was at school, I dropped Felicia off at my mother's and went into town to run some errands. Back then, few if any of Pocahontas's streets had names, let alone street signs, and none of the houses had numbers. If you wanted to find one of those houses, you asked Mr. Tillman Tipton, the town postmaster, a good Christian man who loved his flower garden, never said a bad word about anyone, and knew where they all lived. Pocahontas was a one-stoplight town, and it was as I was sitting at that stoplight, while driving along the main drag, that I spotted a man in an Army uniform, an officer, ducking into the post office for what I assumed was that very purpose; because in small town America, post offices were the first stop for military notification officers looking for directions to the homes of the next of kin. I seized with panic. The air rushed into my ears and my heart drummed against my chest. Then the light turned green. There was a car behind me, and I heard the driver gently tap his horn.

I got out of my car.

"Hey, Miss . . . where you goin'? Miss?"

I hurried into the post office.

The Army officer was over by the main counter, speaking to Mr. Tipton. He had this big sheet of paper rolled up in his hand. It looked like a map or something.

"Are you looking for me?"

He turned around and stared at me as if he didn't know what on God's great earth I was talking about.

"Are you looking for a military wife? Are you a notification officer?"

"No, ma'am," he said finally. "I'm a recruiter."

Then he let the sheet in his hand unfurl slowly on display: a recruitment poster—the one he was just asking Mr. Tipton to pin up on the wall of the post office.

Outside, I got back in my car and started to drive.

The light turned red. The tires screeched as I stopped short. Then I broke down in tears.

I thought my husband was dead.

11

INITIAL CONTACT

Fire Base Moore
October 12, 1968

It was a ten-man overnight patrol.

They had been checking in every half hour from their observation post (OP) out in the jungle. Last time, the radioman could hear the World Series from a civilian radio that one of the grunts had playing in the background—Tigers, Cardinals.

"Bravo-Two, River-Delta-Eight, come in, over. . . ."

I was standing behind him, as he worked the tuner and called for a response, trying to crack the airwaves. I had just walked into the radio hut.

"How many windows have they missed?"

"Three, sir."

"OK. Keep trying."

The next morning, we found them. Still at the OP.

The ten men.

All dead.

I flew out there with our new brigade commander, the legendary Colonel John Geraci, aka *"Mal Hombre."* His predecessor, Colonel Emerson, "the Gunfighter," was recovering off a medevac for burns and other injuries received when the Viet Cong shot down his bird. Geraci more than lived up to his "bad man" moniker. A member of the Ranger Hall of Fame, he was a hard-core cigar-chomping three-war veteran who'd served as a Marine corporal during World War II; then joined the Army to earn two Silver Stars in Korea—and would take home two more from this, his third and last tour in Vietnam.

Lately, I'd been spending a lot more time with my bosses in their command-and-control choppers, running overwatch for ops on the ground. My time as a rifle company commander was winding down. Headquarters wanted me in Saigon, no matter how much I resisted, working the big-picture end of operations. They wanted to make sure I'd stay alive long enough to collect my shiny new DSC. I still saw plenty of action; I had picked up my last Purple Heart, my third one, just over a month ago—on my mother's birthday, no less, which she appreciated about as much as the one I took on my first tour when she said I should have been in church because it was a Sunday. We had flown into an ambush, Charlie Company on one side of the draw, our battalion-brethren in Bravo Company on the other, and an unknown number of Viet Cong between us. I requested fire support from a pair of Cobra gunships and popped a smoke to mark my position. The lead pilot, call sign Silver Spur-36, came on the line. He could see the machine-gun emplacement that I wanted him to take out; but we were danger-close, and he didn't think he could hit it without hitting us. But he was our only chance. That machine gun had us pinned down. "Take it out," I told him. *"Roger that, Charlie-Six. Coming in hot with rockets and miniguns. Keep your heads down!"*

"Heads down!" I shouted down the line.

The lead Cobra swooped in low and fast, riding thunder, and let loose—so low, in fact, that shrapnel from its rockets kicked back up and cracked the windscreen. I was watching through the small V-shaped gap between my rucksack and my radio, which I had set up in front of my position. I felt a sharp pain across the bridge of my nose and blood started pouring out. A piece of shrapnel must have slipped the breech between the two sides of the V. Thank God, it didn't put my eye out. Top Greene heard it all play out over the radio at battalion headquarters; he'd been visiting some of our wounded in the hospital and hadn't gotten back to base in time to saddle up. *"Charlie-Six, I let you out of my sight for five minutes, and there you go and get yourself stung poking hornet's nests."*

Still bleeding from my face, I laughed. "Charlie-Seven, this is Charlie-Six, you are AWOL, over and out!"

<hr>

Geraci always liked to fly no more than eight hundred feet off the deck so that he could keep a close eye on the battle space. When we came in, we came in fast.

As the slick flared on short final, the downdraft from our rotor blades blew the ponchos off the bodies—what was left of them. The image still haunts me to this day. All that mutilation. All the blood where it happened. The bodies stacked up in a neat butcher's heap. No hands, no feet. No heads. Geraci and I took over the OP like a pair of homicide cops working a crime scene, locking everything down. Staring at the bodies, I wanted to retch. I thought I had experienced the worst horrors of war: soldiers—*boys*—all tore up and shot to hell and back, but this was something else. Not combat. Murder. I flashed on a fellow warrior, Maurice Mosher, a Master Sergeant I had helped through jump school way back when. In 1965, while serving with the 5th Special Forces Group, Mosher fell prisoner to the Viet Cong. They executed him as a "war criminal"—but not before skinning him alive and castrating him.

Then I flashed on Widehat. Just a few weeks ago. As he returned from a scouting run to a killing field: "Captain, no one here alive except us, sir. Cobras killed 'em all." The women farmers in the field. "How many?" I asked. "Six, sir." I nodded. "Well, I guess you could mistake an ox plow for artillery." I called it in across the battalion net. "*Any weapons on 'em?*" asked the voice at the other end. I held the handset tight against my mouth and growled: "This kind don't carry weapons."

Bad things happened in war. Our side did things. Like those poor women farmers. Every now and then, you ran into someone who liked to shoot first and ask questions later. Or not ask 'em at all. Or just liked to shoot, period. Call it what you will: fear, boredom. The hair-trigger numbness that comes with an attrition mindset. But I never saw Charlie brave fire or artillery to save even his own, let alone innocent civilians. And just as there were separate categories of crime in peacetime, there were different degrees of atrocity in war. Unlike the Viet Cong, we never sanctioned that sort of thing—torture, mass killings. When our side did it, like at My Lai, or Widehat's death-paddy, it was an aberration. When Charlie did it, it was business as usual.

October 15
11:47 a.m.

I would never get over the smell. Or the flies. The stench and buzz around those ten bodies would stick to my skin forever. It burned me up. It burned everyone up. All we wanted now was payback. Intel got right on it; and through comms intercepts and human sources, tracked down the Viet Cong cell responsible. Charlie Company went out on the hunt. Search and destroy. (With an emphasis on *destroy*.) First day, we poked a dry hole. Second day, we hit pay dirt. From the initial contact, we couldn't tell how many were out there—their size and strength. In the jungle, it could be very hard to tell. For one thing, you can't see, so you have to listen to the volume of fire: small arms, machine guns—the louder and wider the spread, the bigger the unit. This unit was big. Bigger than we expected. Big enough that we almost bit off more than we could chew, getting sucked into a vicious firefight with a much larger force of what turned out to be not just local Viet Cong, but crack NVA regulars. Almost made me wonder whether the VC cell—which, by the way, were hardly a bunch of local-yocals if the NVA were wasting officers and resources on them—had butchered our brothers under orders. To get our blood up, draw us into this very ambush. Or some ambush. I wouldn't have been surprised to learn that they had even let us break their comms to make sure we got to the right place at the right time. Who knows? In the end, it backfired on them, because as vicious as the combat was, we brought in all the force and firepower we needed to put them out of business. This wasn't about keeping count. This was about settling accounts. The tide of war had a big ripple effect.

One of our platoons had captured an NVA officer, a captain, who'd been shot up pretty bad on his left side. Guiding the battle from his command bird, Colonel Geraci and I flew in to grab the guy up, see if we might be able to keep him alive long enough to get something out of him—something that might help us kill more like him. We were on the ground maybe thirty seconds, tops. They slung him onto our slick, and we dusted off fast, our troop doors slammed shut. Laid out at my weary feet, I watched the blood pour out of him, this man, my enemy. I thought of Sergeant Mosher. I thought of the ponchos blowing off those ten mutilated bodies. But as I caught the dying man's bloodless gaze, the dull fade in his eyes, vacant of all but anguish, and let his trembling hand find refuge in my own, the burning faded. Then I wondered: Would this man have done the same for me? Offered me comfort in my final moments? Probably not. But so what? It didn't stop me. Whatever currency there was in blood, the toll was a lifetime of human turmoil. Colonel Geraci was still talking on the radio, but I couldn't hear him—if he was still asking for a medic to meet us on the ground. It wouldn't do any good. The dying man was on his last breath. I held his hand until that moment—until I could see that he was finally resting in peace, as the chopper banked into a steep turn, and the noonday sun flooded the cabin in a wash of golden light.

12

MR. SMITH GOES
TO VIETNAM

Saigon
October 1968

I watched an Army doctor drain fluid from a knee that was about the size of a grapefruit.

The knee belonged to me. I had banged it up pretty bad this tour. Running around in the rice paddies. Jumping in and out of choppers. All that rough mud. Not to mention getting blown up the night I took my DSC. And a decade dropping out of airplanes—on and off—as a paratrooper, along with the five British barrage balloons. My knee looked like a balloon. Hurt almost as bad as my chest wound, too. Sore. Worse than leeches or jungle rot. The doc said enough was enough. "You'll need to stay off it. That means no more patrols. No more combat." Doctor's orders. (Gimme a break, Doc.) As soon as I got back to Moore, I crumpled up those orders and tossed 'em in the Mekong River. Nothing was gonna keep me off the battlefield.

Except my knee.

It blew up again. Just a few days later. Out on patrol. Worse than before: now it was more like a melon. I couldn't walk on it. Widehat and another guy had to carry me back to the chopper while Top Greene took over. The problem was that I was now putting the company at risk by leading patrols. I could no longer remain in command. Headquarters wanted me in Saigon, and Saigon got me. I spent a beautiful week on R and R with Judith in Hawaii, then went to work for Colonel Geraci as the headquarters commandant, setting up B-52 strikes. At least I was still in the fight. One way or another. The biggest aerial bombardment campaign in the history of warfare. Nothing spookier than a B-52 strike. You never see the planes. Or hear them. Just their bombs. When they burst—and that thunder shakes the earth.

One night, just before a strike, a real big one, a radio operator caught a garbled transmission hissing through bursts of static.

"... *Help me* ... *I've been* ... *unit* ... *say again* ... *separated* ... *request search-and-rescue ASAP.*"

A soldier, separated from his unit.

"Says he's with the 3rd of the 39th, sir," the radioman said, then looked at me. "He sounds American." His story—what we could make of it through a fractured frequency—was that the Viet Cong had captured him months ago, but that he'd managed to escape with one of our radios that they already had in their possession. (We knew that Charlie had captured several of our radios and was using them to intercept and monitor our comms.) The story checked out. So far. But we were having trouble keeping up with him. He'd call up, request dust-off, then go suddenly dark.

A couple of times, he said, "*My batteries are running low. I need to recharge them.*"

Whenever we tried to raise him from our end, we hit a wall of static—dead air. It made sense if he was on the move, evading the enemy. But still—

"What's his grid location?" I asked.

The radioman relayed the lost soldier's last position, the only one he'd transmitted so far—and wouldn't you know it: smack-dab in the warpath of our B-52s, about a dozen of 'em in four sorties flying out of Guam. I didn't need to check the map-table to know that. Or to know just how many hundreds of thousands of pounds of explosives they'd be dropping on that entire area in less than five minutes. Enough to vaporize vapor.

"Call 'em off," Geraci barked.

The B-52s.

Shoot.

All that elbow grease, big-time planning. All those moving pieces. It was a damn shame, but Geraci was making the right call. I joined him at the map-table to work the search-and-rescue, vectoring in a chopper via a separate radio link. Except every time we got the bird close to the lost soldier's position, or near enough anyway, he'd just go offline again.

"*I need to recharge my batteries* ... *call you in the morning.*"

"Sir," said someone standing behind me. "Sir. . . ."

Some baby-faced second lieutenant out of the signals section who'd been tugging my sleeve for the last little while now, trying to get a word in edgewise as I shifted between the radio and the map-table, barking orders every which way.

"*Sir. . . .*"

"What is your malfunction?" I snapped at him. "Can't you see we have a major situation here?"

"But sir," the lieutenant blurted out, "field radios don't have rechargeable batteries."

He said it loud enough that the whole room heard him—and went silent.

I looked at Geraci. The bombers had already turned back for Guam, the tankers to refuel them called off.

I shifted my gaze to the comms console.

Dead air.

<hr>

One week later.

The first thing I said to Jimmy Stewart was: "Who shot Liberty Valance?"

With his easy grin and everyman stammer, the screen legend didn't skip a beat: "Why, Duke Wayne shot Liberty Valance! And he used a Winchester to do it!"

Then he shook my hand like we were old friends meeting each other across a great distance, the way he did in the movies. That was another thing I would learn about the great Jimmy Stewart as I got to know him: whenever talking about his old friend John Wayne, he always referred to him as "Duke," never John. And how could you not love the Duke? The man had served in every war Hollywood had ever put on the big screen, including this one (in the well-intentioned but dismal flop *The Green Berets*). Hell, he'd even played Genghis Khan. Jimmy Stewart had fought a real war, earning two Distinguished Flying Crosses and three Air Medals as a bomber pilot on several combat missions over Germany during World War II. And a lot of people were unaware at the time—because he was hardly the type to advertise the fact—that he'd fought this one, too, secretly tagging along on a B-52 run over suspected Viet Cong sanctuaries northwest of Saigon, well within striking distance of North Vietnamese MiG-17s based in Cambodia. By then, he was Brigadier General Stewart, United States Air Force, still serving his country as a reservist. "Mr. Smith" had come to Vietnam to see the troops. A lot of celebrities came to Vietnam, and I had been lucky to meet a bunch of them—Ann-Margret, Bob Hope. "Handshake tours," they called them. Meet the boys. The Army liked to have its heroes roll out the red carpet, so I was ecstatic when they chose me to act as a VIP escort for the Hollywood icon who'd starred in one of my favorite movies, *Shenandoah*, which, he told me, was his favorite, too, if only because he had taken his whole family to the premiere and saw them all moved to tears. With him was his wonderful wife, Gloria McLean, a real lady—as sharp as her husband, with a wicked sense of humor. I spent seventeen days with Jimmy and Gloria, visiting wounded warriors across the war zone. Jimmy knew how to talk to the troops. He had seen the plaque on my desk—*Olé*—and knew about my encounter with "El Toro," the water buffalo that knocked me into a rancid canal. He used the story as an icebreaker at every stop. "Don't worry, though, I understand the Army's taking this water buffalo problem very seriously; so much so that they've assigned Captain Johnson over here to recruit and train a—a special unit of matadors, so if you're interested . . ." (Always got a big laugh.) Jimmy was much more than just a movie star—unlike all the others, we all knew that he was one of us. He even confided in me that he had taken the controls for a bit on that B-52 run, though the Air Force had made sure to keep it out of the press. And even if you didn't know, you knew—just by the way he carried himself, the backbone in his step, the easy esteem in his drawl, as his admiring gaze swept over audiences full of so many brave young faces.

One of those faces belonged to Gloria's son from her first marriage: First Lieutenant Ronald McLean, United States Marine Corps, a platoon leader with the 3rd Reconnaissance Battalion in Da Nang. We spent four days visiting with him at the dangerous frontline post. The eager young lieutenant got one look at my ribbons, and quickly confided in me that what he wanted more than anything was to earn a Silver Star in combat. "Holy smokes, Captain," he exclaimed, "how'd you get three?" Ronald was one of the few rich kids in this war—let alone from old money. His grandmother had once owned the Hope Diamond, which was said to be cursed. Many of his relatives had met bad ends. I just told him to stay aware of his surroundings, look after his men, and always lead from the front. Never hesitate. It was the yearbook answer; but it was the best I could do. Nothing prepares you enough. Not even solid advice.

My friendship with Jimmy and Gloria would last well beyond that one visit. We stayed good friends and kept in close touch. When Gloria passed away in 1994, it was Jimmy alone who personally signed the Christmas cards and letters updating me and Judith on all his latest happenings—until he joined his beloved wife three years later.

A few days after I saw them off at the airport in Saigon, I was back running air ops out of Brigade HQ. I was heading for the map-table when I ran into the baby-faced lieutenant who spotted the con on that aborted B-52 strike: "Oh hey, Captain, you remember that ghost soldier from the other night—Mr. Rechargeable Batteries?"

I frowned. The whole thing had left a bad taste in my mouth. "Yeah."

"Well, Third Battalion finally got back to us on the name check, sir. Turns out he was KIA."

KIA.

Killed in Action.

"When?"

"Four months before he radioed us for help."

It was next June that I saw the news.

I had been back home less than a month, still settling into life as a "Black Hat," an airborne instructor, at Fort Benning, which helped keep the war off my daytime mind, leaving it to blow like a hurricane through my nightmares. I had just sat down with a beer in front of the TV after a long day, the room cluttered with boxes, Judith still unpacking our new home off the move from Arkansas. Cronkite was on—or one of those guys—back from a commercial. I got up again to switch the channel. I wanted the ball game, any ball game. Then the photo popped up, and I froze halfway out of my chair. Filling the TV screen was a military portrait showing a sharp, shit-together Marine, all decked out in his dress blues. I knew the name before I heard the reporter say it, as I turned up the volume: Lieutenant Ronald Walsh McLean. Gloria's son. Turned out he'd gotten that Silver Star, after all—the one he'd always dreamed of earning in combat. He was on a six-man recon mission in the Quang Tri Province when his team ran into a much larger, platoon-sized force of NVA. After killing several of the enemy, Ronald was rendering first aid to a wounded man when they fell under fire. He covered the man with his own body, catching the rounds that would have been fatal to his fellow Marine—but instead were fatal to Ronald. His name was now one of many that I would soon seek out to touch on that black wall. The award was posthumous.

Yours truly, age 3. (Courtesy of Colonel Jesse L. Johnson)

Mom and Big Bro Daily O, 1956. (Courtesy of Colonel Jesse L. Johnson)

High School sweethearts: Judith and me. (Courtesy of Colonel Jesse L. Johnson)

Devil in baggy pants: Me and my very own glass-shined jump boots, with the 82nd Airborne, 1957. (Courtesy of Colonel Jesse L. Johnson)

Pack Mule: Hitting the beach at Qui Nhon, South Vietnam, September 21, 1965. (Courtesy of Department of Defense)

Me (facing camera) in War Zone D: After three days in the jungle with the 173rd Airborne on my first combat op. (Courtesy of Department of Defense)

Gung Ho NCO: 1st Cavalry Division (Airmobile), Central Highlands, South Vietnam. (Courtesy of Department of Defense)

Death Card, front and back. (Courtesy of Colonel Jesse L. Johnson)

Ready for action: M-16 mags taped together "jungle-style" for quicker reload. (Courtesy of Department of Defense)

Presentation of Bronze Star for Valor (Operation Scalping Mustang) by Major General John Norton, Commanding General, 1st Cavalry Division, June 7, 1966. (Courtesy of Department of Defense)

Second Bronze Star, awarded Fort Benning, Georgia, 1966. (Courtesy of Department of Defense)

Back in-country: second tour, just hit the LZ, leading from the front, our "saddle into battle" dusting off in the background (upper left). (Courtesy of Department of Defense)

Charlie Company, 2nd Battalion, 39th Infantry Regiment,
9th Infantry Division, Rạch Kiến, South Vietnam, July 1968.
(Courtesy of Department of Defense)

Major General Ewell field visit: I'm in the foreground,
shouting commands, General Ewell center. (Courtesy of
Department of Defense)

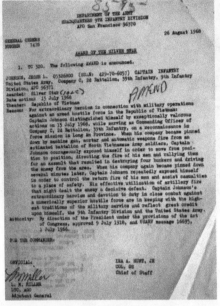

Original citation for third Silver Star.
(Courtesy of Colonel Jesse L. Johnson)

The Chicom MG that killed Sergeant Cowen; I hung it on the wall of my field office. (Courtesy of Colonel Jesse L. Johnson)

On the reviewing stand with General Andrew Goodpaster, Deputy Commander of US forces in Vietnam, future Supreme Allied Commander Europe (SACEUR). (Courtesy of Department of Defense)

Purple Heart from the night I won my DSC, with the rocket shrapnel they pulled out of my chest. (Courtesy of Colonel Jesse L. Johnson)

Me with General and Mrs. Jimmy Stewart, 1968, signed on back. (Courtesy of Colonel Jesse L. Johnson)

Sharing the same birthday with General Goodpaster, Supreme Allied Commander Europe (SACEUR), NATO HQ, 1973. (Courtesy of Department of Defense)

Just another jump—exactly why I went to the 509th Airborne in Vicenza, Italy: to do this every day, all the way! (Courtesy of Department of Defense)

Next stop Desert One: Delta Force mounting up for Operation Eagle Claw, April 24, 1980—that's me looking at the camera. (Courtesy of Colonel Jesse L. Johnson)

Judith's angel pin—all Delta wives wore these "Charlie's Angels," named in honor of Beckwith . . . until he decided they were a security risk and banned them. (Courtesy of Colonel Jesse L. Johnson)

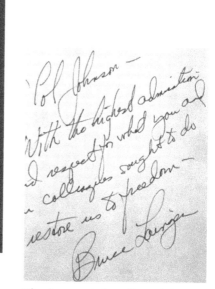

Thank-you note from Bruce Laingen, top American diplomat taken hostage at US Embassy in Tehran. (Courtesy of Colonel Jesse L. Johnson)

Colonel Beckwith promoting me to Lieutenant Colonel, Fort Bragg, NC, July 1981, signed by Beckwith. (Courtesy of Colonel Jesse L. Johnson)

At "the Stockade," Delta's HQ and training facility, with then–Vice President George H. W. Bush, February 1982, just after the Dozier kidnapping and rescue op. (Courtesy of Department of Defense)

With General Norman Schwarzkopf, "the Bear," on the tarmac in Saudi. (Courtesy of Department of Defense)

Talking to the foreign press in the Gulf.
(Courtesy of Department of Defense)

With former Secretary of State General Al Haig
in Saudi Arabia. (Courtesy of Department of
Defense)

The jet that General Schwarzkopf put at my disposal
did not endear me to certain other generals who
didn't like seeing a colonel fly so high. (Courtesy of
Department of Defense)

Proud to be the first one to welcome the Emir, Jaber al-Sabah, back to his homeland at Kuwait International Airport. (Courtesy of Department of Defense)

With General Schwarzkopf, planning special operations in the lead-up to Desert Storm, Saudi Arabia. (Courtesy of Department of Defense)

THE CALLING

13

WHAT CHARLIE WANTS, CHARLIE GETS . . .

Somewhere over the Atlantic
February 1979

The C-141 Starlifter scratched a four-fingered claw of vapor through the sky. I could see the contrails through the little portholes in the jump doors on either side of the empty cargo deck, the starboard side pink under the setting sun, the port side purple against a slate gray storm on the horizon. Lightning flashed, but far off. The Starlifter was a workhorse airlift jet that could carry up to 120 fully kitted-out paratroopers or several tanks and trucks. Or a single Minuteman thermonuclear Intercontinental Ballistic Missile. Or one man traveling under an alias with a blank payload manifest. No orders anywhere that anyone could find them. The Air Force crew acquainted only with the flight plan—the Point "A" to Point "B"—nothing else. Not the why or what for. I was heading to Key West, Florida. The Army was sending me on an all-expenses-paid fishing trip. A top-secret all-expenses-paid fishing trip. Others were heading to the same destination, under the same program. Soldiers. Like me. *Operators* now. That's what we called ourselves. That's what the Army called us. The rest of the team were on commercial flights, wearing civilian clothes—Hawaiian shirts and vacation shorts—with their hair grown out, hauling rods and reels, tackle boxes, fake IDs, the whole shebang, reading *Field & Stream*.

On final approach into Naval Air Station Key West, staring into the distant storm, I remembered that it was a Starlifter called *Hanoi Taxi* that brought the first POWs home from North Vietnam in 1973. I had stayed up all night to watch the coverage from Brussels, where I was working for the Supreme

Allied Commander of NATO, General Goodpaster, as those blessed brave men stepped off the plane at Travis Air Force Base and arrived back on American soil, to kiss the ground at their feet and feel the warm embrace of their families. I remembered that famous photo, *Burst of Joy*, the Air Force captain who was the first one off the plane, his teenage daughter sprinting ahead of the rest of his family to throw her arms around him. I couldn't imagine the culture shock. These were prisoners of war who'd spent most of the last decade in hellholes like the Hanoi Hilton. America had changed. It had changed already by the end of my second tour. I had left under Johnson, come back under Nixon. Martin Luther King Jr. and Bobby Kennedy had been assassinated. Riots had happened. The Chicago 8, or 7, or however many it was. Lots of noise in the streets. But I was able to block it out; first by burying my head in my work, teaching soldiers how to jump out of airplanes as a Black Hat at Benning; then by burying my nose in a pile of books, earning my college degree through an Army-sponsored program at the University of Tampa, where I cemented lifelong friendships with fellow Vietnam vets Captain Ron Ray and Captain Jim Taylor, both Medal of Honor recipients who were classmates of mine. Tampa wasn't like Berkeley or Columbia; it wasn't a protest school, and the students weren't the weekly sit-in kind. My fellow vets and I felt more than welcome on campus. Nobody threw red paint or shouted "baby killer!" at us. The only run-in came when my French professor made sure to tell me how proud she was that she had purposely inflated a failing student's grade to a "C" to save him flunking out and getting drafted to Vietnam. I told her, "Do you realize what you just did? You just put a noose around the neck of some poor kid who can't afford college and is gonna end up taking that guy's place in the draft."

The professor burst into tears.

I didn't mean to make her cry, but there was no way around it: she needed to know the truth. Even the most well-intentioned actions could draw deadly consequences.

Halfway through our second year, Ron Ray and I headed up to Atlanta to visit my old mentor, Tony Herbert. By now, Herbert was a lieutenant colonel; but his career was in tatters, his life upside down. While serving as a battalion commander with the 173rd Airborne in Vietnam, Herbert had claimed to have witnessed several war crimes perpetrated by American soldiers, including the torture and murder of civilians. He reported these allegations to his superiors, who repaid his integrity by smearing him as a liar in the official record. When he refused to back down, the Army brass relieved him of his command and ran him out of Vietnam—but not before his commanding officer locked him overnight in a Conex box. A warning of sorts. Back stateside, Herbert retaliated by going on *Dick Cavett* and giving whistleblower interviews to just about anyone who would listen, which *Time* magazine, the *New York Times*, and many others gladly did. I had never witnessed anything remotely akin to the brutal atrocities that Herbert described in his reports and interviews. Yes, I had stood by as one of my machine gunners burned off a full belt of 150 rounds into a dying enemy soldier; but that was still in the heat of battle, the one in which that dying enemy soldier had just killed young Sergeant Cowen. Anyway, the guy was too badly wounded to be saved and had refused to surrender in the first place. Civilians were a whole different deal. Many times, I had risked my life—alongside my fellow soldiers as they risked their lives—to save innocent women and children, the elderly, anyone caught in the cross fire who didn't belong there. Not rape or massacre them. The soldiers with whom I was privileged to serve always displayed the highest degree of gallantry. But everyone had their own experience. My experience was that Tony Herbert was one of the most honorable men I had ever come across—and had been steadfast in putting forth allegations from which he had nothing to gain. When Ron and I saw him in Atlanta, special agents from CID, the Army's Criminal Investigation Division, were sitting on his home. They had a car down the block and a surveillance team in the house across the street. Intimidation tactics. They were wasting their time and our taxpayer dollars. Herbert had already decided to retire. He would go on to write a book called *Soldier* with James Wooten of the *New York Times*, chronicling his clash with the Army brass over his allegations. While on a promotional tour for the book, Herbert appeared in a segment on the CBS news program *60 Minutes* titled "The Selling of Colonel Herbert," during which journalist Mike Wallace seemed to go out of his way to rake him over the coals, calling into question the validity of his claims and even suggesting that it was Herbert himself who was the war criminal. Herbert wasn't the only one who believed that CBS had deliberately thrown him under the bus to win favor with the Nixon White House. Although he would go on to lose a long shot of a libel case against the network that went all the way to the Supreme Court, if there was ever a more ironic example of just how absurdly off the rails the war had gone—the media helping the government shoot the messenger, who also happened to be a war hero—I'd have been hard pressed to point one out.

Burst of Joy . . .

Not so joyous after all.

The guy in the photo—the Air Force POW whose teenage daughter was rushing to hug him—his wife had already written him a "Dear John" letter that he had received just a few days before he came home. I was lucky. I had my family. I had Judith standing by her man, making a home for us no matter where we went or how many times we moved, reminding the girls not to make any loud noises around me. As I had learned from the many whose service had come before mine, the ghosts of war could haunt even the bravest heroes. Family and the military insulated me from the fallout. At least in the daytime, wide awake.

We had spent most of the seventies in Europe. I had requested an assignment in Bahrain, but instead they gave me NATO headquarters in Brussels. At least it began with a "B." (In the Army, that was sometimes considered close enough.) It was a plum assignment that anyone looking to make general would have been champing at the bit to get, but just because I was career military didn't make me a *careerist*. I was a US paratrooper. I wanted to jump out of airplanes. And I wanted to lead soldiers who liked jumping out of airplanes, too. I guess it was just my luck then when I bumped into a major general who spotted the famous yellow horsehead patch of the 1st Cavalry Division, with Airborne tab, on my right shoulder—and turned out to be wearing the same patch on the same shoulder because he'd commanded an artillery battalion with 1st Cav around the time of my first tour. We got to talking, and he made a point of telling me that he was currently in command of the NATO Southern European Task Force that oversaw one of my old outfits, the 509th Airborne Combat Team, where there just happened to be a spot for one more officer looking to get out from behind a desk and back under a parachute. "What do you say?" asked the general. Without hesitation, I replied: "Yes, sir, I would like nothing better than to get back with an Airborne unit. I love to jump. All the way."

When I put in for the transfer, everyone at NATO thought I was nuts. Who the hell requested a transfer out of what was probably the cushiest gig in the United States armed forces? "Career suicide," they all said. But far be it from me to have expected a bunch of pencil pushers to understand why a paratrooper would be more interested in jumping out of airplanes than bucking for promotion. Since my last run with the 509th, the team had moved its headquarters from Germany to Italy—Vicenza, to be exact, where the bright golden sunshine provided a much warmer welcome than the dismal gray skies of Belgium. We stayed three years in Italy, and loved every minute of it: the food, the people, the weather—and most of all, a crack outfit that loved to jump. My old battlefield mentor General Knowlton, now head of West Point, was elated when he saw that his star pupil, the distinguished cadet he always referred to as "Young David," who also happened to be his future son-in-law, had earned an assignment to the 509th under my command upon graduation. Knowlton asked me to show him the ropes the same way he showed me the ropes in Vietnam. "You're in good hands," he told the freshly minted second lieutenant. "Jesse Johnson is one of the most inspirational young officers I have ever seen. He was one of the most aggressive, effective, and courageous leaders in the Delta."

Still, situations like this could be tricky: What if the guy turned out to be no good? But "Young David" turned out to be way beyond good: he was a brilliant, outstanding officer and an exceptional leader. I had no idea then that he would end up where he did, but his were the only two fitness reports that I ever submitted about someone under my command declaring that person to have the stuff of a four-star general. Over the next thirty years, "Young David" Petraeus would rise through the ranks to receive that fourth star as the mastermind of the successful "Surge" that turned the tide of the Iraq War; go on to become commanding general of Central Command, heading up both the Iraq and Afghanistan campaigns; and serve as director of the Central Intelligence Agency under President Obama. When Congress approved his fourth star, I was pleased to send him a congratulatory email reminding him of my previous statements in his fitness reports from Vicenza. With good humor, the general replied: "Weren't you drunk when you wrote those, Jesse?" (Yeah, probably.) What he did in Iraq with the Surge, authoring the *Army and Marine Corps Counterinsurgency Field Manual*, put him on par with Ike, Macarthur, and Bradley. At least in my book. I was as proud to have him under my command as I was to serve under his father-in-law—and even prouder to call them both friends.

After two fantastic years in Vicenza, we moved back to the States. I did a tough yearlong stretch at Leavenworth—not the maximum-security prison, but at the Army's prestigious Command and General Staff College, where the first thing I learned was that I hadn't already learned everything there was to learn about warfare. While at NATO, I had already picked up a master's degree in international relations from Boston University, and I was pleased to have the opportunity to further my education and charge up my intellectual and military credentials at an institution that was open only to the crème de la crème of the Army officer corps. The General Staff College always welcomed a large contingent of foreign military officers, and it was there that I met Major Sheik Jaber al-Khalid al-Jaber al-Sabah, a member of the Kuwaiti royal family, whose lifelong friendship would prove important in the decades ahead as America awoke to a new dawn of warfare in the Middle East.

From Europe, I had watched the back-and-forth brouhaha and political skullduggery of the Watergate hearings, sat in stone-dead silence at the footage of Navy personnel pushing a Huey over the side of the USS *Okinawa* during the fall of Saigon, and caught my first taste of modern terrorism as eleven Israeli athletes lost their lives in the Munich Olympics massacre. Bob Dylan had sung about times changing—well, they had changed, all right: it almost seemed by several eras in the blink of an eye. Once again, I had left the country under one president and had come back under another. Ford had replaced Nixon, and now Carter had replaced Ford.

Upon graduating from the General Staff College, I took up my next assignment at the John F. Kennedy Center for Military Assistance at Fort Bragg, North Carolina, where I acted as a liaison overseeing the top-secret war planning of our Special Operations Forces. It was in that role that I would become acquainted with a new clandestine counterterrorism unit whose members referred to it simply as "*the* Unit." Established under the command (and at the behest) of Colonel "Chargin' Charlie" Beckwith, the former Green Beret who'd broken the siege at Plei Me; its official name—if it had an official name at all—was the 1st Special Forces Operational Detachment—Delta. The world would soon come to know it as "Delta Force."

LOOSE NUKE

So there I was, touching down at the southernmost tip of our country in sunshine state Florida, USA. Naval Air Station Key West was not only a military airport serving all the branch services; but was also home to the Army Special Forces Underwater Operations School, where Green Berets and Rangers became combat divers—though that had nothing to do with my visit. I wouldn't be barhopping down Duval Street or hanging out with Hemingway's six-toed cats either. Like I said: I was on a fishing trip. Except we weren't fishing for marlin or wahoo or whatever normally swam in these waters—we were angling for a much bigger catch: in this case, a school of well-farmed Eastern Bloc–bred terrorists. Hard-core leftist zealots who'd managed to get hold of a small nuclear weapon and wanted to prove a point.

Against a rising tide of left-wing radicalization, so-called national liberation movements, Islamic fundamentalism, and guerrilla (or "revolutionary") insurgencies tied to all of the above, the seventies had witnessed a nuclear-grade explosion in terrorism. By the end of the decade—while a bunch of US Army "fishermen" were all quietly rendezvousing in Key West with the Rangers who would back us up on our takedown—Israeli assassins were still combing the back alleys of Europe and Beirut in search of the remaining Black September terrorists responsible for Munich. Palestinian and West German militants had orchestrated one kidnapping, hijacking, bombing, and assassination after another, many times working together. The Middle East was a hotbed of sectarian violence. And Carlos the Jackal had become a household name. On the heels of Munich, many Western European nations realized the need to form elite counterterrorist units to deal with this new gathering storm. Some organized these units under their police forces, such as GSG-9 in West Germany or GIGN in France. Others, like the Israeli Sayeret Matkal and the British Special Air Service, were pure military. Always on the cutting edge, and already aware of the emerging threat of the Provisional Irish Republican Army on its home turf, the SAS had already formed its own counterterrorist section years before Munich—much to the surprise of Prime Minister Edward Heath, who only discovered that it already existed when he ordered its establishment in the aftermath of the massacre—and therefore became the model for most of the others, including Delta Force. (Of course, the same night that Prime Minister Heath had made it official, a few of the boys at Hereford decided to beef up the motor pool with the right transport to get them to and from any domestic operations; though rather than go through the tedious process of filing requests, they simply prowled their way down to the local Range Rover factory, broke in, and swiped a pair of brand-new vehicles straight off the assembly line—or so the story went.) Beckwith had served with the SAS in Malaya and remained an honorary member. He had long been a proponent of developing a similar direct-action unit within the US military, modeled on the SAS; but the Army had been a bit slow on the uptake—probably in part due to the *minor* distraction of Vietnam—until the bottom half of the decade, when it became clear that as the East-West pendulum between the United States and the Soviet Union continued to swing back and forth over the Third World, the cancer of international terrorism would only metastasize.

The pushback was predictable: mainly that we already had plenty of special operations units that could fill a role in counterterrorism—Rangers, Green Berets, SEAL teams, Air Commandos—why on earth did we need to create a whole new one? (As if to prove the point, the JFK Center brass had even temporarily activated a subunit within the 5th Special Forces Group code-named "Blue Light" as a stopgap until Delta was fully up and running; but this only created confusion as to which unit was primarily responsible for counterterrorism, not to mention competition for resources that were already scarce enough. What it all really boiled down to was a pissing contest for the chain of command—who would be in charge, who would answer the phone when the president dialed 911 in the dead of night.) Delta specialized in the dark arts: direct action, hostage rescue, clandestine counterterrorism. It wasn't just about kicking down doors and shooting things—although both were Delta specialties. New Delta operators not only became master marksmen with just about every kind of firearm on earth, they also learned how to pick tumbler locks, crack safes, and hotwire cars that they could then drive as if fighting for the win on the last lap at Le Mans. They learned covert tradecraft: how to service dead drops or dry clean a tail. Delta snipers had to maintain 100 percent accuracy on targets up to six football fields away. They learned to shoot center mass to at least put the bad guy down to neutralize the threat, if not kill him outright. As a conventional soldier, a Delta operator could have stood at attention, snapped off salutes, and shined enough boots to pass muster in the most rigorous inspection; but once in the Unit, they didn't need to worry about inspections anymore. They wore civilian clothes and grew their hair out; dispensed with military courtesy officers called enlisted operators by their first name; enlisted men called officers "Boss"—just like in the SAS. They were organized into "Sabre Squadrons"— just like in the SAS. (They even used the British spelling "sabre" with the last two letters reversed.) Anyone unwilling to unlearn, learn and relearn over and over again wasn't gonna cut it. A Delta operator needed to exhibit all the same qualities that it took to earn a Ranger tab or wear a green beret: motivation, attitude, determination; the same physical and mental toughness; all the leadership and command capabilities; all the same tactical skillsets—and then some. They needed to possess the greater will to survive even when there was no chance of survival: the same tough-as-nails-I-ain't-done-till-I'm-dead mindset that got guys like me and Charlie Beckwith through the horrors of Vietnam. I noticed that a lot of the operators came from backgrounds like mine: many of them had grown up dirt-poor and at a young age had to step up as the oldest male in their households to fill the void left by absent fathers who'd either died or gone to prison. This wasn't just something you decided to do. This was a calling.

It certainly became my calling—just as soon as I plopped down in the mud behind Charlie and we started crawling up the coast toward our target, trailing the assault squad. (I felt like I was in the jungle again—and, oddly, it was good to be back.) Behind me was an old friend, Lieutenant Colonel Joe Stringham, commanding officer of the 1st Ranger Battalion, Delta's backup for the day. The bad guys—actually seven bad guys and one very bad girl who was their second-in-command—were holed up in a derelict housing complex on Sigsbee Park, a small island less than a half mile northwest of Key West. There was only one road onto the island, but we had people coming round the back on a Boston Whaler that looked like any other fishing charter. Joe's Rangers were already in place to secure the perimeter, crawling through the vegetation with M-16s and camo paint on their faces. The terrorists were on the second and third floor of the complex. They had stolen radioactive material from a decommissioned nuclear plant and taken the security guards and several workers hostage. They had rigged the material with explosives and were threatening to kill the hostages and detonate their dirty nuke unless we met their demands, which included the payment of an absurdly large ransom and the release of several of their radical German and Palestinian comrades serving time in prisons throughout Europe and the Middle East. They said it wasn't a negotiation. They were right. The days of negotiating with terrorists were long over. We hit them fast and full blast—immediate action. Doors and windows; a breaching charge at the back from the guys on that Whaler. The threat was too big to work a game plan. Not with a nuke on the loose. It was showtime from the get-go. Our covers were just to get us to the door—in case they had people watching the airport or the approaches to the target building. We were using World War II–era Grease Guns because that's all we had available for the moment; but we had added suppressors that reduced the report to a cough, and V-notched the rear sights to make them easier to aim on the fly. On the room-clearing sweep, we threw in nonlethal flash-bang grenades (an invention of the British SAS) ahead of our entry, which temporarily blinded and deafened everyone in the room, giving us just enough time—about five seconds, give or take—to put clean, quiet kill shots into each of the bad guys without harming any hostages. Of course, those bad guys were actually target mannequins standing in for our Eastern Bloc–backed terrorists—and we knocked the stuffing right out of 'em. The hostages were real people—members of the 4th Psyops Battalion doing a good job playing make-believe for us: a little worse for wear from all the close-quarters-combat commotion, equilibrium thrown off from the deafening crash of our bangs, but alive and well. We hurried them out of the building, patted them down to make sure none of them were terrorists playing possum in plain sight (you never knew what kind of real-world twist some planner was gonna throw in the mix); then we moved out, the Rangers covering our dust-off, and called the exercise. Just a practice run on the road to Delta's official validation—this one mainly to evaluate our ability to integrate and operate with the Rangers while responding to an imminent threat.

Delta's headquarters at Fort Bragg was located at "the Stockade," the old post prison. Shortly after we got back from Key West, Charlie Beckwith rang me up and invited me over for a chin-wag. He said he liked the way I handled myself on the exercise. He told me that he'd just lost his operations officer, who'd left Delta to become a battalion commander.

"I know what you did in-country," he said.

I nodded but said nothing.

"You want the job?"

"Yes, sir."

"Think about it."

"I just did."

Except I did think it would probably upset my commanding officer at the JFK Center—a pretty powerful general.

Beckwith told me not to worry about it—he had carte blanche to recruit whomever the hell he wanted for Delta. It reminded me of something Joe Stringham had said down in Key West, as I marveled at how Beckwith had managed to convince the Army to give him a full Ranger battalion on twenty-four hours' notice off a single phone call: "What Charlie wants, Charlie gets."

As Beckwith and I finished swapping stories about the Ia Drang, I got up to leave. "One more thing," he said, as I started out the door. "All those medals you got over there ain't gonna do you a damn bit of good in this outfit."

I nodded again, saying nothing, but I knew he was right.

Most of us had medals, but not one of 'em would stop a bullet.

When I got home, I flicked on the evening news. ABC's Peter Jennings was reporting from Mehrabad International Airport in Tehran, where millions of Iranians were celebrating the arrival of the Air France charter jet that moments ago had pulled up on the tarmac to deliver the person they had all come to see— the quiet, imposing figure with the gray bushy beard and dark piercing eyes, who soon emerged from the aircraft in his signature black turban and flowing clerical robes.

After fourteen years in exile, Ayatollah Khomeini had just come home.

14

EAGLE CLAW

Tehran, Iran
November 4, 1979

The students who stormed the embassy had a plan of action.

Part of it was to make it look spontaneous. They wanted the world to see a popular uprising play out on their television sets. They wanted it to look like a protest that got out of hand, an innocent student sit-in that inflamed a revolution off the smoking tear gas canisters that US Marines fired into the crowd as they stormed the embassy compound. The Ayatollah wanted the United States to return the ailing Shah from exile to stand trial in Iran, but not before he had a chance to use the most intense hostage crisis in history as a smokescreen to unite his people and distract the world as he vanquished his domestic rivals and consolidated power in the new Islamic Republic. What better way to accomplish that than to give a big black eye to the newly anointed "Great Satan," the United States of America, make the motto of the mob Iran's favorite national slogan: *Marg bar Amrika—Death to America!*

As the "students"—and their Revolutionary Guard handlers—prepared to overrun our embassy in Tehran, Delta Force was at a secure location in the southeastern United States wrapping up our final exercise as part of our validation as America's first dedicated (and, to use the old cliché, highly classified) counterterrorist unit. The battery of tests played out over several days and covered both individual skillsets—mostly shooting—and real-world scenarios, culminating in the simultaneous hostage-rescue takedowns of a building complex and a "hijacked" 727. (They wanted to certify us as something more than certifiable.) Delta passed with flying colors and celebrated with a big breakfast at an all-night diner. Most of the Unit was just getting back to Bragg when the word came down: our embassy in Tehran had fallen.

Out of the training-exercise frying pan and into the real-world fire.

I was still a little bit banged up. I had spent the best days of an oppressively hot and muggy summer flat on my back in a hospital bed recovering from surgery. My knee had finally blown out again—all that jumping with the 509th, and then hard charging with Delta. We had spent the last year training round-the-clock—working every skill, drill, and scenario imaginable. We shot nonstop; both on the range and in the shooting house, which we built ourselves. We had Remington design custom rifles for our snipers, who handloaded their own ammo, which was enough of a chore to keep them honest about the number of rounds they threw down range, accurize their shooting. Mornings were for pistol work. Afternoons, we broke out our vintage World War II Grease Guns—until we replaced them with that venerable CT-unit (and Hollywood action-movie) machine-gun mainstay, the 9-mm Heckler & Koch MP5—for close-quarter-combat and room-clearing drills. (One nice thing about the Grease Gun, though, was its slow rate of fire—which made it very controllable—and that big .45 slug that could put a man down without over-penetrating, something that even hollow-point 9-mm ammo sometimes did: no one wanted to shoot through a terrorist and kill a hostage; still, the MP5 proved an excellent weapon for the purpose). We modified and customized our own firearms to match-grade standards; put two-pound trigger pulls on our standard-issue .45s that weren't so standard issue anymore after our gunsmith got done with them. Like our British cousins in the SAS, we developed and innovated a lot of our own gear. We liked their flash-bangs; they went gaga for our state-of-the-art comms package, a neat piece of kit that we could hook up to any phone in the world and gain access to a dedicated secure satellite uplink to headquarters. When it came to the counterterrorist game, America had definitely arrived late to the party; but then it wasn't *our* athletes murdered at Munich or *our* Olympic Games that suffered such a brutal atrocity; and despite all the Soviet-inspired animus toward Western capitalism and democracy, along with our burgeoning alliance with Israel, no terrorist or terrorist group of any serious international note—not the PLO or the Red Army Faction or Carlos the Jackal—had hijacked our airlines or bombed our buildings or taken Americans hostage. Until now.

All the major Euro nations already had counterterrorist units up and running—British SAS, West German GSG-9, French GIGN, Italian GIS—and the terrorist groups to go with them: Irish Republican Army, German Revolutionary Cells, French Action Directe, the Italian Red Brigades. We ran several advanced training exchanges with our European partners—swapping intel, techniques, skillsets—mostly with the British, French, and West Germans. A couple of years back, GSG-9 had stormed a hijacked Lufthansa jet on the ground in Mogadishu, Somalia, and rescued ninety-one passengers and crew, killing three of the terrorists and wounding a fourth in a textbook aircraft-hostage-rescue takedown. Leading the operation, code-named Magic Fire, was their commanding officer and founder, Colonel Ulrich Wegener, a hostage-rescue pioneer and good friend of mine who personally attended Delta's validation exercise as an observer; along with the legendary Christian Prouteau of the French GIGN, another friend; and a top British SAS officer who shall remain nameless for security reasons. (Forty years later and the Brits are still touchy about their Official Secrets Act—*quite rightly so, old chap*, as my old SAS friends would say.)

In the Middle East, the PLO, with its several groups and factions, were the big boys on the terrorist block. Black September sent advisors to train the Iranians, but it was the Iranians—through this one act of belligerence masquerading as brinksmanship—who consummated the marriage between what the Ayatollah called "Revolutionary Islam" and jihadist extremism, both Shiite and Sunni, ushering in a whole new era of modern international terror. What was before the favorite ideological hissy fit of overwrought college-age Marxists and militant fedayeen transformed into a much deadlier brand of terrorism that, in the wake of its Revolution, would emerge as Iran's go-to tool of statecraft in pursuit of its national interests. Iran would become the world's number-one state sponsor of terrorism—a title it still holds to this day—midwifing the birth of jihadist groups across the Muslim world, whether through direct sponsorship, as with Hezbollah, or as a counterweight to undermine Iran's own influence, as with Saudi-backed al-Qaeda. The events this set in motion would impact our military commitments for generations to come—especially on the special ops side of things—as Saddam Hussein launched the Iran-Iraq War to become the Arab Gulf's favorite foil to the Ayatollah, only to later stick his thumb in their eye with the invasion of Kuwait, and Osama bin Laden rose out of the ashes of Soviet-scarred Afghanistan to top Iran's own devastating two-decade-long campaign of mass-casualty suicide bombings to launch a series of "spectaculars," as they would come to be called, culminating in the biggest "spectacular" of them all—so far anyway—9/11.

But it all began with the one flash point that lit the fuse on the jihadist powder keg: the takeover of the United States Embassy in Tehran.

Charlie Beckwith assigned me to be Delta's liaison to a special joint task force (JTF) that the big brass in DC had set up to run any rescue—which was something the White House, and certainly President Carter, sought to avoid at all costs. General Edwin Meyer, the Army chief of staff, wanted Delta to spearhead any attempt. General Meyer's nickname was "Shy," but we called him "Moses" because of the way he cut through the Army red tape as if parting the Red Sea and freed the Unit from the shackles of military politics, bureaucracy, and most of all petty jealousies—which had almost killed us in utero via Blue Light and two years of roadblocks and resistance from the conventional brass and other special ops units. Charlie Beckwith was as tough minded, determined, and smart as they come, a man who knew how to stand his ground in a room full of four-star generals without ever throwing anyone under the bus; but as a colonel, even a full-bird colonel, there was no way he would have ever gotten the Unit up and running without Shy Meyer as his rabbi. Now the internecine dust had settled, and Delta was officially our country's "break-glass-in-case-of-emergency" solution to terrorism—and boy, was this just such an emergency.

Back when I was in the hospital getting my knee fixed, Beckwith had come to the ward to visit me. As he looked around the room, he was a little perturbed. "Where are your damn flowers?" Huh? "We sent flowers. Someone must have ripped them off. Anyway, you made light-colonel." Despite all the painkillers they were pumping into me, I suddenly jumped wide awake. I had no idea I was even up for consideration, but it turned out that out of four thousand majors, I was one of seventy-eight selected for early promotion. The selection board hadn't even released the results yet, but Beckwith had the inside track.

I arrived in Washington, DC, wearing silver oak leaves on my uniform, though I would be working in civilian clothes for most of the op from here on out: a formal but incognito three-piece suit—because everyone in DC wore three-piece suits back then, and the brass and political bigwigs still expected you to look sharp. I went straight to the Pentagon and set up shop under the man in charge of the JTF, Major General James Vaught, a tough old-school three-war veteran who was proud of the Ranger tab on his shoulder and had just finished a stint as the commanding general of the 24th Infantry Division. Vaught was in it to win it, so we got along just fine.

Delta was already relocating to "Camp Smokey," our secure training site in the deep backwoods of North Carolina. As the home of the 82nd Airborne and Special Forces, Bragg was too visible, and a big target of surveillance for the Soviets and even the Cubans, who turned their commercial flights into spy planes by packing them with enough eavesdropping gear to hear a worm fart from six feet under. Beckwith ordered everyone to split into small groups and drive up in rented cars whose trunks were packed with ammo and automatic weapons. (Good thing we didn't get pulled over, even with the cards from the Bureau of Alcohol, Tobacco and Firearms authorizing us to carry and transport what for everyone else would be illegal—we didn't need some statie or local sheriff compromising us either.)

I spent the next several months shuttling between DC, Smokey, and various other classified locations throughout the United States as we gamed every scenario imaginable to come up with a farmable plan to present to the Joint Chiefs and the president. This wasn't some cowboy deal; go in guns blazing, get everyone killed. This was a precise military operation. President Carter was under immense pressure to act. The longer the situation carried on and the diplomatic options were exhausted one by one, the more he himself became a hostage to the crisis, as it played out every night on the six o'clock evening news—Cronkite keeping a running tally of *this* many Americans held for *this* many days. Apart from the briefest of respites to ponder images of Soviet tanks rolling into Afghanistan—another debacle with historic reverberations, this one prompting President Carter to boycott the next Summer Olympics in Moscow—and maybe the five-day forecast, all the press cared about was Iran and the hostage crisis. You couldn't turn on a TV without seeing the hostage takers and their annoying mouthpiece, "Screaming Mary," the Iranian "Tokyo Rose," who spoke English with an American accent because she had lived in Philadelphia as a child, spewing vitriol against the United States in her effort to propagandize and justify the takeover. Intercut, of course, with images of Iranian Revolutionary Guards parading blindfolded Americans in front of unruly mobs chanting "Iman! Imam! Imam!" with headshots of Ayatollah Khomeini taped to the front of their shirts, or "*Marg bar Amrika!*" (*Death to America!*), as they burned our flag. After all the division that grew out of Vietnam, Watergate, and who knows what else, Americans suddenly became united in our outrage.

The biggest hitch in our planning was distance. As General Sir Michael Rose, then-commanding officer of the British SAS, would later tell me: "When we hit Princes Gate"—the SAS takedown of the Iranian embassy in London in May 1980, just a couple of weeks after our own op in Iran—"all we had to do was pop on the tube and there we were. Your lot had to fly more than halfway round the world." Then infiltrate about a thousand miles across an empty desert into the heart of enemy territory—one of the most denied areas on earth. With about four million locals who, for the most part, weren't exactly fans of Uncle Sam. A few years earlier, as America celebrated its bicentennial, the Israelis had pulled off their own long-distance rescue mission at Entebbe, saving over a hundred hostages whose Air France flight had been hijacked by a mixed bag of German radicals and Palestinian militants. I met with one of the Sayeret Matkal shot callers who planned it, Ehud Barak, the future prime minister of Israel, who, with his red commando beret tucked under the left epaulette of his uniform in true Israeli fashion, told me that surprise, and therefore speed, had been key components of their success. But this operation would eclipse all those before it—more complex, more daring, more dangerous than any hostage-rescue mission in history.

We code-named it "Eagle Claw."

The training was the most demanding that I ever experienced. Delta worked round-the-clock, refining the assault plan, practicing it, then refining it again. How to get in. How to get out. Where the bad guys were. We built a full-scale mockup of the embassy. We studied photographs of the hostages until we could recognize each of them at a glance. We consulted psychologists to develop workups on their possible states of mind. It was safe to assume they were being tortured: isolation, beatings, Russian roulette, mock executions, all of which turned out to be the case. We wanted to know if any of them might take up arms in defense of their captors just as much as we knew there were others—Marines and CIA—who would take up arms against them, which was no less a danger, considering that our orders were to kill anyone with a weapon; and in the dead dark of night, even with all those faces committed to memory, it wasn't like we were going to be checking ID before squeezing the trigger, with that light two-pound pull. We watched tape of all the news coverage we could get our hands on. Round-the-clock real-time drones weren't a thing yet, but we had a daily batch of bird's-eye shots of the twenty-seven-acre embassy compound with its fourteen buildings and surrounding streets from the NRO, the National Reconnaissance Office. We monitored the traffic patterns along our infil and exfil routes—we didn't want to get stuck in rush hour on our way in or out. We scoped out any additional security or crowd-control measures in the area that might get in our way—roadblocks, checkpoints. We checked points of entry, what kind of locks they had on the gates, where we could set up covering fire for our exfil. We counted the guards, marked any sentry rotations, though they were pretty ragtag. We clocked their weapons, a hodgepodge of H&K G3 assault rifles, Uzi submachine guns (Israeli made, of course), and various other small arms. We ran dossiers on the Revolutionary Guard ringleaders and their militant helpers. We had the CIA pumping us full of the same intel they were providing the Joint Chiefs and the White House, but most of it was garbage. Despite the Ayatollah painting the embassy as a "den of spies," the Agency had only three officers stationed there, who didn't even speak the language, and zero sources on the ground, since the Church Committee and the new Director of Central Intelligence, Admiral Stansfield Turner, had stripped the Operations branch bare of the kind of rough-and-tumble experienced field officers who knew how to cultivate agents in the backstreets and bazaars of the world's most dangerous countries—the knock-on effect of Watergate and a whole bunch of other dirt that the Agency had gotten into up to its eyeballs, including Operation Ajax, the 1953 coup d'état that had given the Shah absolute power and whose nuclear-grade blowback had fanned and fueled the fires of the Iranian Revolution (and the takeover) in the first place. We read message traffic with snippets of intel from anyone we could pin down going into and coming out of Tehran—mostly Europeans: German industrialists, Swiss bankers, French journalists, British diplomats, whoever. Anyone who could give us the new lay of the land, whether it was airport procedures, street traffic, popular sentiment. We studied architectural diagrams, schematics, blueprints. Delta already had some of those on hand because just before the crisis, we'd volunteered to assess embassy security at sites considered at risk around the world, only to run into a State Department refusal to cough up the dough to pay the airfare for our operators—not that money was the issue: the idea of allowing a bunch of gunslingers to sniff around their embassies made Foggy Bottom's palms sweat. Tehran had been at the top of the list. We spoke with experts on construction; stone walls; doors and doorknobs of all shapes, makes, and sizes, based on what we had gleaned in thorough debriefs of those who had firsthand knowledge of the embassy complex, including the thirteen hostages that the regime released early on as a "gesture of goodwill." (That's how we discovered that three of the hostages were being held off-site at the Ministry of Foreign Affairs, including L. Bruce Laingen, the chargé d'affaires, a class act who wrote me the kindest thank-you note for our efforts when it was all said and done.) We blew out windows, walls, doors, then built them back up only to blow them out again until we figured out exactly how much C-4 plastic explosive we would need to pack, and how to set up the charges. We practiced stealth climbing and set up our gear and loadouts to remain noiseless as we breached the embassy complex and swept toward the target buildings. In addition to over a hundred practice drills covering different parts of the operation, we conducted ten full dress rehearsals with support aircraft—C-130s, choppers—and the Ranger company that was coming in with us to secure Manzariyeh, a small airfield outside Tehran where the choppers, having picked up the hostages and assault-team elements at a soccer stadium across the street from the embassy complex, would cross-load everyone into waiting C-141 Starlifters for the final flight out of Iran. Covering our final flight would be several fast-air attack craft off the USS *Nimitz* and USS *Coral Sea*, all of which would be wearing special markings to distinguish them from the American-made F-14 Tomcats that our government had sold to the Shah but were now in the service of the new regime.

We ran everything under a heavy veil of secrecy; we even had a skeleton crew back at the Stockade whose role was strictly to keep up appearances with the usual Delta routines: lots of shooting, door kicking, explosions, cars coming in and out of the parking lot at the expected times of day to make it seem like we were all still there doing the same-ol' same-ol'—though all that cloak-and-dagger would later come back to bite us and draw some very unwise criticism from the armchair brass who didn't much understand how this type of deal worked and had never been big fans of the Delta concept or Charlie Beckwith to begin with. (Some of these guys were so locked in their own box, they might as well have worked for UPS.)

In February 1980, God blessed Judith and me with another bundle of joy, our daughter Shannon, and we couldn't have been more over the moon to welcome a third miracle into our lives. But here I was, preparing once again to go to war—on a mission more dangerous than anything I faced in Vietnam. Only this time, it was so secret, I couldn't tell anyone. For the several months that I was away between training and the mission itself, Judith had no idea where I was. She thought I was in California on just another boring military exercise; unlike my tours in Vietnam, she had no idea where I would be going or why—what could go wrong and probably would. None of the wives did—not until it was all over. They never really knew what their husbands were getting up to, which was probably one of the biggest reasons why the Unit, and others like it, had such a high divorce rate. They knew what we did was dangerous; but if they knew just how dangerous, they probably would have killed us themselves. Early on in Delta's infancy, someone—I don't know who—dubbed us "Charlie's Angels" in reference to Colonel Beckwith's Christian name and the hit television series. We didn't like it, but our wives did, so they all started calling themselves "Charlie's Angels" and went out and bought these angel pins to wear around town—until Beckwith put the kibosh on them for security reasons. (Judith still kept her pin in a drawer; but never wore it again, at least not while I was with Delta.)

Late April, I returned to DC to prepare for deployment. While holed up at the Marriott with my team, I got a phone call from a CIA officer who requested that I meet him at the River Entrance to the Pentagon, where he handed me a brown paper bag stuffed with $100,000 in US currency—emergency funds for any further contingencies. Anything we didn't spend we would return after the mission. That was nothing new—I had received the same amount in a briefcase as part of that Key West exercise. Judith had found it under the bed and went wide-eyed as she opened it. When she showed it to me, I just told her to put it back and not worry about it. She knew better than to ask.

We had our final huddle, prepping Beckwith, who then went to the White House to brief the president. It was a hard sell. Carter was willing; but still a bit gun-shy, sweating the risk, the danger, losing people. Finally, he gave the green light. Eagle Claw was a go.

"Godspeed," the president said.

15

DESERT ONE

Wadi Qena Air Base, Egypt
April 24, 1980

I needed wheels.

It was a last-minute thing. After all the planning, it wasn't until just before zero hour that I realized that our first LZ was so big that I would need some sort of transport for my team to get around while on the ground waiting for the choppers. Beckwith had put me in command of the road watch team that would go in with him on the first plane, an MC-130 Combat Talon with Delta Force's B Squadron for the main assault, a team of Air Force combat controllers to guide in the follow-on aircraft, and a six-man squad of Rangers for extra muscle. Our mission was to secure the flanks and set up roadblocks at either end of a barely there road along a salt flat in the Lut Desert that would double as a makeshift runway and refueling point—code-named "Desert One."

We were staging out of Wadi Qena, a vast, shoddy Soviet-built airbase not far from the pyramids that the US Air Force had been using for years to run all kinds of black ops that the world probably would never know about. We'd arrived on the twenty-first, a Monday, and taken up residence in one of the main hangars, whose décor revolved around a pockmarked concrete floor caked in human excrement—until we scrubbed the hell out of it—along with a buzzing swarm of flies that was biblical in proportion: the nasty biting kind that never quit. From here, we'd be hopping a C-141 to Oman and cross-load into the MC-130, one of three, that would fly us to Desert One.

But first I needed those wheels.

Didn't take long.

I spotted an Air Force colonel driving a big long-haul jeep around the base and flagged him down.

"Gonna need to commandeer your ride, sir."

I was standing there in my commando gear, with my CAR-15 assault rifle slung across my chest, fresh off the range where I'd just zeroed it, sweating bullets in the boiler-room Egyptian heat.

The colonel stared a moment, blinking at me in the tangerine light of the setting sun. He didn't know me or my rank from Adam or Shy "Moses" Meyer. He just knew that "Charlie's Angels" had full pull to get what we wanted when we wanted it.

"I'll need you to sign a receipt."

With the further demand that I return the vehicle in mint condition.

He looked worried.

I promised him that I would do my best.

And I meant it.

(No, really.)

⟺

I briefed General Vaught on our final preparations, and he swung by my crew's little corner of the base to check out our range-work and practice drills—an array of "what-if" scenarios. As in, "what if we run into civilians at Desert One?" A goatherd or whatever. You never knew who or what you might run into in the middle of nowhere. Even a desolate nowhere. About a month earlier, our lead USAF combat controller, Major John Carney, went into Iran in a small Twin Otter prop plane with two CIA officers to mark the runway with several infrared beacons that could only be seen with night-vision goggles and that the pilots would be able to activate on approach with a Sears garage door opener modified for the purpose. While on the ground, Carney twice had to lie flat as trucks rushed past within minutes of each other—like it was Route 66. That barely there road seemed to see some pretty heavy traffic. Still, Vaught thought we had our drill wired tight enough to handle any surprises. His parting words were, "Let's pray for good weather."

Amen.

⟺

A few hours later, we were ready to go, locking and loading as we prepared to board the Starlifter that would take us to Masirah, a small island off the coast of Oman, where we would transfer to the lead Talon for the flight into Tehran.

There was just one problem—a CIA officer we'll call "Harold," a real cover-your-ass company man who demanded that his agent, or "asset," as he liked to call him, an Iranian we only knew as "Al," one of the Shah's former bodyguards, go with us. Now, most of the guys liked Al, even Beckwith, who could be a tad prickly, but something about the guy rubbed me the wrong way. He had a big mouth and kept telling anyone who would listen that he was a wanted man with a price on his head. Then why the hell would he want to go back? That didn't sit right with me, and I didn't want him anywhere near me on the op. Harold was having none of it, throwing a hissy fit. We were really going at it. I think some of my operators were taking bets. Vaught pulled up in his jeep and waved me over. "What's the problem, Jesse?" he asked, as I plopped down in the passenger's seat.

"I don't want that guy with me."

"Which guy?" Vaught asked, eyeballing Al and the apoplectic Harold, who looked like his head was about to explode.

"That guy," I said, jerking my thumb at Al.

Vaught looked at him, then back at me. "Why not?"

"I don't trust him."

"Oh, that's ridiculous," Harold scoffed.

Vaught was nodding, taking this all in.

Then, still eyeballing Al, he said, "He goes."

Vaught had wanted me to ride with him to the Starlifter so we could get one last briefing in before I took off, but I almost jumped out right then and there. I was pissed.

Vaught could tell. A small smile formed on his caveman-like face. "Hey, don't worry about it, Jesse," he said in his loud, gruff voice. "If he does anything you don't like, just shoot him."

I looked back at Harold and Al, both now pale with shock.

"OK," I said.

Then Vaught mashed the gas, and we drove off.

For years, I heard stories about Harold telling anyone who would listen that he'd been at Desert One. Baloney. I had no idea where he went after we left Qena, but it sure as hell wasn't anywhere near Iran.

As for Al, he was a no-show at takeoff. Shocker.

I never saw him again, but that was just fine with me.

The Talon flew into Desert One low and fast.

Under the radar.

As we crossed into Iranian airspace, we were hugging the terrain, flying barely four hundred feet off the deck. We had already refueled in-flight, coming out of Oman, and now we were on the homestretch. This was it. We were behind enemy lines. No going back now. It sure was a bumpy ride, the plane rolling, pitching, plunging all over the damn place, its cargo deck awash in the red glow of our blackout lights. Other than that, we were flying completely dark, the pilots relying on the night-vision goggles that they were sharing back and forth to navigate the desert and mountains. A couple of the guys were throwing up into barf bags. The Air Force loadmaster, a master sergeant, had secured my commandeered jeep at the rear-ramp of the aircraft. I was sitting on the hood—the only space left—with Major Logan Fitch, commander of B Squadron. With each plunge of turbulence, our heads bounced off the roof of the cargo deck, then we'd land back down hard against the hood of the vehicle. I was worried we might dent it and cost that Air Force colonel back at Wadi Qena. Besides the two or three guys barfing, everyone was quiet. Colonel Beckwith was up front near the cockpit so he could talk to the pilots, though he was leaving them alone for now, as they sliced and diced through the narrow gaps and glided down the passes between the razor-sharp ridges and peaks of the Zagros Mountains, the whole world doused in the grainy green haze of their goggles. With Beckwith was Colonel Jim Kyle, who was heading up the aviation side of the mission. This was the command craft.

Our attire was a civilian-military mix of jump or jungle boots, Levis, field jackets with extra pockets sewn on to carry all the bits and pieces of our personal loadouts, and navy blue watch caps. Plus, on our shoulder sleeves, we each wore an American flag with a piece of black Velcro over it that we would remove as soon as we hit the embassy. Anyone who saw us could have easily mistaken us for an impeccably well-equipped, if not well-dressed, guerrilla army, but the flag would at least allow us to argue that we were in military uniform and therefore protected as soldiers under the Geneva Convention. (Yeah, right.) Our weapons were a mixed bag—we were kitted out more like the Viet Cong than American soldiers, though with much better gear: a hodgepodge of Grease Guns, some MP5s, with or without suppressors. I was running my trusty CAR-15 because I liked the range it offered and it had served me well in 'Nam—well enough to keep me alive.

We expected a hard landing, but the pilots brought it in like they were landing on butter, due to a powdery ankle-deep layer of sand that had dusted over the runway in the weeks since Carney and the two spooks had prepped the previously hard-packed landing zone. My team were gonna be the first ones out so that we could secure the site as soon as possible. Five more planes would follow within the hour. Two with the rest of the assault unit, topping off the total at 132 men; and three bearing giant fuel bladders two apiece—that would gas up the eight choppers, RH-53D Sea Stallions, big heavy-lift sumbitches that in non-swabbie Air Force trim were called "Jolly Green Giants," already en route along their six hundred-mile sea-to-land flight path off the USS *Nimitz*, stationed in the Gulf of Oman sixty miles off the coast of Iran. Once the thirsty Sea Stallions refueled off the pregnant bladders at Desert One, they would ferry the assault elements to Desert Two, the secondary staging area.

Days earlier, an undercover CIA and Special Forces advance party had already infiltrated Tehran to put eyeballs on the embassy and other key locations, double check all the infil and exfil routes, and secure the transpo that would collect the assault squads from Desert Two. The team leader was Dick Meadows, code-named Esquire. A Special Forces legend, Meadows had earned his own DSC as a member of "Blueboy," the fourteen-man team that, in November 1970, had spearheaded the famous Son Tay Raid, the attempted rescue of American POWs from a North Vietnamese prison camp that turned out to be a dry hole. The commanding officer of that operation, code-named Ivory Coast, had been Colonel Arthur "Bull" Simons, another Special Forces legend who'd just led a successful private operation financed by billionaire H. Ross Perot to extract a pair of his executives imprisoned in Tehran during the revolution, using a strike team comprised solely of employees from Perot's company, EDS, all civilians who had volunteered to be trained up by Simons for the job. It was Bull Simons, already long retired, who'd early on urged Charlie Beckwith to require our snipers to handload their own rounds and helped set up their bullet shop. Meadows had entered Tehran posing as an Irish businessman, the others as West Germans because they spoke the language. He had been retired for a couple of years now himself, but had come back shortly before Eagle Claw to work with Delta and ended up going in with the CIA advance team. The team's drivers would link up with the assault squads at the separate hide-sites around Desert Two, both situated in the mountains just outside Tehran, which was where the Sea Stallions, draped under camo-netting, and the assault team, waiting for darkness to fall, would lie low until the next evening, when six Mercedes trucks—already stashed in a warehouse in the city—would arrive to transport everyone to the embassy complex, while a separate thirteen-man squad from Detachment-A, a clandestine unit of Green Berets out of Berlin, would hit the Ministry of Foreign Affairs to extract the chargé d'affaires, Laingen, and the two other Americans being held there. Det-A, as it was often called, was well versed in many of the same skillsets as Delta, including counterterrorism, though normally detailed as a stay-behind deep-cover unit to conduct unconventional warfare in the event of World War III. Det-A's piece of the mission was code-named "Storm Cloud."

When the loadmaster dropped the ramp, the first in line was my good buddy, Delta intelligence officer Captain Wade "Ish" Ishimoto, who'd quipped as we prepared to go in: "The only difference between this and the Alamo is that Davy Crockett didn't have to fight his way in."

Ish had done monumental work handling the Herculean task of vetting the reams of intelligence that had come in daily over the last several months. Much of what we were able to accomplish to date was due to his tireless efforts.

As he started down the ramp, I called out to him: "Wait, Ish! Look out!"

Ish froze, probing the dead dark desert with his rifle, searching for a threat.

I jumped out ahead of him, my weapon at the ready, my feet landing in the soft chalky sand.

Ish cried, "What is it?"

I looked at him and flashed a big grin, shouting over the din of the plane's turboprops: "Oh, I just wanted my boots to be the first on Iranian soil!"

Ish shook his head with a smile. "Asshole!"

Then he jumped on a Yamaha dirt bike with a Ranger called Rubio and headed off toward the south to get on with the business of running the road watch, per plan, as we had rehearsed many times.

A burst of light seared through the darkness.

I turned around and squinted against a pair of headlights as they blazed through the sandy cream-colored grit of the sand squall raging in the backwash of the plane's propellers.

It was a bus.

A passenger bus.

Speeding right toward our position along the runway.

Shit.

The bus itself was unexpected, but we had also prepared for this possibility. We knew that a lot of smuggling operations used this stretch to move whatever they were moving.

Everyone was still unloading from the plane.

I could hear Beckwith barking orders and getting on top of things.

"Stop that vehicle," he shouted.

I was already on it. I raised my CAR-15 and fired about ten rounds over the top of the bus. One of the Rangers thumped a grenade off his M-79, the explosion—as the 40-mm round struck home in the dirt—drowned out to a dull thud by the noise of the propellers. A warning shot. It was enough. The bus squealed to a heavy halt.

It sat there, idling.

I climbed aboard.

Forty-three faces glared back at me with frightened eyes.

I couldn't imagine what they must be thinking. With my own expression, I tried to strike some sort of balance between humane and intimidating. I didn't want to frighten them any more than I already had—but I also didn't want them to think that I wasn't the one in charge.

Man, taking hostages on a hostage-rescue mission—now, there's a first.

These were mostly women and children.

An old woman tried to give me her baby. Even in Vietnam, I had never had anyone try to hand me their kid—at least not before we'd been properly introduced. I told her no thank you. It was the only Farsi I knew. The bus driver started chattering away at me. I couldn't understand a word he was saying; but neither could he understand me, so we were even.

A couple of Logan Fitch's B Squadron boys came over with a Farsi linguist to relieve me so I could get on with the road-watch work. As far as the passengers were concerned—yes, for all intents and purposes, they were our hostages now. In fact, President Carter would order us to fly them out on one of the C-130s and hold on to them until we had the hostages clear of Iranian airspace and the rescue was complete.

As the rest of my team deployed to set up the roadblocks, two more vehicles appeared: a pickup truck and a tanker—fuel smugglers.

Ranger Rubio came up next to me, seeing what I was seeing; except he had also whipped out an M72 rocket launcher, otherwise known as the LAW—as in, light antitank weapon.

"Take it out," I told him.

"Yes, sir," Rubio said sharply. He pulled the safety pin on the LAW, yanked the inner tube out to full extension, making it live, shouldered it, and fired. The rocket struck home. The explosion lit the night on fire. The driver must have had some good karma, because he managed to get out looking unscathed, and hopped in the pickup for a quick getaway. We tried to give chase, but Ish's bike got bogged down, and my jeep wasn't exactly built for high-speed pursuits. Anyway, they were smugglers—it wasn't like they were gonna tip off the Ayatollah's police and explain that they had been smuggling stolen fuel. They'd be imprisoned or executed right along with us.

In a moment, the second Talon, A Squadron's bird, arrived and taxied to our end of the runway. Bucky Burrus, a major and fellow Vietnam vet, was one of the first guys off the back ramp. Beckwith thought he was a dead ringer for Robert Redford, but I always imagined him as more of a California surfer dude—looks-wise anyway. Bucky was all jazzed up, ready to go. Preparing to mount up out of Wadi Qena, after one of the other operators read a prayer about David and Goliath from the Book of Samuel, Bucky had broken into a proud rendition of "God Bless America"—full blast like he was auditioning for a Broadway musical. Everyone joined in. It was stirring, if only because there were photos of all the hostages pinned to the wall behind him. I still get goose bumps thinking about it. We sang our hearts out.

Now he looked around and immediately saw the tanker engulfed in flames. How could you miss it? The whole LZ was lit in a flickering orange haze. "Holy shit, Jesse, what the hell are your trying to do, start World War III?" Then he turned to the others coming off the ramp of the third 130 that had just come in behind his aircraft and shouted: "Hey everyone, welcome to World War III!"

The bladder birds were next. Once on the ground, Jim Kyle, John Carney, and the rest of the combat controllers directed them to the other end of the runway to do their mating ritual with the choppers when they arrived, not an easy job with all the tornadoes of sand that those propellers were kicking up. In his book about Eagle Claw, *The Guts to Try*, Kyle would later write that he had a hard time tracking me down at Desert One. I found that funny because before departing Wadi Qena, I had gone out of my way to offer him a secure brick radio tuned to my team's frequency, but he flat turned me down. "I don't need people jawing my ear off," he said. "If I want to talk to someone, I'll find them." If he'd taken the radio, he would have been able to speak to me at any time. Without having to find me. Oh well. Kyle and the Air Force personnel under him were outstanding throughout the whole operation, start to finish. They certainly weren't the reason it went sideways.

The fuel truck was still burning bright and high. At least it would make a good visual reference for the choppers, which indeed were having trouble navigating in the low-vis conditions—and were now running late. Very late. Charlie Beckwith was beside himself, gripped with tension over the whole deal.

We all were.

Waiting.

Wondering.

Everyone checking their watches.

Was this thing gonna happen?

Where the hell are these guys?

DEVIL WIND

The problem was the Marine pilots flying the Sea Stallions.

This wasn't their usual gig. Their original training had prepared them only for minesweeping duties. At sea. It was as simple as that. They had never flown a mission like this. A special operation. It was way above their pay grade—and that was no fault of their own. They did their best, but as hard as they worked on the technical aspects of flying through all the exercises we ran, it always seemed that their hearts weren't in it. And for this kind of mission, flying nap-of-the-earth, no light, first-time navigating with night-vision goggles in real-world warfare, you had to be willing to go *beyond* all the way. You had to maintain a special operations mindset—a *Delta* mindset—and that's a rare thing. Make the impossible *possible*.

No slight on them. At least they had been brave enough to try in the first place. They were Marines. But I had no idea whose bright idea it was to use guys who'd never flown any type of mission even remotely close to this one. Why not use guys who flew slicks or heavy-lift missions in Vietnam, people who would fly with their rotors duct-taped together if necessary. The Pentagon sometimes was more like a Rubik's cube whose colors never matched up.

But that was all above my pay grade.

Thankfully.

Poor Charlie Beckwith: he had the weight of an entire nation on his shoulders under the direst of circumstances.

In the aftermath, there would be a lot of finger-pointing and dispute about when those choppers actually arrived at Desert One; but I knew our timetable like the back of my hand. I was running the overwatch at Desert One, so I was paying attention to everything coming in and going out, every piece of the puzzle as it got put in place or left a gap. We had arrived on time and handled the bus and the smugglers with cool precision. We had the passengers under calm control and were ready to go forward with the mission despite any hiccups. The bladder birds were on the ground, revved up and ready to do their mating ritual with the thirsty choppers when they finally started to arrive at Desert One.

Hearing the *whump-whump-whump* of those rotor blades took me to back to the elation of all those times in Vietnam when our slicks rode in to save the day. More so because I knew we could now proceed with the business of rescuing our fellow Americans and making sure no one got left behind. That elation would be short-lived.

The first Sea Stallion—call sign "Bluebeard 1"—arrived exactly one hour and forty-five minutes behind schedule—which meant the assault teams and the choppers themselves wouldn't have gotten to their separate hide-sites at Desert Two for the layover until well after daylight, putting the mission at risk. It was a risk that Beckwith was willing to take.

Until more problems arose.

Of the eight Sea Stallions assigned to the mission—flying in four pairs, along a different flight path than the one that the 130s had followed, though still as demanding and dangerous—two had already been lost on the first leg of the journey. One chopper had returned to the *Nimitz* with electrical issues, and another had ditched in the desert due to a cracked rotor blade. A third chopper—*Bluebeard 8*—picked up the stranded crew. That left six. OK. We could go with six. Our plan allowed for it. The Delta assault teams began to load up and board.

But then there were the pilots.

By the time they got to Desert One, they were frazzled.

On their last nerve.

Maybe past it.

Fried.

Their mental state hung at the exact opposite end of the edge of where it needed to be. They were exhausted, dehydrated, nursing vertigo headaches from the night vision, and they'd just gotten through flying into and out of a violent thousand-foot dust storm that was probably the icing on the cake for the worst conditions any of these men had ever had to face while flying at such a dark and dangerous low altitude. Dust storms in this part of the world were notorious. Big white clouds of granular doom. They swirled up out of the ground out of nowhere, like someone had rubbed the wrong genie's lamp. The locals called them haboob—the devil's wind. The pilots had never flown through anything like it, zero-vis and dust so fine that it permeated their cockpits and coated their skin.

On the other hand, outside the haboob, one of the pilots had felt comfortable enough, despite running behind schedule, to take time to eat a snack on the way in, while another had to urinate so badly, he set his chopper down in the desert to take a leak. *Really?* Why not just go in a bottle, or in your flight suit, for that matter? The hostages were going through a lot worse.

We could have gone with six.

But not five.

And that sixth bird—wouldn't you know it—sitting on the ground, suddenly had its own mechanical issues. Most of the accounts of that night—written by people who weren't there—note the problem itself: that a hydraulic pump had failed. What they would omit—probably because they didn't know—was what caused the failure: some bright light had left a flight jacket draped over an air intake valve of some kind. Whatever. Either way, it was done.

And so were we.

I know I would have gladly carried on the operation.

I know the Delta assault teams would have gladly carried on the operation.

Gone in with only five of the eight choppers.

Hell, we would have gone in on unicycles if we had to; fought our way out on foot, too, against four or five million angry Iranians. But Beckwith wasn't having it. His plan had always called for six choppers minimum to make the mission work as is. Otherwise, he would have had to cut twenty operators from the roster to make space for the hostages, and there was no way that was gonna happen. No wiggle room on this.

Damn.

Beckwith relayed the message to the White House via a secure satellite uplink. The order came back from the president himself: *Abort.*

We had a plan for this.

The exfil.

In the event that we had to abort at Desert One.

It was simple: the assault team would go out on one the remaining 130s, the chopper pilots on their own Sea Stallions. (Two of the Talons were already on their way back to Masirah, and the other was parked a few football fields away on the far end of the LZ.) We'd head back to Egypt; they'd head back to the *Nimitz.*

My team would be the last to board. We would run the road watch to the very last, policing the area to make sure no one was left behind before we bugged out. Because my "loaner" jeep was the only available means of transportation to get back and forth across the sprawling LZ, I assumed the role of the airport shuttle, racing around picking up guys and equipment and making sure that nothing and no one got left behind.

B Squadron commander Logan Fitch ordered his boys onto a fuel-bird that had just finished topping off one of the Sea Stallions before the abort came down. The chopper was still sitting behind its fuel-bird, but now that fuel-bird needed to taxi for takeoff. The abort plan called for all the 130s to get off the ground before the choppers. The topped-off Stallion had damaged its nose gear, so the pilot would have to air-taxi it out of the way. One of Carney's combat controllers moved into position to guide the first chopper away from the tanker, but the downdraft off the Sea Stallion's own massive heavy-lift rotors was whipping up its own kind of devil winds, and visibility dropped to near zero around both the fuel-bird and the chopper, the controller like a small black smudge that the chalky white dust wiped from view. That left the pilot of the chopper disoriented as he tried to maneuver, lurching forward and to the left when he should have slid back and to the right.

I was sitting next to Lieutenant Colonel Carl Savory, the Unit's senior surgeon, in my "loaner" jeep, watching it all go down, when we heard a loud metallic crash, like Godzilla chomping down on some steel girders, as the chopper's rotor blades clipped the top of the fuel-bird just behind the crew compartment, and the giant Sea Stallion dipped its dying nose and rammed into the 130's cockpit. I had been danger-close to plenty of napalm strikes, close enough to cook my bones, but the fuel-lit explosion at the tail end of the chain reaction that came out of that impact produced a blaze like nothing I had ever seen before: fireballs of red, blue, and orange ringed around a twirling high-rise of blinding white light that stood like a towering inferno over the crash site.

Without hesitation, Doc Savory said, "Get me over there."

As we sped toward the wreckage, we could see men coming out of the burning plane. Some of them were on fire. We were more than a football field's distance away and the heat felt like it was out of hell's own blast furnace. There were thirty-six Delta operators on board, plus the crew, and then the eight who were on the chopper. My God. The impact of the collision had jammed the fuel-bird's ramp and all but one of the paratroop doors. The operators and crew were trying to escape through any hatch they could get open. Still mashing the jeep's gas, I saw two other black silhouettes running toward the burning airframe. The two men were Master Sergeant Paul Lawrence, a Delta Force operator, and Sergeant First Class Stu O'Neill, one of two observers that the British SAS had sent to tag along with us. Both would receive the Soldier's Medal for their heroic actions in pulling men off the plane. But not everyone. Between the chopper and the fuel-bird, eight brave men would perish in the blaze. Five Air Force personnel from the C-130 crew, and three Marines on the Sea Stallion.

Doc Savory began triaging the wounded. We were losing the cover of darkness as an early dawn threatened to break across the horizon, and we still had to get everyone the hell out of here, including those requiring more intensive medical care. The flames were starting to mellow out, but then I heard the familiar Jiffy-Pop crackle as the heat started cooking off ammo and other munitions left aboard the aircraft. Red streaks licked skyward. The Rangers had brought with them Redeye shoulder-fired missiles to take out any enemy aircraft that might pose a threat to us. Now every single one of those Redeyes popped off and shot up into the night sky. It was like a demonic version of the Fourth of July. No one panicked. Everyone kept on their game faces. We still had to get whatever was left of the job done—but inside, we were all gutted. It would be hours before the fires died and the wreckage cooled enough for us to retrieve any bodies. We had no choice. We had to leave our dead behind. Now, not only were we abandoning the hostages; we were abandoning our own people. Dead or alive, it didn't matter. We were United States soldiers, and the idea of leaving anyone behind went against every last strand of our DNA. But we had to do what we had to do.

I hopped back in the jeep and drove off to continue rounding up any stragglers. We had cut the poor folks on the bus loose and I could see them huddled together a safe distance away from the mayhem. I hoped they were enjoying the show. I found Fitch way off by himself approaching one of the choppers that still had its rotors running. He had been rounding his men up and sending them to the remaining 130s for extraction.

"Yo, dummy, what the hell are you doing?" I shouted.

"Fixing to take off on this chopper."

"Look inside, Einstein."

Fitch poked his head into the troop compartment. It was empty.

I waved him over to the jeep.

"Come on, we're dusting off."

I was the last one off the ground.

Beckwith was holding the plane for me.

As I bounded up the ramp, I saw him staring at his watch and shaking his head.

"Where the hell you been, Jesse?"

"I had to take care of something."

The jeep. There was no room for it on the bird, so I had no choice but to ditch it. I had abandoned it out on the runway—but not before wiring it with a pair of claymores.

16

HOT WASH

The Farm
Camp Peary, Virginia
April 27, 1980

We were in the sticks.

Way out in the backwoods of Virginia, not far from historic Colonial Williamsburg, where aspiring CIA officers sometimes secretly intermingled among the tourists and period-correct historic interpreters, putting their newly acquired surveillance detection routine skills to the test in invisible games of cat and mouse with their instructors, because Camp Peary was their covert training ground, where the Agency sent all its future clandestine officers to learn how to be spooks.

They called it "the Farm."

We called it "the *Funny* Farm."

The spook school was just one part of the place. The Agency also maintained a secure safe-house complex within the sprawling compound where they debriefed defectors and the like.

It was there that we would spend the next few days conducting our own debrief—what in the lexicon of Delta, we called a "hot wash"—warts and all, on Eagle Claw. The disaster of Desert One had begun to sink in and sting from the moment we dusted off from Iranian soil. A collective numbing effect that we all observed and endured in solitary silence. The public fallout would be worse. Possibly the coup de grâce to President Carter's reelection bid—though I'm not so sure it wasn't the economy that did him in, just as it would later do to Bush

41 only one year after he had earned a 90 percent approval rating for winning the Gulf War, not to mention both the fall of the Berlin Wall and the collapse of Soviet Communism happening on his watch. The men of Delta did not care about politics. Our hot wash wouldn't be about that old Beltway parlor game of CYA—"Cover Your Ass"—though you could bet your own ass there'd be plenty of that going around.

We cared about the Americans we left behind.

The hostages we failed to bring home on our inaugural outing as America's premiere counterterrorist unit. And our war dead.

Bitter pills are hard to swallow, but this tasted more like tainted beef. I wanted to vomit. The journey home had been the longest of my life. Longer than when I last left Vietnam—which covered about twenty-four hours with all the connector flights and layovers—if not in duration, then certainly emotion. We were frustrated and angry—even more so after Colonel Beckwith chewed our asses out on our return to Wadi Qena. He went after us for all sorts of nitpicky things—leaving gear and weapons and a bag full of cash behind on the burning fuel-bird. The men were furious with him—some had even given it right back for complaining about such a thing while everyone had been trying to avoid being burnt to the bone. Some of those guys still smelled like smoke and av gas. Those that had caught the worst of the fire had flown on a C-9 that contained a special burn unit. Eight men had died.

History would cast Beckwith as a man who lost his cool after rolling snake eyes on one big gamble. I was the only one who knew the truth because the colonel had confided in me as our Starlifter flew us back across the Atlantic to a blacked-out corner of Andrews Air Force Base near the hangar that housed Air Force One. "Chargin'" Charlie Beckwith had given his men an ass chewing they didn't deserve so they would turn their hatred on him instead of themselves. It was quirky and esoteric, maybe cheap pop psychology, but it worked. By the time we landed, the guys weren't beating themselves up so much.

Eagle Claw was a bust, but you had to suck it up, move on.

Anyway, as far as we were all concerned, we were going back.

That was the first thing people had started asking as soon as we touched down in Wadi Qena: "When are we going back?" The mission would be even harder now, maybe impossible—the Iranians would triple security around the hostages, spread them across several different locations. But we wanted to take another shot at it. Not to prove ourselves. This wasn't about us—our guts, our glory. It was about bringing home our fellow Americans. When General Vaught came to the Farm to address the Unit, he told us this was just the first quarter of the game, and there were still three to go. When we got back to Bragg, we would start planning a second rescue mission in earnest. What we didn't know was—planning or no planning—the notion of a second rescue op was already a dead horse, and we wouldn't even get a chance to beat it. Feeling the heat from the media, their political rivals, and the public at large, the powers-that-be had other ideas.

Our hot wash at the Farm was just the first in what would be a long line of after-action debriefs, reviews, reports, hearings, rebukes—and all-out finger pointing. The media would portray the mission as a failure—a *disaster*. They could have all gone and jumped off a collective cliff as far as we were concerned. Head-first. I knew it could have been a lot worse. Shit, I had been in the worst of Vietnam—that whole war was a decade-long clusterfuck. I was well acquainted with the dangerous mental minefield of "what-ifs." *What if* things had gone sideways at the embassy—during the takedown? *What if* that devil wind had caught us on the dust off out of Tehran or at the soccer stadium, and downed the choppers with a whole army hot on our tails? *What if* we had lost all the hostages? What kind of disaster then?

Eight men had died.

I could have been one of them.

I kept thinking about that. I had never thought like that in Vietnam—it could have been me. But there was something different about this one. I didn't know what. Maybe I was just getting old, starting to feel my mortality. Or wising up. Judith hadn't even known where the hell I was—or that I was even out of the country—until a phone call woke her just after daybreak back in the States. It was Colonel Dean Darling, my former commanding officer at the 509th in Vicenza. "Sorry, Dean, Jess isn't here," Judith told him matter-of-factly. "He's in California training." Because that was the cover story we gave the wives. All of us sitting by the pool at Twenty-nine Palms for the last six months. "No, Judy, he's not. Turn on your TV. They went in." Judith knew instantly that he was talking about Iran. Where else would we have gone? She turned on the news. It was breaking all across the airwaves—an aborted rescue attempt, reports of casualties, people killed. Was I one of them? Judith didn't know. None of the wives knew. They had no one to call, and no one had called them. For her, it was Vietnam all over again, watching the wounded being loaded onto choppers, scanning the litters to see if any of them was her husband because she knew that the ones in the litters were the worst off. It wasn't until the next day that someone from the Pentagon finally reached out to let her know that I was OK.

Washington had no shortage of armchair generals and Monday-morning quarterbacks to throw the blame around. I got my taste when the Director of the

CIA, Admiral Stansfield Turner, a man who had no prior background in intelligence or special operations, sat down with me and Charlie Beckwith to share with us his conclusion that the operation had been compromised by a leak or spy penetration within Delta. I wanted to reach across the table and put the guy in a chokehold, but that would have been impolite. If there had been any risk of penetration, it would have come from his Agency working with a Pahlavite pimp like "Al" and his half-assed handler Harold. But I kept it simple and just told him straight-up: "Sir, a compromise isn't what stirred up that devil wind that took down our choppers."

Turner dropped the issue.

On the second night of our being sequestered, a VIP arrived under the cover of darkness to meet with us. I could hear the rotor blades thumping through the night sky and stirring the pines in the chill air. The chopper was a Sikorsky Sea King, painted black and unmarked; but its call sign was still "Marine One" because on board was James Earl Carter Jr., the thirty-ninth president of the United States. With him—other than the two Secret Service agents who seemed magnetically attached to his flanks—were Harold Brown, his secretary of defense, and Zbigniew Brzezinski, his national security advisor.

We fell into formation on a small back lot where a podium had been set up. We were in civilian clothes, but we stood at attention anyway. This was our commander in chief. The visit was under a strict media blackout—the Secret Service had sneaked him out through a secret White House entrance, put him in an unmarked chopper, and flew him to the Funny Farm under the cover of darkness.

The president thanked us for our efforts, expressed his genuine sorrow and concern for the hostages, and said we needed to continue our efforts to find a way to bring them home. It made us feel good that he still believed in us and didn't blame the Unit for what happened.

When he finished speaking, he went down the line and shook each man's hand, including mine. "Thank you, Mr. President." He offered a small smile, but his eyes looked hollowed out and sunken. This was the closest I had been to a president since John F. Kennedy had come to inspect my outfit back when I was under Tony Herbert's command at the 505th. But the Kennedy thing was just a parade-ground review; he didn't shake our hands. Brzezinski was following the president down the line. One of our guys who was of Polish heritage, spotted his footwear, which looked like a pair of moonboots, and as Brzezinski shook his hand, the operator said in Polish something along the lines of: "I like your shoes, sir." The national security advisor's eyes lit up. "You speak Polish!"

he exclaimed, and then switched to his mother tongue to continue the conversation, chattering away for several minutes.

Later, when everyone else had gone back to their quarters, Beckwith invited me to join him to brief the president in private, along with the secretary of defense and national security advisor. We went through some more of the details concerning the operation; what went right, what went wrong. I could see that Brzezinski and Brown were driving toward the consensus that circumstances beyond our control had doomed the mission from the start, but I didn't quite buy into that. Decisions were what doomed us. Every service branch getting their shot at glory off the bench. Air Force flying the planes, Marines flying the choppers, Navy mechanics servicing those choppers despite being totally unaware of their purpose, and therefore failing to prep them properly. There should have been a tighter whip on who got to play first string.

Carter seemed despondent. He'd put on a good face out in front of Delta, but now he looked almost broken.

I felt bad for him—until we adjourned, and as we were all getting ready to head out, he draped his arm around me and said: "I'm just glad you didn't kill anybody."

I stared at him for a long moment, and the president back at me. I was stunned but said nothing. I had to bite my tongue. I couldn't believe that our commander in chief would say such a thing. Eight Americans had just lost their lives. What the hell was he going on about? Their lives didn't matter? He might not have meant it that way, but that's the way it came off. I gave him the benefit of the doubt and put it down to exhaustion and left it at that. "Yes, sir, Mr. President."

Out in the hallway, a CIA officer that I knew, a hard-nosed instructor who'd worked with the Phoenix Program in Vietnam, one of the lucky few to avoid Turner's purges, took me aside. In-flight to Masirah, Beckwith had requested an air strike to take care of the five choppers that we'd ditched at Desert One; but the White House had put the kibosh on the idea, fearing that we might kill the passengers from the bus. It was unfortunate because we had carried special incendiary explosives with us to blow up the choppers upon our escape with the hostages, but we didn't have time to place them after that fuel-bird blew. Now, the Iranians were all over Desert One, picking over the wreckage and excited to check out their five brand-new, made-in-the-USA Sea Stallions, packed with a treasure trove of classified mission documents that the crews had failed to destroy. Some of the scraps off the wreckage—mechanical bits and pieces—would be integrated into exhibits that still stand to this day, one of them on proud display outside our old embassy complex, now the main headquarters for the Revolutionary Guard, a grand statement in and of itself. The docs the Iranians pulled off our choppers compromised Meadows and his infiltrators, but thankfully they had managed to slip out of Tehran by the skin of their teeth on commercial flights, using their Irish and West German passports. (Hope our Euro allies didn't mind.) I was relieved. Meadows was a good man who'd done a great job the whole way through Eagle Claw. He'd take a lot of flak down the road after giving a cover-story interview on the mission to *Newsweek*. That didn't so much become a thing until much later, during the War on Terror, talking out of turn. By then, it seemed like any special operator who'd put a boot down in-country for five minutes had a tell-all war-glory book to write.

"Something else," the CIA man said. "Intel's picking up chatter out of Iran. Apparently, an Iranian Army patrol that was the first to reach Desert One tried to start a jeep that had been left behind and ended up tripping a pair of claymores that blew them off the damn map." A sly smile drew across his face. "You wouldn't happen to know anything about that, would you?"

I stared at him a sec, expressionless, then said, "Who me? Nope."

INAUGURATION DAY

Within one hour of Ronald Wilson Reagan taking the Oath of Office as the fortieth president of the United States, the Iranian government released all fifty-two of the remaining American hostages. They came back to an America that welcomed them home as heroes, awash with relief on a wave of patriotic fervor. But there was one more hostage whose legacy would never escape the crisis—or its aftermath. The fifty-third hostage—President James Earl Carter Jr.

In loving memory of the eight servicemen
who lost their lives on Operation Eagle Claw

Major Richard L. Bakke, USAF
Major Harold L. Lewis, USAF
Captain Lyn D. McIntosh, USAF
Captain Charles T. McMillan, USAF
Sergeant Joel C. Mayo, USAF
Staff Sergeant Dewey Johnson, USMC
Sergeant John D. Harvey, USMC
Corporal George N. Holmes Jr., USMC

17

BRIGATE ROSSE

Location Classified
February 5, 1982

I was sitting in an old prison.

That's where they had me stashed—the two terrorists breathing down my neck, tight on my flanks, as I sat at the small table in the dark room where they would interrogate me. I could barely make them out from the shadows. There must have been an opening somewhere, though, because I could just detect a wedge of light glinting off what appeared to be a large window to my left that had been blacked out. I was Zen-calm. Statue-still. I didn't flinch an inch or bat an eyelid—not when the door suddenly burst open. Not when my Delta brothers stormed the room in their black commando kit and frog-eyed night-vision gear, MP5s at the ready, and blew away the terrorists with perfect double-taps to the head and chest. Not when the lights came up in a blinding flash to reveal the two "dead" mannequin terrorists to either side of me. And the window that was not a window at all, but a bulletproof partition that the Secret Service had insisted upon after much arguing about the use of live ammo in the first place around their protectee—the Vice President of the United States, George Herbert Walker Bush, our VIP guest for this very special demonstration. A standard room-clearing drill. Hostage rescue 101. Live ammo instead of lip-gunning—shouting "bang-bang!" And yes, with me playing the hostage in the line of fire, a role that I often took, whether here in the Stockade's Shooting House, our "House of Horrors," as we sometimes called it, or even as a live passenger in the Boeing 727 that we used for airplane takedowns.

Coming around to greet me and shake hands as I stood from the table, the vice president complimented me on what he called my "steel-eyed nerve"—to be able to sit like that, in the dark, live rounds cracking past my ear, thudding into the targets at my flanks, blowing the stuffing out of them. "I didn't know which one was the mannequin," said the vice president and former naval aviator who'd earned a Navy Cross in World War II, his steel-rimmed glasses glinting in the overhead lights as he cast a congenial smile. "I understand you're the man that led Operation Winter Harvest. The hunt for General Dozier. You want to tell me a little bit about that?"

YEARS OF LEAD

Dozier.

They grabbed him in Italy.

At his apartment. A week before Christmas.

Got in posing as plumbers. (I always wondered if that was a nod to the Watergaters.)

It was the Brigate Rosse, the Red Brigades. Hard-core Italian leftist radicals. Terrorists. Of all the bloodthirsty Euro-militant commie groups of the era, the Red Brigades were certainly among the most active. And lethal. These were people who'd been expelled from their local Communist Party organizations for being *too* extremist. They didn't just talk the talk. The Brigades had proven well schooled in the methods of mayhem and murder. Not the spectacular two hundred-plus dead in truck bombings that were months away from becoming a signature of the so-called Islamic Jihad Organization, a front for Hezbollah, in Beirut; but rather, dozens of smaller-scale targeted kidnappings and killings, along with the bank robberies and sabotage bombings that had come to define the MO of similar leftist radical groups like the Red Army Faction and the Irish Republican Army. By the time they grabbed up Dozier, they had kidnapped God knows how many and killed at least fifty people over the last half decade or so, including the abduction and murder of Italian prime minister Aldo Moro in 1979. As a target, Dozier made sense. The Red Brigades had stated many times that they intended to seize power through "violent revolution" and upon doing so, pull Italy out of NATO. Dozier was the deputy chief of staff for NATO's Southern European land forces, a Vietnam veteran who'd earned a Silver Star and Purple Heart in-country. When they kidnapped Moro, they held him for fifty-four days before convening their own mock Stalinist-style kangaroo court, then put him "on trial," sentenced him to death, and executed him—all in one go. No doubt anyone hunting these guys would be racing against the clock before they did the same thing to General Dozier.

This was Italy in the Cold War.

These were the "Years of Lead."

I was at home, sitting by a warm, crackling fire as I watched reports of the general's kidnapping break on the evening news. Judith and I had just gotten back from the mall, where we'd finished our Christmas shopping, most of it anyway. I was looking forward to being home for the holidays, kicking my feet up by the fire and enjoying some rare downtime with my family.

I was now the number-two man at Delta Force—deputy commander. It was Beckwith who'd promoted me, one of the last things he did before he left the Unit. The weight of Eagle Claw's failure had crushed his spirit. A lot of people in the Beltway tried to throw him under the bus, but he walked tall and gave 'em hell on the Hill, stood his ground as always, and made sure the right remedies were prescribed to address the very real blind spots that undermined Eagle Claw from the get-go: first, the establishment of JSOC, or Joint Special Operations Command, to bring together under one roof all the other service-branch units tasked with special missions, mainly counterterrorism—no more spur-of-the-moment joint task forces that put way too many cooks in a dozen different kitchens. (Now, we were a one-stop shop.) And second, a dedicated elite force of hot-shit chopper-jockeys who could get us in where we needed to go no matter where it was or what the conditions. Dust-off in a dust storm. People who didn't worry about losing daylight, but instead owning the night. Which led to the formation of what would eventually become the 160th Special Operations Aviation Regiment (SOAR), the mythical "Night Stalkers" of *Black Hawk Down* fame. And no joke, these guys were badass. I know firsthand because I advised on its formation. These were the guys who would fly in the Red Squadron SEALs who zipped Bin Laden. That was Charlie Beckwith's true legacy—not the failure of Eagle Claw, but the success of the changes that he fought for in its wake—changes that would save many American lives over the next four decades. He never got over it, though—Desert One. The whole deal left him feeling busted flat. I remember one time I was over at his place with Judith for dinner when she produced a scrapbook that she had put together with all the news clippings on Eagle Claw. He wouldn't even look at it, told her to put it away.

"You think they'll send you?"

It was Judith, watching the TV talk about all the devil's work that the Red Brigades had done in Italy over the last decade, culminating in the "Moro Case"—*Caso Moro*. And now this.

"Not a chance," I told her. No way. This was an Italian job—something for their state police and its counterterrorist unit, the NOCS, one of the best in the business, to handle.

Then my pager beeped.

The only guys who had pagers in 1981 were doctors and Delta—not even drug dealers yet. And ours were the only kind—still not even on the market— that had a display. I checked it: CALL THE UNIT.

Judith said, "I'll get your Go Bag," and calmly walked off down the hall toward our bedroom. "If we're lucky you'll be home before Christmas."

=====

Rome
December 19

They flew us out the next day on a commercial flight.

I was traveling on a diplomatic passport but under a different name. I think we were supposed to be State Department so-and-sos, which would have probably marked me as CIA to anyone watching as CIA anyway. You had to be careful traveling around Europe. The Red Brigades and all the other loony-left terrorist groups were all Eastern Bloc trained and had hooks in with the Stasi and the KGB. You never knew what kind of intel those fine and friendly folks might be feeding them. Moscow Center wouldn't lose any sleep over the kidnapping of a top NATO general—and an American, no less. As long as their fingerprints weren't on it, good riddance.

I had a layover in Germany that was long enough for me to head into Stuttgart, home of the Porsche factory and headquarters of the United States European Command, where I checked in with their J-3, or operations officer, Vice Admiral Thomas Kinnebrew. Right out of the starting gate, Kinnebrew struck me as one of these "by-the-book" guys who seemed to write the rules as he went along and whose pomposity was more a product of his rank than his record, which meant he liked to throw it around. He was uptight and snarky, focusing on anything and everything that had nothing to do with getting General Dozier back before his captors killed him, making little side remarks about my nonregulation Delta haircut, or lack thereof, and complaining that I was out of uniform. I didn't sweat it. One additional skillset Delta had learned on the fly during both our formation and Eagle Claw was how to bust through bureaucratic roadblocks, put down any pencil pushers manning the checkpoints. So as the admiral fired his warning shots, I just nodded and smiled, even as he mentioned my uniform yet again for good measure, then thanked him very much and made my exit—but not before he took one last shot at my attire. It was a refrain I'd hear about a half dozen times over the next few weeks while dealing with him—mainly from others with whom he'd lodged the same complaint about me—so when this thing was all said and done, I made sure to break out my best Class A's with all my ribbons decked out on colorful display, including my three Silver Stars and my DSC, as I appeared before him for the last time before heading home—*in uniform.*

Arriving in Rome, I went straight to our embassy and met with Deputy Chief of Mission Peter Bridges, who informed me that Kinnebrew had already dispatched Colonel Norm Moffitt, commander of Special Operations Forces-Europe, a special-ops planning cell, to Rome to brief our ambassador, Maxwell Raab. Kinnebrew—via Moffitt—had insisted that Det-A, coming out of Berlin under the EUCOM chain of command, would handle the hunt for Dozier. Detachment-A had done a superb job on Eagle Claw, but they were not the right outfit for this kind of work. In a pinch, yes, maybe; but no unit was as focused on counterterrorism as specifically or intensely as *the* Unit—Delta Force. I realized right away that I was once again standing in the middle of a minefield, but this one sprawling out before me amid a turf battle that was about to light off over my presence and was way above my pay grade as a dime-a-dozen—and very expendable—lieutenant colonel. No matter how highly decorated.

I thanked Bridges for the update, left the embassy, and found the nearest pay phone. I slotted just enough change into the phone to open the line, then attached my little Delta Q-Branch gizmo to the receiver, instantly turning it into a secure satellite uplink. I punched in a long series of digits that would never be mistaken for a telephone number anywhere in the world, more akin to an automobile VIN, heard the static break across the connection and then a series of beeps that stood in for a ringtone. It was on the fourth beep that the voice at the other end came on the line. The voice belonged to Colonel Rod Paschall, the new commanding officer of Delta Force, an excellent leader who'd served two tours in Vietnam—earning a pair of Silver Stars and a Purple Heart—and years later would go on to write military doc scripts for the History Channel and A&E's *Biography.* I was honored to serve as his deputy; but sadly, that service would hurt my friendship with his predecessor. Upon leaving the Unit, Charlie Beckwith had rung me up and asked me point-blank where my loyalties would lie: with him or the new guy. It was an unfair and loaded question, and I was surprised that he would even ask it, but Charlie was mercurial that way sometimes. I told him the truth—that my loyalty would always remain with the current commander that I was sworn to serve. He hung up on me, and our friendship was never quite the same after that. Oh well. I still would always think the world of him—but I also had a job to do.

I gave Paschall the rundown: Delta had no mission in Italy. EUCOM wanted Det-A to be the embassy's tango partner on this one. (*Let the turf war begin!*) At least I'd be home for Christmas as planned. But Paschall had other ideas. He told me to hang tight: he would take care of it—and boy, was that an understatement. Paschall must have had quite a strong foot, because he kicked this thing all the way up the chain to the Joint Chiefs; the Chairman of the Joint Chiefs of Staff himself, General David C. Jones, put out a very firm and not-so-friendly reminder to all those involved that the US government had created Delta Force for this very role—counterterrorism—and Uncle Sugar had spent tens of millions of dollars on its formation, training, and equipment so that when terrorists, say, kidnapped one of our generals, Delta would be the ones to deal with it.

That settled that.

(Well, kinda.)

Moffitt split for Stuttgart, leaving Colonel Chuck Vossen, our defense attaché in Rome, with the awkward task of informing Ambassador Raab that there had been a mistake: Delta had control, and I was the man in charge.

I had already booked a flight out of Fiumicino, and was sitting in the airport lounge, still unconvinced that this would get resolved in any short order, when I heard my alias being paged over the airport PA. I avoided the courtesy phone and called into the embassy on a pay phone. Just in case it was an attempt to bust my cover.

The embassy switchboard patched me through to Vossen, still choking on all the crow he'd had to eat on Kinnebrew's behalf. I could sympathize: Vossen, like me, was just another colonel trying to keep his head out of the political cross fire, to avoid being turned into a scapegoat or sacrificial lamb or whatever animal metaphor the Pentagon was using these days.

"Get back to the embassy," he said, and clicked off before I could even issue a "Yes, sir." So much for being home for the holidays.

I caught the first cab back into the city.

It was Sunday evening.

General Dozier had been missing for three days.

Reagan's man in Rome, Ambassador Maxwell Raab, was a political appointee.

That could be a good thing, or a bad thing.

Ambassadors were tricky.

On the one hand, career foreign service officers, the guys who'd spent their whole careers at Foggy Bottom climbing the diplomatic ladder while suffering one backwater posting after another, until finally achieving their dream of a marquee post like Bonn or Moscow, could be problematic. Insofar that they tended to be too infected with the gun-shy culture that seemed to define the State Department in situations like this one, even at their most dangerous postings. (Hence, Benghazi.) Too much so to countenance action, even when it was the only option available and absolutely necessary—as in when facing murderous terrorist groups like the Red Brigades or others who might only respond to force. Sometimes you had to take a life to protect many more lives—or take several lives to protect your own. Some very good-natured and smart people strangely had trouble reconciling that simple but hard truth. On the other hand, political appointees, who acquired their ambassadorships through high-roller presidential campaign donations—in amounts over $250,000—the kind that came in bundles and were funneled through PACs, could be risk-averse simply because they were too ignorant to know better, that avoiding risk was often the riskier proposition when it came to counterterrorism.

Ambassador Raab displayed none of these hang-ups—and nobody on the civilian side of the Dozier Affair exerted more effort to secure the general's release than him. It was a pleasure to work with him, and it would spoil me down the road when I worked with other senior diplomatic officials who proved much less helpful under even more dire circumstances.

I brought in a Delta assault team, along with a small crew from a new clandestine military intelligence unit that, when established in the wake of Eagle Claw, had been called the Field Operations Group, or FOG—a fitting name, considering that they seemed to operate in the cloudy mist that often enveloped covert operations. Without a doubt, they were the spookiest outfit in the US armed forces—spookier even than Delta. Since renamed the more innocuous-sounding Intelligence Support Activity, or simply "the Activity," its baptism-by-fire inaugural op had been to infiltrate Iran to gather intel on the ground in advance of a second rescue attempt—code-named "Snowbird"—after the Revolutionary Guard had already beefed-up security to the max in the wake of Desert One. Though Snowbird ended up a nonstarter, the Activity had proven their chops, slipping in and out of the most hostile territory on earth without a trace. They were code-breaking commandos, infiltrators, every single one of 'em a ghost; like their unit, they didn't exist. Their specialty was advance force intelligence gathering—including human and electronic—and operational support. At all times operating undercover, like Delta, they wore civilian clothes and haircuts—which probably would have made Kinnebrew's head explode more than anything if he'd known they were even in Rome.

The good admiral was still buzzing around, auditioning for his role as the official bureaucratic fly in the ointment, now arguing that—because I was military—I had no business working directly for the ambassador and must report to him at EUCOM. Raab handled it like a seasoned pro, firing off an official top secret memo that reaffirmed our working relationship: that I had carte blanche to take any action I deemed necessary, and that I would report those actions to him or his deputy, Bridges, when and if I was able to do so, whether before or after. In other words, he shut down Kinnebrew for good.

We were in business.

After all the unnecessary delay, it was time to find Dozier.

We set up shop in the warren of basement offices that made up the CIA's Rome Station, if only because it made intelligence sharing easier and was the most secure part of the embassy, reinforced against the electronic eyes and ears of the KGB and every other Eastern Bloc spook-house running round-the-clock surveillance on the place.

Day One, I sent some of my guys up to Livorno to co-locate and coordinate with our counterparts in the Carabinieri, which, like the French Gendarmerie Nationale, was a military force that acted as a national police agency with powers of arrest. The Carabinieri had its own counterterrorist unit, the GIS, and had taken the lead from the Italian side in the hunt for Dozier. They were very aggressive, chasing down leads, kicking down doors, hauling in suspects; they had even set up round-the-clock roadblocks along every route from Verona to Venice. But they were dealing with their own turf battle; and when the shoe finally dropped on the Red Brigades, it would be Italy's other national police force, the civilian Polizia di Stato, and their own in-house counterterror unit, the NOCS, that would win out on handling any takedown. We worked with both units, observing their infiltration techniques and room-clearing drills. Several of our friends in other European CT units—German GSG-9, French GIGN, and as always, our old mates in the British SAS—called in to offer support and assistance: manpower, intel, equipment, anything we needed; just say the word kinda thing. "But not weapons," said Colonel Ulrich Wegener across a secure line. "We can't do weapons." I said: "Nah, I don't need weapons, Colonel. I got plenty of my own. *Danke*." Weapons or no weapons, it was nice to know they had our backs the same way we would have theirs under similar circumstances—but there wouldn't be any takedown if we didn't find Dozier first.

The Red Brigades had issued a series of communiqués, one even loonier than the last. The first paid homage to the German Red Army Faction, whose operatives Italian intelligence suspected of participating in the Moro abduction, and referred to Dozier as "a Yankee pig of the American occupation army," saying that he was being held in "a people's prison." Another announced the start of a "proletarian trial" for "the assassin and hero of the Vietnam massacres," and included a photograph of the general with a badly swollen eye, likely from the beating he took when they grabbed him, as he sat in front of a red banner emblazoned with the group's communist gold star emblem. (According to Dozier's wife, also named Judith, the general had only stopped fighting when one of the "plumbers" put a silenced pistol to her head.) But the most demented dispatch had to be one that demanded the removal of the entire Sixth Fleet from the Mediterranean Sea in exchange for his safe return. (Yeah, not a chance.) Even crazier was the army of psychics that our own people in the Defense Intelligence Agency (DIA) sent our way out of this bogus experimental "remote-viewing" project they had going out in California that even involved a TV magician who claimed to have telekinetic powers or some jazz like that—"Project Stargazer," they called it. (Because there wasn't a hokier New Age name available, I guess.) Some of these nutjobs had even convinced the Pentagon to send them—all-expenses paid, of course—to Rome to "help" us. I thought it was all a bunch of hocus-pocus crackpot-crap, and refused to even let them near our command post in the embassy. When Ambassador Raab asked for my thoughts on the matter, I told him, "Mr. Ambassador, I may be just a good ol' country boy, but I think these so-called fortune-tellers are nothing but a bunch of fortune hunters looking for a free trip to Italy." Raab smiled and said, "I couldn't agree more, Colonel," then remarked on what a shame it would be if all the United States contributed to the recovery of one of its own was a bunch of crystal-ball-rubbing clairvoyants sitting around a Ouija board.

Christmas and New Year's came and went, and I had that lonely feeling in the pit of my stomach that I had felt on both my tours in Vietnam, and a couple of other times since with Delta—but at least I was free. I imagined General Dozier and his wife would remember this as the most unpleasant holiday season of his life.

The Brigades weren't bashful; they were brazen. While we hunted them, one of their hit squads used gelignite to blast a hole in the wall of the maximum-security women's prison at Rovigo and bust out four of their members, who raked the guards with suppressive fire from the submachine guns that their comrades had thrown to them through the hole—just fifty miles from where they'd kidnapped Dozier. Right after the New Year, they attempted to kidnap Nicola Simone, the deputy chief of the Polizia di Stato's counterterrorism and organized crime intelligence branch, a man with whom I had been working closely. When he resisted, the attackers, posing as mailmen, shot him twice in the face, but Nicola managed to pop off a round that winged one of them as they fled, before collapsing at the doorstep of his Rome apartment. It was a miracle he survived.

What we thought might be our first big break in the case came in the form of a proposition from a source, a cutout or go-between, connected to the Red Brigades, who offered to give us Dozier's location in return for a $450,000 "reward"—what was really a ransom. Word on the Italian street was that the United States would cough up big-time to get the general back, but the reality was that the embassy didn't have those kind of funds on tap, and we sure didn't have time to machete through all the red tape that the Pentagon was sure to throw our way before releasing them.

But I knew someone else who might be able to help us.

Some months after Eagle Claw, I had been sitting in my office at the Stockade when my phone rang. I was filling out paperwork and snatched up the receiver without lifting my eyes from my desk. "Hello?"

"Hi there, is this Lieutenant Colonel Jesse Johnson, deputy commander of Delta Force?"

"Who the hell is this?"

The voice, with its nasally Texarkana twang, sounded familiar; but I couldn't quite place it.

"This is Ross Perot."

I laughed. "Yeah, right, bullshit," I said, and hung up the phone. I thought it was one of the guys pranking me; they loved to do stuff like that. Whoever it was sure as hell had a future in Hollywood as the next Rich Little because he did a damn good imitation of the guy. That's because it was the guy—*Perot*. As I soon found out when he called back and established his bona fides.

"My apologies, sir. What can I do for you?"

I knew that this was the man who'd tried to bring Christmas to our POWs in North Vietnam and had personally arranged to get his people out of an Iranian prison during the hostage crisis.

He said, "I understand that there were eight men killed at Desert One. Is that accurate?"

"Yes, sir," I replied.

"And I understand that they left behind seventeen children between them, and that there is a scholarship fund being established to help them with their education?"

"Yes, sir."

"Now I also understand that y'all are just getting started with it and haven't raised very much yet. Correct?"

"That is correct, sir."

"OK," he said. "Well, you're gonna be the first to hear it, but I'm gonna tell you: every single one of those kids is going to college—on me. I've already arranged to donate the necessary funds."

To what would become, thanks very much in large part to Perot's own extremely generous donation and future fundraising efforts, the Special Operations Warrior Foundation, a fantastic nonprofit organization that would go on to fully fund the education of over four hundred surviving children of fallen special operators and Medal of Honor recipients to date.

Before ringing off, Perot had given me his direct line, where he said he could be reached at any time, day or night, if Delta ever needed anything. I called it now, from the embassy, and gave him the rundown. I was just glad he didn't hang up on me the way I had hung up on him. He told me to give him one hour, then go to the Banco di Roma on Via Veneto, ask for the manager, and tell him a "Mr. Brown" had sent me. That was it. An hour later, I did exactly as instructed. As soon as I introduced myself to the manager, he showed me to a back room and, without saying a word, handed me a small valise with a half million dollars of cash stuffed into it. As I walked back to the embassy with a jackpot-score dangling from my fingertips, I was sure glad I was packing my .45.

Anyway, the whole thing turned out to be a dead end—the cutout never rang back at the appointed hour—so I returned the money to the bank. But Perot never hesitated—that's the kind of guy he was—always ready to help out his fellow Americans, especially soldiers. (Looking back now, maybe it's too bad we didn't elect him and Admiral Stockdale to the White House back when he ran against Bush and Clinton in '92, after all.)

The leads started pouring in, the Activity spinning the little dials on all their slick gear: multiband scanners that could trap and track radio signals—even the encrypted, frequency-hopping kind that the Red Brigades favored—and electronic direction finders to triangulate location. A lot of this stuff was homebuilt inside the outfit, ten years ahead of anything in the movies. We packed it into a Huey helicopter to overfly areas where we believed the Brigades were operating or holed up. Mobile units—Activity guys dressed up as painters or delivery drivers in white panel vans, with Delta and GIS or NOCS shooters covering their six—worked the ground routine, mirroring the chopper overhead while phantom-tapping phone lines and snatching electromagnetic transmissions and radio waves out of thin air. Most of the grid mapping was done in our basement command post and came off intel gleaned from the Italians after several raids, arrests, and interrogations that boxed in the Brigades' cutout and courier network. The ground teams used new voice-match analysis technology (that they created) to ID Brigade members from their speech patterns. Everything we grabbed—frequencies, wavelengths, whatever—got kicked back to the National Security Agency (NSA) and its geek squad of signals experts and computer scientists at "the Puzzle Palace" at Fort Meade, Maryland, who re-tasked one of their Aquacade satellites flying high over the Med to stay on top of the trapped signals and track them to the Red Brigade's safe houses. It was a full-court commando and computer nerd press. We even helped the Italians muscle the local Mafia, who feared the extra heat over allegations that they had sold the Brigades the weapons they used to conduct their terror operations, including Dozier's abduction. Word went out on the street to every low-level hood, drug dealer, and criminal informant out there to give up any leads on the general's whereabouts or go take a swim with the fishes. Wherever and whenever the Brigades surfaced to communicate, we trapped the signals. Off this, we'd locate a possible safe house where they might be holding Dozier, and we'd mount up with NOCS and jump on board the choppers and hit the rooftops *Black Hawk Down*-style, only to end up hitting a dry hole—at least as far as Dozier's whereabouts were concerned. But we knew we were hot on the trail, and with each takedown, getting one step closer. We also knew that it was only a matter of time before they decided to call their kangaroo court into session and sentence him to death. The Red Brigades had taken many hostages over the last several years, and not one had been found alive.

I started working the streets, trying to chase down some of the leads that were coming out of the Activity; maybe even see if I could draw these bastards out. I knew the embassy was being watched—KGB, East German HVA, take your pick. So, money or no money, I took precautions—alternating routes to dry clean my tail, double-backing at random, window shopping to spot any surveillance reflecting off the glass—all the little tricks of the trade that I had learned during several Delta-sponsored visits to the Funny Farm. And I was always armed. One night, as I was crossing a bridge on the way back to our safe house, an apartment within walking distance of the embassy, I noticed a black Fiat pacing me. Black Fiats were a dime a dozen in Rome, but I knew the Red Brigades favored them. I walked faster. Yeah, I had my .45 and a spare mag, but I had seen how they'd taken down Moro and the arms caches—automatic weapons, RPGs, gelignite, like they used in that prison break—that we'd pulled out of a couple of those "dry holes." If they were coming at me strong, I knew it would be with Beretta submachine guns. They'd already tried to kidnap and kill Italy's top counterterrorism cop; what a coup it would be for them to kidnap the American Army guy responsible for finding the other American Army guy that they'd kidnapped—even better, another "assassin and hero of the Vietnam massacres." The car crawled at my flank. I dropped my hand low at my side, fingertips brushing the edge of my sport coat, ready to sweep it back and slap the .45 from the waistband holster riding my hip. Up ahead, a small gang of prostitutes was warming their hands over a burn barrel, looking to turn a trick. I glanced over the side of the bridge. Thirty-foot drop. If I had to jump—

Then the Fiat's engine howled.

I ducked down fast, almost to my knees, whipped out my pistol from under my jacket, tracking the vehicle as it sped past in a sudden blur, my heart racing as I watched it pull fast over to the curb up near the burn barrel. Then the driver said something to the campfire girls trying to stay warm, engaging in a bit of back and forth, until one of them casually strutted over to the car and leaned seductively into the window to get down to business. Just a john looking for a cheap date. I holstered my weapon.

BALLIAMO?

At long last, we bagged the intel we needed to connect up the missing dots that allowed us to track down our man and the bad guys who took him. A pair of snap-raids outside Rome had yielded the arrests of several Red Brigade operatives and a jackpot of intel on the cell that had kidnapped Dozier, and its leader, Antonio Savasta, whose mug we had up on our crazy wall back at the embassy command post. This, combined with our own triangulation of Red Brigade radio nets, had tightened the fix down to three possible areas around the Veneto region between Padua, Vicenza, and Verona. We had the Brigades' comms networks cold and were picking up a lot of chatter from a run-down section of Padua called Guizza, which tracked with some of the street intel that the Italians were getting off their informants in the Mafia, but they were careful to talk around Dozier's exact location. Then the Activity caught a signal from a yacht off Venice that had several times pinged Red Brigade radios in the same neighborhood. The yacht belonged to a local doctor, a respected lung disease specialist, who also happened to be a Red Brigades sympathizer. I had the Activity get their geek on, tap into the electrical grid, and track all electricity usage in the same area for the last several weeks—until they noticed a sudden spike that occurred in a shabby, second-floor apartment above a supermarket at no. 2 Via Pindemonte on the same day Dozier was kidnapped. But that wasn't all. It turned out that the owner of the apartment was the same doctor who owned the yacht with the transmitter that had been pinging all those Red Brigade radios. *Bingo*.

We linked back up with the Italian Five-O and set up full-sweep surveillance on the place, photographing and tracking every face that went in and out, even the supermarket. Sure enough, some of those faces belonged to Red Brigade bad guys, the same mugs we had up on our crazy wall. The next morning, NOCS moved into position to execute the takedown. The Italian newspapers called them *le teste di cuoio*, "the Leatherheads," because of the leather balaclavas they wore back then. My Delta door kickers had already advised them on a general action plan for this exact scenario. The first thing was to create a distraction. As NOCS prepared to strike, a team of undercover policemen dressed as construction workers fired up a loud bulldozer on the street fronting the supermarket. I was in the command post across the street with the NOCS commander, both of us watching through a pair of long-focus lenses that our people had been using to photograph the bad guys. When everything was in place, the NOCS commander looked at me. Both of us had on our war faces, and his was as cold and hard as steel, someone who had seen action taking down some of the Cosa Nostra's most vicious crime bosses in Italy's Mafia Wars.

"*Balliamo?*"

I didn't *parlo italiano*, so I had no idea what he'd just said. It was only later, when I looked it up in a foreign-language dictionary, that I would discover that his one word actually translated to three: *shall we dance?* But I got the gist: Dozier was an American flag officer, the only one ever kidnapped by terrorists. If his people were going in, the NOCS commander wanted sign-off from the senior American in charge—and that was me. Hitting him with my own cold stare, the thousand-yarder that I'd carved in the Ia Drang and the Suoi Ca and the Mekong Delta, I nodded once and answered: "It's a go—take 'em down."

They hit from front and back, all armed with the same Beretta submachine guns that the Brigades favored. Six guys up the front stairs, four up the fire escape at the back. They found five bad guys inside, one a former railway worker who was still carrying the two bags of groceries that he had just purchased downstairs. They took him down with a hard chop to the back of his neck and— before he even knew what the hell was going on—bound his wrists with a pair of the brand-new plastic flex cuffs that we'd loaned them for the purpose because they weren't yet widely available. Three others surrendered right away. The last was Savasta, who realized they were being hit and raced to the bedroom where they were holding Dozier under a tent to disorient him between night and day and put a silenced Beretta pistol to his head. Whether he was going to kill him or use him as a bargaining chip, we would never find out. One of the NOCS operators had already gotten in through a window from the fire escape and pistol whipped the hell out of the little commie bastard before he could shoot. It was all over in less than two minutes. A perfect takedown. (*Forza Italia!*) Dozier was a little worse for wear, a bit ashen, slightly gaunt—understandable considering that he'd been kept shackled by his ankle to a bed with music blaring in his ears from the headphones they had made him wear for the entire forty-two-day duration of his captivity—but otherwise in good health. It would take a lot more to break any man who'd earned a Silver Star and Purple Heart in Vietnam. I congratulated my Italian counterpart, and once the general was safely transferred to Caserma Ederle, my old Army post in Vicenza, I called into Bragg and requested a C-141 Starlifter to get me and my team back stateside ASAP. Dozier was going home to celebrate the Christmas that he'd missed, and so was I.

Our tree was still up when I got home, Judith waiting to welcome me with her warm embrace. But one small hitch: Judith had been glued to the news coverage of Dozier's rescue, including the moment that he was reunited with his wife and presented her with a belated Christmas gift: a beautiful gold Medallion of St. Mark, no less—something Judith herself had wanted ever since we lived in Vicenza.

Gazing with her soft eyes into my own, she said, "*He* was kidnapped."

"Yes, he was," I replied. I could see where this was heading, but I knew it was probably best to go along.

Judith said, "And still he found time to get his wife a lovely Christmas gift like that. . . ."

"He did do that, didn't he?"

"*Hm-mmm. . . .*"

I gave a shrug. "Whoops."

"Yes indeed," Judith said, nodding with a smile. "*Big* whoops."

"Did I ever tell you how beautiful you are?"

"Uh-huh. . . ."

INTO THE STORM

18

INTERNAL LOOK

Washington, DC
June 9, 1990

I said one more prayer before the Wall.

It wasn't a formal prayer, like the Lord's Prayer, just my own. But I said it for every last one of them—the over fifty-eight thousand names carved into its sloping black-granite expanse. Our war dead from Vietnam—both those declared so and killed in action. I came to this place often. Whenever I was in our nation's capital. I was drawn here. Always. I had attended the dedication back in '82; on a cool, crisp November day, the bright sunshine of autumn battling a smoky chill that signaled the restless stir of a cold hard winter. I remembered walking the entire length of the Wall, decked out in my Class A's, ribbons and patches on proud display. I remembered the knee-deep sea of mementos from one angled end to the other. Photos, dog tags, jungle boots, C-rat cans. Medals. Purple Hearts. Last letters home. Liberated from dusty old attics and freed from fireplace mantels to convene here in collective memoriam. You could smell the flowers a mile away. I remembered the one fellow veteran who picked me out of the crowd when he spotted the silver oak leaves on my uniform and asked me to do him a favor. He told me that no one had ever properly decorated him with the six medals that he'd earned fighting in the jungles of Vietnam. "Sir, would you award them to me right now?" He was a young man, much younger than me, couldn't have been more than eighteen when he was in-country. He was wearing his old combat fatigues and carried his decorations in a small olive-drab canvas bag that he held out before me and looked as timeworn as the war and all the men who fought it—even the younger ones. Like him. "I would be honored to present these awards to you," I replied. With him was another veteran, a war buddy, also in fatigues but missing a leg. I appointed this man my adjutant, and one by one, as he read the appropriate citation, his voice quavering but undaunted, I pinned each medal to the young veteran's chest. A crowd gathered around us. Cameras whined as people started snapping photographs. Some were crying. On the last decoration, the young man stayed standing at rigid attention, face awash in tears, as he tried to choke them back just long enough to tell me: "Thank you, sir. I have waited fifteen years for this moment—and now I can finally rest in peace." Then we shook hands and saluted each other in solemn soldierly grace—and then it was I who felt at peace.

The memory of that moment faded but never died. It lived and breathed and swirled over this place, sunken into the sacred ground under each polished panel. With all the other memories. All those names. Private Stirpe and Lieutenant Colonel Schroeder. Sergeant Cowen.

I looked even further back in time: to a letter I received while still on my second tour. The letter was from one John Cover, a former coach of the Pocahontas high school football team, asking after his brother, Specialist-4 Bobby Cecil Cover, who was stationed with us at Fire Base Moore, serving with the 9th Infantry Division for just two weeks in August 1968 before he was killed in action. Coach Cover had read about my "gallant action," as he put it, in our hometown paper, the *Pocahontas Star Herald*. The Army had told him that his brother had died in the Delta, but nothing more. He wanted to know if I might be able to *"shed some light on his loss of life."* Bobby had only been with us a short while and hadn't made enough war buddies yet to write home about him, so there was no one for me to ask. I didn't know him myself, and I never did find out what happened to him. The details of his death had died with him on the battlefield. There was no scar tissue between the hand-scripted lines of the letters from the loved ones left behind. Just open wounds that would never heal. All those severed souls piled high in the wake of such great loss. How do you shed light through so much darkness? I found him now, Specialist-4 Bobby Cecil Cover, at Panel 46-West, Line 47—and I touched his name. I touched all their names. The brothers who had died at my side. Or under my command. Somewhere else in the same hell. Many had no children. They had died too young.

SOCCENT
Special Operations Command Central
MacDill Air Force Base
Tampa, Florida
June 10, 1990

I arrived at MacDill Air Force Base as a full-bird colonel, coming off a fantastic two-year run as the commanding officer of the 10th Special Forces Group, where I had earned a second Legion of Merit for my leadership. I had picked up my first as deputy commander of the Unit.

My last tango with Delta had been Urgent Fury.

The October 1983 invasion of Grenada.

I had already gotten tipped for a command position in the 82nd Airborne Division and had gone to Leavenworth to take a refresher course in our latest infantry training and tactical doctrine. One day, I got pulled out of class to take a call, and the voice at the other end said: "We miss you at the Stockade, Colonel. So much so, we want you to come back. ASAP."

Click.

I figured it must be Beirut, where a new Iranian-backed group that called itself the Islamic Jihad Organization—but was really an embryonic front for Hezbollah—had detonated a car bomb outside our embassy the previous April, killing sixty-three people, including seventeen Americans, among them several CIA officers, including the station chief. As we tooled up for Urgent Fury, Hezbollah would again strike in Beirut, ramming a pair of explosive-laden trucks into two separate barracks buildings belonging to a multinational force of peacekeepers, killing 58 French paratroopers and 241 US military personnel, most of them Marines. The attack would prompt President Reagan to pull all US forces out of Lebanon—except Delta. Beirut was definitely one of the hottest spots on earth. I had never even heard of Grenada. Until they flipped us the score—that a Cuban and Soviet-backed communist coup threatened to paint another piece of our backyard permanently red, not to mention the threat to about six hundred American medical students and other US citizens trapped on the island. Back in those days, our leadership had a bit more backbone when it came to bringing our people home. Ronald Reagan wanted to nip the situation in the bud before it turned into another Iran hostage crisis—and to contain Soviet and Cuban influence in the region.

My role in it was no big deal. The whole thing was over in three days—a weekend jaunt. I missed most of the early action, including the parachute drop at Point Salines, and flew in with the spare parts. On arrival, I hooked up with a CIA team from the Special Activities Division, the Agency's in-house spook-commando brigade, and conducted reconnaissance and surveillance to put eyes on any enemy activity. Most of the Delta and JSOC elements were already heading back to Bragg, leaving a small contingent under my command. On the first day, Delta had taken down Fort Rupert, where coup leader and self-proclaimed "General" Hudson Austin had been holed up. I flew out on a chopper to ID Austin against photographs from the dossier we had on him. To my surprise, the pilot who flew me out turned out to be none other than Colonel Billy J. Miller, one of the Cobra jockeys that had flown air cover for me on my second tour in Vietnam. (It was Billy's Cobra flying mate, Jerry Thiels, call sign Silver Spur-36, who'd taken out a machine-gun emplacement with rockets that sent a fragment ricocheting into my nose and got me my third Purple Heart.) Small world, even smaller war. Before Urgent Fury was all said and done, I'd bump into a couple of other old war buddies who'd stayed in the service. Grenada turned out to be a regular ol' homecoming.

Two months later, I signed out of Delta after five tough but glorious years and reported to my new assignment at the 2nd Battalion, 325th Infantry Regiment, 82nd Airborne—the cream of the paratrooper crop, and another homecoming for me. The 325th was where I had begun my military career over twenty-five years earlier. I had started as a private; now I was returning as a lieutenant colonel and battalion commander, with my old Vietnam buddy, Lonzo Peoples, as my command sergeant major. It was great to be back, jumping out of airplanes, leading maneuvers and live-fire exercises, teaching young soldiers who might one day go to war the lessons of the Central Highlands and Mekong Delta the same way the World War II and Korean War guys had taught me the lessons of Normandy and Bastogne and Wonju. The times were definitely changing, more women rising through the ranks, fighting their way to the front lines. Fine with me. As long as you could do the push-ups, crawl through the mud, fire your weapon (in the right direction), carry someone almost twice your body weight, you were OK in my book—it didn't matter if your Class A's might involve an optional skirt. I was proud and honored to come to know and mentor an outstanding and talented young captain at the time, Ann Dunwoody, who would go on to become not only the first woman ever in the 82nd Airborne to command a battalion herself, but also the first female four-star general in the history of the US armed forces—quite an amazing accomplishment, though no surprise. She bore many of the hallmarks of all the other great four-stars I had ever come across; many of them, like her, in the making: smart, tough, determined, selfless, with a natural talent for strategy and logistics.

Still, a lot of grumbling from the old guard about females among us. A decade later, in the aftermath of the Gulf War, I would receive an invitation, along with General Wayne Downing, a fellow Vietnam veteran and counterterrorism legend who at that time was in charge of Army special ops, to brief members of the Senate Armed Services Committee on the success of Desert Storm. When General Carl Stiner, commander in chief of SOCOM (Special Operations Command), heard about it, he decided to invite himself as well. On the flight up to DC, Stiner was going over the list of questions that the committee's staff had sent us in advance, when he bumped on one that asked whether women should be permitted to fly with Task Force 160, the Night Stalkers. Stiner instructed both me and Downing in no uncertain terms to answer "No," and when the committee chair, Senator Sam Nunn, asked us the very same question, that's exactly what Stiner said: "No, Senator, they should not." He went on to argue that women simply do not possess the experience necessary to fly special ops missions. Nunn replied: "That's because you won't give them the experience, General." (Kind of a catch-22.) Downing was next, and went right off script, saying that he had no problem with women becoming Night Stalkers. As a colonel, I was grateful to have him running interference for me, so that when Senator Nunn finally turned the issue my way, my response was: "As long as they maintain the same standard for everyone, let 'em fly." Stiner's frown indicated his deep displeasure, to put it mildly—but oh well. It wasn't the first time.

After I left the 82nd, the bottom half of the decade had turned out to be pretty vanilla—no big wars, no secret missions to far-off places that I would never be able to confirm or deny. Despite kicking off on the heels of the Iran hostage crisis, a new and frightening dawn of state-sponsored terrorism, and brutal Soviet aggression in Afghanistan (and many other parts of the world, though less obviously so), the relative peace and unprecedented prosperity of the Reagan era had ushered in a renewed sense of optimism and national purpose that bled through our military in the tumultuous wake of Watergate, the Misery Index, nuclear missile charts on the nightly news, and of course Vietnam. President Reagan had demanded that Mr. Gorbachev tear down the Berlin Wall, but it was the people of Eastern Europe who did that for him, weaving a freedom-loving fabric of Velvet Revolution that wrapped itself around the Warsaw Pact like a funeral shroud.

But still, new threats were emerging from the old along a darkening horizon.

I arrived at MacDill eager to take up my new position as commanding officer of SOCCENT—Special Operations Command Central, responsible for some of the world's biggest, baddest hot spots. Mainly the Middle East, North Africa, and Afghanistan. My new boss, the commanding general of Central Command

(CENTCOM), was a combat veteran who, like me, had earned three Silver Stars in Vietnam. I had no idea that before the end of the summer, General Norman Schwarzkopf would become a household name—a national hero on par with Marshall, Eisenhower, Bradley, MacArthur. Right now, his fame only extended as far as the troops under his command—who affectionately referred to him as "the Bear," a play on both his hefty, defensive lineman's frame and short temper, both of which belied a brilliant strategic mind. His rise to prominence would come as he led a military campaign that—even more than many wars before it—would set in motion in its wake waves of history that would long outlast its short duration and put in place the pieces on the global chessboard of the twenty-first century.

Right out of the starting gate, as we sat down in his office for our first meeting, the Bear wanted me to draw up my end of a major military exercise—code-named "Internal Look."

I knew the scenario.

"Soviets invade the Middle East, sir?"

Schwarzkopf shook his head. "Forget the Sovs. They just had their Vietnam in Afghanistan. They're not going to invade anyone." The general envisioned a more real-world scenario. "Iraq invades Kuwait," he said. "Let's game that out."

Something that might actually happen.

That *did* happen.

Internal Look lasted the month and change, ending on July 29, 1990. Four days later, on August 2—as Judith unpacked the last few boxes in our new family home in Tampa, marking her twenty-seventh and final move as a military wife—Iraqi dictator Saddam Hussein sent his tanks into Kuwait and declared it the nineteenth Province of Iraq.

The Gulf War had begun.

19

SNOWFLAKES
IN THE DESERT

King Fahd International Airport
Damman, Saudi Arabia
December 23, 1990

I hated interviews.

All these years in special operations had made me camera shy. We were supposed to be "quiet professionals," which meant avoiding the limelight. They didn't call us "shadow warriors" for nothing. Not to mention I had work to do. We were only a month away from the opening kickoff to all-out war, but the media didn't know that yet. Like Vietnam, this war was getting heavy airplay across the big-three networks—ABC, NBC, and CBS. Except this time, the American people could get their packaged fix well before the six o'clock evening news; tune in 24/7 to cable upstart CNN, catch Bernie Shaw and Peter Arnett reporting "Live from Baghdad."

Unlike Vietnam, the overwhelming majority of Americans and our allies supported our mission to liberate Kuwait—and by any means necessary. The White House wanted to keep it that way. That meant the Pentagon playing along with the press—or rather giving them just enough access to make the whole thing seem like an open book when really it was the brass writing the script. No more losing Middle America to Walter Cronkite. (Hell, he was retired now, anyway.) Control the message, control the war. As commanding officer of SOCCENT, it was not only my job to prosecute that war, but sometimes deliver the message right along with it, which explained this little sit-down with NBC reporter Linda Vester for a piece she was doing on Desert Shield: the massive buildup of

US and allied coalition forces to defend the Kingdom of Saudi Arabia from any further Iraqi aggression and "eject Saddam's forces" from Kuwait.

I had been in-country with my troops for almost four months; holed up at King Fahd International Airport, our base of operations, which I had taken over upon our arrival in the kingdom. It turned out to be a stroke of luck. On landing in Riyadh, USAF Lieutenant General Chuck Horner, Commander of Coalition Air Forces, had informed me that the Saudi capital was getting too crowded with American troops, and I should find a home elsewhere. Horner had been the acting commander in chief while General Schwarzkopf finished getting everything tooled up out of Tampa. This was mid-August, right at the beginning of this thing, but space in the kingdom was already at a premium. I was getting a fast education in grand-scheme command logistics. Horner suggested I take my people to Dhahran. "Why not King Khalid?" I asked, referring to King Khalid Military City (KKMC), located in the Hafra Basin fifty miles south of the Iraqi border. General Horner stared at me deadpan and asked if I knew what lay between KKMC and Iraq. I replied: "Yes, sir, nothing—that's why I want to go there." He flashed his fighter pilot's grin at me. General Horner had flown F-105s over Vietnam. "No, go to Dhahran," he said, "and find a proper billet to bed down your forces." I gave him a "Yes, sir," with a crisp salute, and he sent me on my way, but not before adding: "I don't care if you get killed, but I don't want to lose your command."

The next morning, I flew out with an advance party to Dhahran and found King Fahd Airport just up the road in Damman. Dhahran, Damman—what difference did it make to me? Fahd was still under construction, but its runways were all ready to go, and there were more than enough buildings and hangars up to service our needs. The best part was that no one had claimed it yet, and the Saudi general in charge was more than happy to accommodate me. I sent a message back to Riyadh that we had found a home and that all units under my command should prepare to move out pronto. Then I headed back to Dhahran to catch my return flight to Riyadh, a C-12 puddle jumper that I had already put on standby. But when we arrived at the airfield, it was a ghost town, no one around—until finally, about an hour later, we bumped into a lieutenant colonel who informed us that none of the Army flight crews were available to fly because they had all been drinking.

I came unglued.

Thirty years as an NCO, commanding officer, and especially a Black Hat instructor at the Army Airborne school had taught me the fine art of chewing people out. One time, at 10th Group, I was leading an exercise with our forward-deployed battalion in Bad Tölz, Germany, and upon hearing a couple of guys who should have damn well known better discussing sensitive information near an open window, where a civilian worker who turned out to be Polish (this was still the Cold War, after all) was hanging around without the proper credentials, I flew into a fury and kicked the door to their office off its hinges. A few weeks later, I was visiting another unit when I noticed that the doors to all of their offices were missing. When I asked why, the major in charge smiled and said: "We heard about what happened at Bad Tölz, sir, so we thought it might be a good idea to remove them—just in case."

On the matter at hand, it wasn't operational security I was concerned about, but "General Order No. 1" from the commander in chief of Central Command, which banned the consumption of alcohol by all US personnel stationed in the Kingdom of Saudi Arabia. The pilots in question had violated a direct order from General Schwarzkopf himself, one derived out of respect to our hosts. This wasn't Vietnam, where we could have our slicks running Operation Cold One, flying beer into our LZs for a little Miller Time at the end of a hard day's combat. Saudi Arabia was a dry country where drinking alcohol was against the law. Maybe it stuck in my craw all the more, if only because, just a few hours earlier, as we drove to Fahd, I had stopped off to watch as the brave young soldiers of my old outfit, the "White Falcons" of the 2nd Battalion, 325th Infantry, 82nd Airborne—among the first American combat units to hit Saudi soil—dug out their fighting positions under a blazing Arabian sun. At the time, had Saddam decided to invade the kingdom, which many thought he might, those few lightly armed soldiers would have been the only thing standing between all of us, including those drunk pilots, and an onslaught of Soviet-made T-72 tanks—our first and last line of defense. The lieutenant colonel from the flight detachment said they could fly me back to Riyadh in the morning, but I had a meeting scheduled with General Horner for that evening. I told him to keep his airplane and his drunk pilots; I'd drive back to Riyadh instead. "Sir, it's very unsafe to drive this time of night," he said. I shouted back, "If you're so damn concerned about my safety, you should have kept your pilots sober. I know how to take care of myself. You worry about your sad-sack flight detachment." This wouldn't be my last run-in with the same Army aviation boneheads. The final straw came when I missed a briefing with General Schwarzkopf in Dhahran after they once again left me stranded. After that, the general ordered an Air Force Learjet to be put on standby for my personal use—a privilege normally reserved for three-star generals, which didn't exactly endear me to a lot of the guys who wore that many stars on their collar-tabs and cover. Schwarzkopf didn't care. Neither did I. As I told the general: "I'm not running for office."

Fahd turned out to be a prime piece of war-fighting real estate, strategically located and with plenty of room to accommodate my command and then some. The "then some" being the 101st Air Assault Division and two operational wings of A-10 Warthogs, tank-busters whose six-barrel 30-mm rotary nose-cannons could turn a T-72 into Swiss cheese off a single rip. Not to mention hundreds of helicopters and other airplanes—Black Hawks, Apaches, MC-130s—along with several staff headquarters, including those for the 3rd and 5th Special Forces Groups. Everyone wanted in on the place, their slice of frontline paradise. Within seventy-two hours of my arrival, an unfinished airport that no one had ever even heard of had suddenly become one of the busiest in the kingdom, with a big ol' Iraqi bull's-eye painted right over it, considering we were within twelve hours striking distance of those T-72s. They even had to send me an Air Force colonel to act as the base commander and take over the full-time job of running the place so I could focus on preparing for war; though the Army still considered me the honcho whose ass would be on the line if anything went sideways. Some of the troops had started calling it "King Jesse Airport"—and the next thing I knew, a few of them were even receiving mail at that address:

Sergeant First Class John or Jane Doe
c/o King Jesse Airport
1st Battalion, 101st Aviation Regiment
APO NY, NY

The buildup was massive. A US-led coalition of thirty-nine countries was going to war. The biggest military alliance since World War II. The day I moved in, I had 50 people with me. By the time Desert Shield became Desert Storm, Fahd would be home to over 35,000 military personnel, 11,000 of them in my fold alone—not just fighting on the front lines, but deep behind them, too.

By winter, my forces had become the tip of a long Coalition spear, already running recon missions, embedding with the Arab members of the alliance. Like our advisory program in Vietnam. My idea. "Don't laugh," Schwarzkopf told the conference room back in Tampa when his fellow generals laughed off the suggestion. "I was an advisor in Vietnam." The general would later refer to the Special Forces as "the glue that held the Coalition together" and "the eyes that were out there." On the ground. In Kuwait. In Iraq. Watching. Waiting. Feeding back intel. My people, my pipeline. Ready to strike.

Schwarzkopf told me: "I will personally approve all your missions. But you will not cross into Iraq or Kuwait unless I authorize it."

I said, "Sir, you have my word that none of my people will cross into Iraq or Kuwait without your authorization."

Schwarzkopf shook his head: "I'm not talking about your people. I'm talking about *you* personally. You will not cross into Iraq or Kuwait without my express authorization."

I smiled. "Sir, who me . . . ? Do that?"

"Yes, you. I read your file. I know your background. I know what you did with Delta. Iran, Red Brigades. . . . I need a commander, not an operator. Those days are over."

I nodded once. "Yes, sir."

With the general's blessing, I set up two operational areas running ten klicks deep along the Saudi frontier all the way east past the border town of Khafji. The first, I code-named "Shannon"—after my youngest daughter. The second was "Cochise"—my Delta call sign. No one operated in either sector without my say-so. The day after my meeting with General Schwarzkopf, I took a chopper up to the Iraqi border. I would go several times in the lead-up to the war, but this was the first. I wanted to see for myself what we were up against. I had orders not to cross out of Saudi territory, but nothing wrong with me putting my own eyes on the enemy—conducting reconnaissance. I could see them over there, Saddam's troops, digging into their half-assed positions. These weren't the elite Republican Guard or special operations forces that he'd used to take Kuwait. These were conscripts, cannon fodder: sloppy, ragtag, armed with twenty-year-old AKs, looking malnourished enough to star in their own late-night charity ad. We had good intel that they had no food. Back in Baghdad, Saddam was living the high life on beluga caviar and champagne on ice, while his troops went hungry. They were starving, living off scraps, so I found a nice spot on the berm in full view of the two sorry souls watching me from their rickety guard shack with a pair of old Soviet-made field glasses; and under the 110-degree heat, I rolled out my picnic blanket and dug into a lavish spread of cold chicken, potato salad, and flatbread that I had packed for myself before coming up. Washed it all down with an ice-cold Coca-Cola. Psyops. I thought it'd be a good morale boost for them to see how well American soldiers ate. The truth was I felt sorry for the poor bastards. I really did. If only because I knew what kind of ass-whooping they were gonna get if their boss refused to pull out of Kuwait and we went to war. Then when I finished, I packed everything up, folded the blanket, marched right up to the edge of no-man's-land, unzipped my fly, and took a nice long leak all over the Iraqi side of the line—but never crossed it.

By giving me more pull than most generals, the Bear was making good on a promise—that a colonel with that kind of juice was going to rattle those higher up the food chain who thought they should be leading the charge. (The Learjet was just the tip of the desert iceberg.) I had always been a quick study, and it didn't take long for me to realize that holding that level of command—especially as the only component commander who was a full-bird in a room full of two-, three-, and four-stars—was as much about negotiating political minefields as crawling through real ones. General Schwarzkopf had my back. This was the guy who had earned his third Silver Star pulling one of his own men out of a minefield back in Vietnam.

Case in point: General Carl Stiner. Good ol' "Country Carl," as we called him, hadn't gotten his fill commanding the XVIII Airborne Corps during Operation Just Cause, the invasion of Panama. He knew this was a much bigger deal, our first—though certainly not last—war in the Middle East. Now, as the four-star commander in chief of Special Operations Command, he was desperate to get in on the action, so much so that he flew a good two, three times into Saudi Arabia and had me give him frontline tours of our special ops deployments, just so he could lobby the Bear, one four-star to another. Which was exactly what General Schwarzkopf neither wanted nor needed—another four-star, someone who had the juice to buck his authority, going off the reservation to run his own show trying to take down a whole bunch of cowboy scores on the special ops side of things. Among his many hare-brained schemes was the idea that a team of Delta operators should infiltrate Iraq only to let themselves get captured so they could report back from the other side. *Report back?* From where, an Iraqi prison? How? Sneak out at night between torture sessions? At every one of Stiner's suggestions, all of them designed to see me benched and to make him the star quarterback of special operations, General Schwarzkopf would respond: "If I want that done, I'll have Jesse do it." Already, before a single shot had been fired, I was dodging bullets. A whole different kind of *friendly fire.*

In their 2002 book, *Shadow Warriors: Inside the Special Forces*, Stiner and author Tom Clancy, though complimentary of my overall background and service, would write dismissively of my ability to command SOCCENT in a time of war—just because I was a colonel who, as Clancy put it, would fail to command the necessary respect from the upper brass. (Never mind that within days of my arrival in the kingdom, the Army chief of staff himself, General Carl

Vuono, had sent word to me that he, like Schwarzkopf, also had my back no matter what, whatever I needed.) Of Schwarzkopf, Stiner and Clancy would say that the general neither trusted nor understood special operations forces, which was straight-up bullshit that would later go on to saturate—and bastard-ize—many accounts of the war. Maybe that was the only way Stiner's ego would let him explain away why he was the one who ended up sidelined—in favor of a lowly colonel. General Schwarzkopf understood special ops as much as any of the other units under his command, conventional or otherwise—and gave me all the support I needed to get the job done and achieve our mission objectives. And plenty of respect. He would go on to heap praise on our contribution as vital—both privately in top-secret memos back to the Pentagon during the buildup, and publicly after the war. He would also make a point of decorating me in front of all his other component commanders, all generals, with the Defense Distinguished Service Medal, normally reserved for people with three or four stars on their shoulders, after lobbying to get it approved personally by Secretary of Defense Dick Cheney via the Chairman of the Joint Chiefs himself, General Colin Powell.

But Country Carl, God bless him, was relentless. With Schwarzkopf giving him the four-star cold shoulder, he took his case to Powell at the Pentagon. I heard about it through my old friend, General John Abrams, who worked in Vuono's office. John was the son of General Creighton Abrams, who'd replaced Westmoreland to command our forces in Vietnam. I had been honored to meet his father by chance at a hotel bar in Saigon back in '68, where he was having drinks with the commander in chief of Pacific Command, who also shook my hand: Admiral John McCain, Jr., father of future Senator John McCain III, who at the time was a POW at the Hanoi Hilton. Anyway, John Abrams told me how Stiner had bent Powell's ear to let him send a Delta squadron out to Ar Ar to hunt the mobile SCUD missiles that Saddam was firing into Israel in an attempt to draw the Israelis into the war and disrupt the Arab end of the coalition. Powell was reluctant, to say the least; but Stiner insisted until, finally, Powell got fed up with him jawing his ear off. "Fine," he said. "Send them. Now get the fuck out of my office."

The good news was that Delta's current commanding officer was my old pal, Pete Schoomaker, a future four-star general who would go on to command SOCOM—where he would famously call out the threat from al-Qaeda long before 9/11—and then come out of retirement at the request of President George W. Bush to take on the role of Army chief of staff during the Iraq War. Pete had headed up A Squadron on Operation Eagle Claw and had been at Desert One. He knew his men would be in good hands with me, an alumnus of the

Unit. I visited them several times and coordinated some of their activities with our old friends in the British SAS, who were working an area called "SCUD Alley," while Delta worked "SCUD Boulevard," calling in air strikes on suspected mobile launchers and blowing up the fiber-optic cables that the Iraqis relied on for command and control of the missiles. Whether their ops had any measurable impact on the Iraqi SCUD arsenal itself remains a matter of debate, but their presence behind the lines, the fact that they were hunting them at all, helped assuage the Israelis and not only kept *them* out of the war, but also General Stiner. (A nice twist—since it was his idea in the first place.)

Bob Hope was back in town.

The town being a war zone. Fifty years of USO tours. The one-man morale machine, as he was known. I got to have lunch with him that afternoon when he and his crew rolled into Fahd to spread some Christmas cheer to the troops. The last time I'd seen him was back in '68 when he came out with Ann-Margret and the Golddiggers to do a show at our fire base, and I arranged his security. I remembered there was an explosion and he looked at me and said: "What was that?" I replied: "Don't worry, outgoing." And with a deadpan look and his usual dry aplomb, he answered: "Well, tell me when it's incoming and I'll be the one outgoing—real fast." I couldn't help but laugh. Bob still had it, and the troops still loved him, even the ones brought up on *Saturday Night Live*.

This time, he'd brought along hall-of-fame baseball catcher Johnny Bench, who once signed my hat back when I was at the University of Tampa and I used to go see the Cincinnati Reds in spring training for free with my military ID card—a rare thing at a time when a lot of people in the country were treating Vietnam vets like garbage. Made me a Reds fan for life. Twenty years later, sitting with him at lunch in, of all places, Saudi Arabia, I told him how I'd asked him to sign my hat "to a good Cherokee," knowing that he was part Choctaw, and he'd answered, "There are no good Cherokees," with a big grin. We shared a laugh about that now—and the mutual Native American heritage behind our tribal rivalry. It was a great afternoon, nice not to think about the war, even if only for a couple of hours.

Now this PR thing, a puff piece.

Christmas in Saudi Arabia on the Eve of Conflict.

Something like that.

Interviews weren't my thing, and I was hardly a fan of the press. They had ripped Delta and Beckwith after Desert One. In Vietnam, my usual response to reporters had been either "no comment" or "get that microphone out of my face." Just another minefield. I had already done a couple of interviews, more like sparring sessions, with the tenacious Molly Moore of the *Washington Post*, who kept trying to pin me down on rumors about special ops training the Kuwaiti Resistance, something I was neither willing to confirm nor deny, certainly not while we were still preparing for the war, let alone fighting it. One wrong word, or even a misquote, could get people killed, the ones we might have working behind the lines. Ms. Moore kept referring to the trainers as "Green Berets," which would eventually become part of the modern lexicon of post-9/11 Army Special Forces, just because everyone called them that. (The same way that British MI6 would inevitably throw in the towel on pushing back against that false moniker and adopt it as a genuine one, even though they had always officially been the Secret Intelligence Service, or SIS.) But back then, we were still old school, and as I advised Ms. Moore in true Special Forces fashion: "A green beret is just a hat. You need a quote? Quote that."

Newsweek had sent retired Colonel David Hackworth to cover the war for them. One of the most highly decorated vets in US history, who'd started his illustrious combat career in Korea, "Hack," as he liked to be called, had led the "Hardcore" Battalion (Recondo) in Vietnam, 4th of the 39th. I had no beef with him, and if they were going to send anyone to cover the war, better a battle-hardened veteran than some bespectacled Deadhead fresh out of journalism school; but back in '69, while I was still in 'Nam, I had heard that he'd put in a request to Division to have me transferred into his outfit. When the reply came back that I was a short-timer with only two weeks left on my tour, his response was: "Perfect! That's just enough time for me to get him killed."

A little . . . jungle humor.

(Still made me smile.)

Even as I sat down with Linda Vester, I spotted Hack on one of the monitors in the background, doing a hit for some network. Maybe hers. Linda was good people. She knew the Middle East, had studied in Cairo, spoke fluent Arabic. The soft soap was simply because it was Christmastime, and NBC wanted to lighten things up a bit, which was fine with me—and with General Schwarzkopf, who was determined to keep a tight whip on the press, if only to prevent them from degrading morale the way they had in Vietnam. Nothing to do with politics—everything to do with protecting our soldiers. That's why the Bear had no problem embedding Joe Galloway, a man he trusted as "the finest combat correspondent of our generation—a soldier's reporter and a soldier's friend," and, according to the *New York Times*, "the most unlikely of antiwar activists," with General Barry McCaffrey, another highly decorated Vietnam vet, and the 24th Mech Infantry as they stabbed into Iraq. Not to mention that Galloway—

and reporters like him—were known competent quantities that you could trust would put an embargo on any details that might compromise our operations to the enemy. So, there was that, too. As to the others . . . well, they could direct their questions to General Schwarzkopf at any one of the regular press conferences that he convened for the distinct purpose of mollifying the Fourth Estate while controlling the information flow—and the narrative.

Access?

Of course.

Free rein?

Hell no.

The Vester interview went well. Picking up where I left off with Ms. Moore, I made sure to get it out there that Special Forces soldiers were not the "Rambos" that everyone had seen in the movies, although Chuck Norris surfing on a motorcycle in *The Delta Force* was always good for a laugh. That's not who we were. Every last one of us—Delta, Special Forces, SEALs, Combat Controllers, whatever—lived by the code of the "quiet professionals." We didn't advertise in real time. We did a very difficult and dangerous job for God and country, and we did it with little or no recognition on purpose. We also didn't go looking for fights. Yes, we were lethal beyond measure; but most of the time, our missions required us to avoid the enemy, not engage him.

"Shannon and I are watching it right now," Judith later told me over the telephone. That was another thing. In Vietnam, it had been all about letter writing; and if you were high speed or lucky enough, or had a good reason, maybe one or two phone calls via a radio handset with everyone listening in and your wife having to say "Over," every time she finished speaking (or shouting, more like it) across the scratchy line, as if calling in arty or air support. Now, I had access to a direct-dial commercial phone line and an ATT card. Most of the guys would get to call home maybe two, three times before the war was over, but pen and paper were still the main means of communication with the home front. Still a long way off from email, Skype, and Facetime, or whatever our soldiers would end up using in Afghanistan and Iraq after 9/11.

"You look good," Judith said, her voice clear through the static-edged line. "They're calling it 'Snowflakes in the Desert.'"

20

BACK TO SAIGON

Over the Saudi Desert
December 17, 1990

"I'm coming down to pick you up at King Fahd."

General Schwarzkopf wanted to see the border.

We flew up in a Black Hawk.

Two Vietnam veterans.

Riding a chopper along the front lines of a war zone.

Déjà vu—but this time in a desert. Whoever said the dry heat beat humidity?

Flying with us were the general's two Delta bodyguards, old buddies of mine, including Sergeant Major Mike Vining, another Eagle Claw guy, and the Unit's first explosive ordnance disposal (EOD) specialist, who could disarm a nuke blindfolded. Mike stuck out a bit in the background of Schwarzkopf's press clippings due to the civilian clothes and Army-issue "birth control" glasses that he always wore—along with his M4 assault rifle. I was sure there were terrorists or tyrants somewhere in the world taking note of the faces closely protecting the commander of the allied coalition. But I was also sure that they'd be sorry if they tried to test the men who owned those faces, Mike in particular.

On the ground, we toured a Saudi border post. Some Iraqis had crossed over and given themselves up to the guards there. A trickle in advance of what would be a tidal wave of defections. Schwarzkopf got an up-close look at the POWs that the Saudis had taken into custody, examined their gear, noting what was there: light ammo, tattered uniforms, crap AK knockoffs. And what wasn't: *gas masks.* Saddam had dropped chem on the Kurds. Killed five thousand innocent civilians. He had promised "the mother of all battles." The only way he could make good on that promise was to unleash the WMD that he definitely did have on tap back then. His invasion of Kuwait was the act of either a fool or an irrational madman or both. Either way, we had to assume the worst once we engaged his forces. Already tens of thousands of NBC (nuke-bio-chem) suits had arrived in-country for our soldiers to wear in the scorching desert heat in the event of chemical attack.

And something else, also by the tens of thousands: *body bags*.

Saddam was already letting his guys starve. Would he drop tabun or sarin or mustard gas upwind of them, too? Without giving them protective gear? Sure. Why not? As Secretary of State James Baker would make clear to Iraqi Foreign Minister Tariq Aziz as war became imminent, if Saddam used chem, we had the means to exact vengeance—in other words, nuke Baghdad. The Iraqis had taken the SecState's threat seriously enough that they had started running mass evacuation drills. But if it did come to that, the war would already be lost for both sides, no matter what the outcome. Yes, we had NBC suits—but fighting in a chemical pea soup? While wearing a nylon and charcoal foam-layered suit and rubber mask in 120-degree heat? As brave as our soldiers were, I held little confidence that they were ready—that *I* was ready—for that kind of mass-grave warfare, people vomiting up their intestines. Suits or no suits, those body bags were sure to fill up real fast.

"We're not getting into body counts, enemy KIA's," Schwarzkopf said through the static off his headset mic. As we flew back to Fahd.

The general was concerned only about American losses—and preventing them as much as possible. The White House was estimating thirty thousand US casualties, 170 deaths per day. That was without WMD. Iraqi casualty estimates were three times that.

"We're not keeping score," Schwarzkopf said. *"And if anyone wants to know, tough shit. That's not how we're gonna run this thing."*

Amen. Powell Doctrine. Overwhelming force. Clear exit strategy.

No numbers.

No bean counting KIA's to stack up a victory.

No clash of ideologies. No moral crusades.

No bullshit.

And no more Vietnam Syndrome.

Fifteen years since the fall of Saigon, choppers airlifting the last Americans off the roof of our embassy, the last Huey getting kicked overboard off the *Okinawa*, and the ghosts of Vietnam still haunted our nation. As President Bush would later declare: it was in this Arabian desert that we would soon bury those ghosts. We had plenty of guys still with us who had made their bones in the Ia Drang and the Suoi Ca and the Mekong Delta. A little older, a little grayer, perhaps a bit wiser for their higher rank and all the scar tissue they wore—inside and out. Guys with CIB's and Silver Stars and Purple Hearts preparing now to tune up Saddam. They had been ready, willing, and able to search and destroy from Saigon to Hanoi. And now they were champing at the bit to kick ass for Kuwait. It wasn't the politics or morality of the moment. This was about redemption, a catharsis for our entire military, including the new generation who'd never seen combat and grew up watching Walter Cronkite call out stalemates between episodes of *Gilligan's Island* and *The Brady Bunch*. Heinous Hollywood depictions of the war—from the profanely cartoonish to the pro-communist, from Chuck Norris to Oliver Stone. None of which matched my experience of it, or that of all the others that I knew who served there: General Schwarzkopf and General Moore, Charlie Beckwith and David Dolby, Ron Ray. Joe Galloway. And so many others.

There would be no stalemates in this desert.

No dragged out, decade-long conflict.

"*We are sending American soldiers into battle,*" the general told me. To kick Saddam out of Kuwait and hobble his ability to make war. "*And when those soldiers accomplish that mission, they will go home.*"

"*Yes, sir,*" I replied.

Amen to that, too.

The Black Hawk came in fast and flared on short-final, setting down softly on a heat-hazed patch of tarmac at Fahd.

Schwarzkopf grinned, enjoying the ride.

"Could have used these in Vietnam," he said. "Like a Cadillac."

Damn straight.

Black Hawks were a cut above—far more formidable than the venerable slicks that they'd replaced. Beefed up ballistic tolerance, armored seating, twin engines, run-dry transmission, better maneuverability, more than twice the payload capacity, electronics up the ying-yang. Purpose built for hot LZs. At least the guys who designed these things had learned a lesson or two from Vietnam, even if most of our politicians never had. When it was GO time, the "Screaming Eagles" of the 101st Airborne would launch 300 of them against the enemy in what would be the largest and deepest heliborne air assault in history as they stabbed 90 miles behind Iraqi lines to set up Forward Operating Base Cobra—almost within spitting distance of Baghdad.

"I'm gonna drop you here," Schwarzkopf said, now shouting as I removed my headset to hop out. "I gotta get back to Saigon."

My feet hitting the ground, I turned back to look at him. "*Saigon*, General?"

Schwarzkopf blinked and shook his head with a smile, realizing his mistake. "Whoops! I'm in the wrong country. Make that Riyadh!"

I smiled back and snapped off a quick salute.

Then Sergeant Major Vining threw me a nod, slamming the door shut, and the chopper pulled fast off the deck.

21

RESISTANCE

Kuwait City
August 31, 1990

The young lady, who had chosen the *nom de guerre* "Zahra," strode toward the intersection with a confident catwalk calm.

Her sleek, silky gait was a ruse—like the misdirection of a born magician, a deception to fool her audience, the four Iraqi soldiers manning the checkpoint, get them looking at the wrong thing. Her. Looking at her. Both to entice and frustrate them. She hoped they would react as they had reacted with a friend of hers. The one they had raped and beaten to death. She wore her hijab—really an Hermès scarf, a gift from her mother, pulling double duty—set loosely back about her head to expose much of the dyed blonde hair underneath, the bangs framed perfectly around her big black Jackie O. shades. She wanted them to think she was a rich bitch, maybe dripping in jangly gold rings and diamonds, or veiling soft skin beneath the chic beige abaya with its ornate lioness-patterned embroidery, clinging to her frame just enough to accentuate the contours of her body, another contradiction. Everything about her "modest" dress belied extravagance, if only to entice and frustrate them all the more. She knew that Saddam's occupational force, outside of the more professional—and proficiently vicious—Republican Guard, were nothing more than conscripts of backwater peasant stock. The leader of her "cell," another woman, whose husband, an officer, was still missing in the aftermath of the invasion, had told her as much.

"Hey, hey, hey, look at this one." said one of the wolves of the lamb, grinning, leering, laughing as she entered their sandbagged emplacement. Of course, they would need to search her, said another, and started pawing at her curves, the others closing around her. Perhaps they would have exercised more caution had they noticed the movement beneath her fluttering robe, as the two grenades slipped out from under each armpit, where she had hidden them, the spoons flying off with a metallic ping. "*Allahu akbar!*" All of the men realized their fate, seeing the grenades clunk to the ground and roll out from beneath her abaya, but only one was fast enough with his scream to be heard before the explosion that killed the four occupiers—and the young lady whose *nom de guerre* was "Zahra."

"*She martyred herself. . . .*"

King Khalid Military City
Saudi Arabia
September 2

Jaber's eyes filled with tears.

"She gave her life for her homeland," he said.

Jaber was General (Sheik) Jaber al-Khalid al-Jaber al-Sabah, my old pal from the General Staff College at Leavenworth, a member of the Kuwaiti royal family who now headed up KSS, the Kuwait security service, the tiny emirate's version of the CIA. That was the thing about the General Staff College: one of its greatest benefits—apart from the superb education in the art of war—was that it counted among its alumni so many foreign military officers from armies around the world, giving us the opportunity to cultivate relationships that could prove vital in a time of war. Such was the case with Jaber, who'd stayed behind in Kuwait during the Iraqi invasion, rallying his nation's tiny military force to mount a courageous defense against the fourth-largest army in the world. He recounted the heroism of the Kuwaiti 6th, 15th, and 35th Brigades, along with the pilots of the Kuwaiti Air Force, as they made their gallant stand, refusing to retreat. Jaber had been the last one to get out—and only by the skin of his teeth after the emir himself ordered him out, disguising himself as a Bedouin to slip past the Iraqi lines and cross the desert into Saudi Arabia. He was lucky. The Iraqis had put prices on the heads of all members of the royal family, and their special forces had killed Jaber's cousin, Sheik Fahd al-Sabah, outside the Seif Palace on the first night of the invasion.

I had been trying to track him down for several days when I finally got a call from the CIA's Saudi station chief, a guy we'll call "Barry," who'd served with the 5th Special Forces Group in Vietnam. Barry had tracked down Jaber at the

Sheraton Hotel in Taif. When I phoned over there, I spoke to the front-desk clerk, who had a thick British accent, and informed him that I was looking for a Kuwaiti general. "He's also a sheik, a prince," I said. "If that's any help in locating him." The desk clerk replied: "Sir, the whole bloody hotel is full of princes." It turned out that the Sheraton had become the home away from home for much of the Kuwaiti royal family. The ones that had made it out, anyway. Many of Jaber's friends and family members were still stuck inside Kuwait, their fate unknown.

"I want to set up a Shahid Brigade," Jaber told me, as he finished his story of "Zahra," the young lady who'd blown herself up at an Iraqi checkpoint and taken four soldiers with her. Shahid was the Arabic word for martyr. "She and those like her are the light for all Kuwaitis," he said, wiping the tears from his proud face as we stood inside the shabby doublewide trailer now serving as his office, not exactly fit for a prince. "We must honor them."

I flashed on a pair of soldiers vanishing in an explosion of light as one of them pulled a VC flag off a nipa palm bush somewhere far away and long ago. I realized what Jaber wanted was his own Viet Cong—an insurgent force of civilians conducting asymmetrical warfare behind the lines. Seemed like a no-brainer.

"She is the light," I told him, nodding my head. "But I can train your people to do the same thing *and* survive. And kill even more Iraqis while doing it."

The CIA would supply the weapons and equipment, flying it all in on a C-130 into King Khalid. My SF guys would provide the training on how to use them: small arms, explosives, frequency-hopping radios, the whole shebang. These were civilians we'd be working with, so basic tradecraft, surveillance, intel gathering: how to ID armor and armaments, how to spot rank insignia. Jaber was adamant that no American Special Forces should try to work with the Resistance inside Kuwait. The country was too small, and everyone knew each other. They'd never be able to blend in with the populace. We didn't even go near his own people in the Kuwaiti security service, just in case anyone was captured, so it didn't kick back to us: if it came out that they were working with the Americans, it'd mean an automatic death sentence, summary execution. Jaber already had the networks up and running in-country. He would be their cutout on the Saudi side between us and them. He would run the network. The Brits got in on the act, sending one of their spooks from Century House, then-headquarters of the Secret Intelligence Service, before they moved into that modern sandstone and green-glass monstrosity at Vauxhall Cross, and a four-man "brick" from our old friends in the SAS, who were dying to get in on the fight. They helped train up the fighters, including one "Sheik Mishal," a former Kuwaiti karate champ and nephew of the emir who wore Coke-bottle glasses that we had to replace with custom contact lenses, and had volunteered to go back in if only so the royals could claim to have one of their own on the ground.

My Deputy Director for Intelligence (Special Operations), Lieutenant Commander Mike Williams, a veteran Naval Intelligence officer and expert in counterterrorism, who would later go on after 9/11 to do an almost ten-year stint with one of the FBI's Joint Terrorism Task Forces, where he hunted some of the world's most wanted terrorists, would provide the tasking orders—"grocery lists." We called the program "Open Door." Between the Resistance and my Special Forces A-Teams behind enemy lines conducting special reconnaissance, or "SR" as we called it, my command would provide the lion's share of the intelligence vital to the success of the war. Schwarzkopf's "eyes."

Of all their capabilities—unconventional warfare, direct action, special reconnaissance, counterinsurgency—training foreign armies and insurgents was the bread and butter of US Army Special Forces, the so-called "Green Berets." As we prepared for war, I embedded operators from the 5th Special Forces Group with the regular forces of Egypt, Syria, Oman, Qatar, Saudi Arabia—and those that escaped Kuwait. Washington wanted the Arab armies to lead the liberation, so we were gonna make sure that even if they didn't speak or dress like US soldiers, they could at least fight like them. The Special Forces guys that I assigned to the task did a superb job, not only getting all those Arab armies trained up and on the same page—*our* page—but as Desert Shield became Desert Storm, leading them into battle. Schwarzkopf's "glue."

Khafji
On the Kuwaiti-Saudi Border
September 12, 1990

A ghost town. All tumbleweeds and dust devils and windows boarded up.

Even more desolate from above. Like flying over Mars.

Our Black Hawk looked enough like an alien spacecraft to round out the effect over such a primitive landscape. Riding with me in the chopper as we surveyed the border was my liaison to Saudi special ops, Captain Fahd bin Turki. *Fahd. . . .* Same name as the airport where I kept my main HQ, when it wasn't being called "King Jesse." (I wondered what the airport code for that would have been—KJA?) The Fahd connection hadn't hit me until I picked him up at KKMC and got a good look at his triple-wide trailer, all decked out in the finest Persian rugs, antiques, and luxury accouterments, not to mention the elegantly mannered Indian valet who greeted me at the door and referred to Fahd as "the Prince." Captain Prince Fahd was the nephew of the current Saudi ruler, King Fahd. His full name was Captain Prince Fahd bin Turki bin Abdulaziz al Saud. His grandfather was the first monarch of Saudi Arabia. It was the war that brought Captain Fahd and me together. I wouldn't have known him otherwise, but ours was a fast friendship that would turn lifelong over the decades to come, as he rose to become the commanding general of the Saudi special forces. (By 2021, Fahd would fall victim to the murky, byzantine and cutthroat political machinations of the royal family on charges of "high treason and an attempted coup" against the regime, after falling out of favor with Crown Prince Mohammed bin Salman, aka "MBS," the same MBS who allegedly ordered the brutal assassination of *Washington Post* journalist Jamal Khashoggi. A Saudi military court would sentence him to death, an extraordinary step considering Fahd's lineage as a grandson of the country's first king. The sentence has yet to be carried out. I only pray that my old friend will somehow secure a reprieve.)

"This is like the one on the cover of the Clancy book." He meant *Clear and Present Danger*, Tom Clancy's latest bestseller. Captain Fahd was referring to our chopper. His English, even in the static-wash of the headset mic, was impeccable. "I just read it, the book—it's very good."

Fahd and I had spent the day flying up and down the border, getting a good look at the Iraqi forces waiting to greet our men in Kuwait. An ill-equipped, ill-disciplined rabble. We'd set down to tour one of the border posts, where the commander made a show of radioing the Iraqi unit on the other side, advising them that they didn't stand a chance and should therefore defect. Then he served us tea and, with the elaborate courtesy of a true Saudi, insisted that we remain for lunch, a lavish spread of chicken and rice and homemade flatbread that he had obviously arranged in preparation for hosting the grandson of his country's first king.

I wondered about that: how Fahd reconciled being both a prince and a soldier, considering that his military rank was far beneath the royal one that explained the extravagance of his basecamp billet. It seemed that in Saudi Arabia, princes lived like princes first. But I didn't know him well enough to ask. Jaber seemed less inclined to the trappings of his royal bloodline—especially in a time of war, while his fellow countrymen suffered under a brutal occupation. When I asked him about it, his response was: "If you want to be a sheik, be a sheik. But if you want to be a soldier, be a soldier. The two don't mix."

⊷◆⊶

Alarm klaxons buzzed.

The sound reminded me of the "controlled crash" back in Happy Valley, the day I earned my first Bronze Star. And many other near misses. An Iraqi missile battery on the Kuwaiti side of the line had painted our bird. The pilots took evasive action, banking hard in fast tight circles, dropping flares and chaff. I didn't flinch. Just rode it out, glancing out the window, looking for a missile trail, the serpent-tongued desert sun glinting off my black Ray-Ban aviators and my reflection in the small square of polycarbonate glass.

The klaxon died. No missile.

"Goddamn Iraqis," said the prince over his headset mic.

I laughed. "You're a Muslim and a member of the royal family," I told him. "That's no way to talk."

Fahd smiled. "Ah yes, but it's OK because I am a graduate of both the US Army Ranger and Special Forces schools."

I gave him a thumbs-up. "Fair enough."

We landed at KKMC, where I bade Captain Fahd farewell, then flew on to the airport named for his uncle. The next morning, the prince sent word: Those Iraqis at Khafji—the ones that the Saudi border commander had radioed to break ranks? They had defected that same evening.

22

TASK FORCE
NORMANDY

TF Normandy
Near the Saudi-Iraqi Border
January 17, 1991
12:33 a.m.

"Five minutes out."

The squadron of eight US Army Apache attack helicopters flew in tight single-file formation as they approached the Iraqi border in the dusty dead dark of night. They would be the first coalition aircraft to strike the enemy, kicking off the most intensive bombing campaign in the history of modern warfare. Ahead of them were four Air Force Pave Low special ops choppers. The Pave Lows were the pathfinders. They carried the latest terrain-following radar and GPS avionics, allowing them to hug the deck at speed while guiding the Apaches. No navigation lights. No comms. Just night vision. The twelve choppers would fly nap-of-the-earth for the entire two-hour journey, gliding at fifty feet above the desert floor to avoid detection by the very targets they were on their way to destroy: a pair of Soviet-made early-warning air defense radar sites located deep inside Iraqi territory. A joint task force, they had been rehearsing for months, running low-level stealth infiltration along the border, night flying by thermal imaging, tandem-target acquisition and elimination, live-fire exercises. This was the opening kickoff that would set our whole tempo in motion. Ensure our air supremacy as we degraded and wiped out the enemy's key forces in preparation for our ground game. This was the most daring and decisive covert mission of the war.

Coalition HQ
Riyadh, Saudi Arabia
September 13, 1990

"Well, can you do it?"

That was the question that US Air Force Brigadier General Buster Glosson posed to me in the labyrinthine suite of war rooms buried five stories below ground in the subbasement of the Saudi Ministry of Defense off the Old Airport Road in Riyadh. Glosson was Horner's chief planner for the air campaign that would obliterate Saddam's war machine—on paper, the best aerial attack plan General Schwarzkopf said he'd ever seen. We had just finished poring over top-secret satellite photos that showed the Iraqi radar sites in question, each covering the main flight path for Glosson's jets to hit Baghdad. If the jets got "painted" before they reached their targets, they would lose the element of surprise—or worse, get shot down. One of the primary missions of my forces was to conduct CSAR—combat search-and-rescue—in the event that American or coalition pilots crashed behind enemy lines. As prepared as we were, it was a job that I hoped never to undertake. The ripple effect of losing that element of surprise would not only put those pilots at risk but also likely throw off our entire game plan, and could easily drag out the conflict, leading to greater casualties. We had no intention of repeating Vietnam in the desert. (Maybe later, in Iraq 2 and Afghanistan—but not under this command, not on this watch.)

"Can you knock out those sites?" asked Glosson.

Without hesitation, I answered: "Yes, sir, we can."

The real question was *how?* I had all sorts of assets at my disposal, plenty of special ops people, and more on the way. Earlier that afternoon, I had briefed the Chairman of the Joint Chiefs himself, General Colin Powell, in the main conference room, after he'd tacked on the trip to Riyadh after attending a NATO meeting in Madrid. General Powell had a very easy way about him, down to earth and straight to the point. No nonsense, and not one to traffic in two-dollar words to win a ten-cent argument, because he had no need to impress anyone. Those four stars on his shoulder were shiny enough on their own.

General Schwarzkopf had been unable to attend the meeting. I offered to pre-brief him, but he told me to just go ahead without him. It was nice to know my boss trusted me enough not to make an ass of myself in front of his boss, the man who stood directing traffic at the intersection between the White House and the Pentagon. I would have the honor of briefing General Powell twice more before the end of the war, even making it into a group photo taken in that same conference room, which ended up in his own memoir with Joseph Persico, *My American Journey*.

Up to that point, I had been having trouble with some of the folks back in the Pentagon securing the personnel necessary to accomplish the special ops mission, which was fourfold: special reconnaissance, training the Arab armies (along with the Kuwaiti Resistance), combat search-and-rescue, and direct action. I wanted more of the guys who wore those nifty green beanies in-country. At my last request, the one Pentagon pencil pusher bottlenecking me the most had cabled back: YOU ALREADY HAVE MORE SPECIAL FORCES OVER THERE THAN IN VIETNAM.

My response was: GOOD, I WANT TO WIN THIS TIME.

A Vietnam veteran himself, General Powell agreed. Problem solved. No more pencil pushers from the Pentagon blocking my requests for personnel or resources.

So, when it came to Buster Glosson's radar sites, I had plenty of options on the table: commandos on the ground with explosives or missiles, cruise missile attack, low-level jetfighter air strike. It was General Schwarzkopf who solved it: "Get yourself some Apaches," he said, right off the cuff, as he sat back in the big leather executive chair behind his desk.

Attack choppers.

Good idea.

I took a ride in one belonging to the Screaming Eagles' 1st Battalion, 101st Aviation Regiment, under the command of Lieutenant Colonel Richard "Dick" Cody, who would go on to lead the operation. The Apache was a waspish beast: armed with Hellfire missiles and rockets and a 30-mm chain gun slaved to a helmet-mounted display that allowed either pilot or gunner to point it wherever they turned their head and looked—like Roy Scheider in *Blue Thunder*, but even more high tech than Hollywood could imagine. See a tank, pull the trigger, instant Swiss cheese. A squadron of eight would definitely pack the firepower to get the job done. Cody chose his best people to join him in manning the Apaches. The Pave Lows and their crews came from the Air Force's 20th Special Operations Squadron, one of the best combat search-and-rescue outfits on the planet.

The only sticking point was the distance—well out of fuel range for a round-trip on a full weapons loadout. It looked like we might have to insert special-operations guys behind the lines to set up a refueling point somewhere on the way to the target, like we did on Eagle Claw, but we had learned our lesson the hard way. The last thing anyone wanted was for Desert Storm to turn into another Desert One. Cody and his team came up with an alternative solution: wing tanks with extra fuel, something that had never been tried before. It put the aircraft well over their usual combat weight, heavy enough that each chopper went with only half its usual rocket loadout, taking nineteen instead of thirty-eight, but gave them the range necessary to make the roughly 450-mile round-trip nonstop. The mission was so secret, it carried no code name of its own; but Cody dubbed the joint Army-Air Force heliborne strike team "Task Force Normandy"—in honor of the D-Day landings. Sounded good to me.

⎯⎯◆⎯⎯

King Fahd Airport
January 17
2:36 a.m.
H-Hour minus 24

I was at my forward headquarters with my team, watching a console of satellite feeds showing a live-action mug-book of news anchors back home on the evening broadcasts. One of the monitors showed CNN, and then cut to Bernie Shaw reporting live from Baghdad.

"Turn it up," I told one of my crew.

Just in time to hear Shaw tell the people back home in Atlanta: "I'll be departing Baghdad tomorrow. . . ."

I laughed. "Oh, no you won't, Bernie!"

Because the Apaches and their Pave Low escorts had already entered Iraqi airspace and were three minutes from their targets. At five miles out, still beyond the range of the radar sites' air defenses, the Apaches broke formation and spread out in a hover, surveying the targets on their FLIR screens. The Pave Lows had already peeled off to drop back behind them, switching from pathfinder to search-and-rescue mode in case one or more of the attack choppers went down. Timing was everything. Coalition fast-air strike fighters were already taking to the skies on their way to bomb Baghdad. The Iraqi radar sites had direct lines to four air bases and a major operations center. If the Apaches failed to destroy the two targets simultaneously, the Iraqis would get the jump on activating their ground air defenses and send up their MiG-29s to intercept our jets.

At 2:38 a.m., Saudi time, one of the lead pilots broke radio silence to give the go order: "*Party in ten.*"

Ten seconds later, the Apaches of Task Force Normandy launched the opening salvo of the war in the form of twenty-seven Hellfire missiles. The flight time for the missiles was twelve seconds. As soon as they struck home, the choppers moved to within three miles of the exploding targets to unleash one hundred of their flechette rockets and take out the air-defense guns still out front. Closer in, they opened up with their 30-mm chain guns, firing off over four thousand rounds that proved even better than Mr. Clean for doing a mop-up. The total time on target was four minutes. When it was over, all that remained of the radar sites were massive swathes of black sand, scorched earth, and charred metal.

Cody radioed my HQ at Fahd to confirm that the Iraqi early-warning sites were out of business, opening up a twenty-mile-wide swathe of sky for coalition aircraft to use for their bombing run. As the choppers headed back to base, the pilots could see the first wave of over nine hundred fast-air jets flying just one thousand feet above them on their way to Baghdad.

From King Fahd, I called General Schwarzkopf, poring over maps in the war rooms at the Saudi Ministry of Defense. "How'd it go?" asked the Bear. "All targets destroyed, sir. All choppers coming home." Schwarzkopf's response was crisp: "Outstanding. Let me know when they're all back." I did so a few minutes later, after the choppers had all landed safely at Al Jouf. "OK, tell the guys good job," Schwarzkopf said, and hung up.

I turned to the monitors. Special reports were breaking all across the networks—and Bernie Shaw was hiding under his desk as the whole of Baghdad went *boom*.

Desert Storm had begun.

23

THE MOTHER
OF ALL BATTLES

Our strategy to go after this army is very, very simple. First,
we're going to cut it off, and then we're going to kill it.

— General Colin Powell

Khafji
January 29, 1991

The ground war began at Khafji.

It was the first major battle of the conflict.

And one of the bloodiest. Twenty-five Americans dead.

The most in combat since Vietnam.

Iraqi losses totaled approximately seven hundred captured or killed. It was the only time Iraqi forces would cross into Saudi Arabia or preemptively attack US troops. My special operators were on the ground, directing air power that pulverized Saddam's infantry and armor and kicked their asses back across the border.

I was supposed to be visiting Khafji with General Jaber that same day; but he'd canceled at the last minute. Just two days earlier, I'd been watching the Giants beat the Bills by a single point in Super Bowl XXV from Tampa, delighted to see my youngest daughter, Shannon, among the fifty military children participating in a special halftime tribute to the troops in the Gulf. Watching home from a war zone. Live. It was a bizarre feeling. I couldn't tell whether it helped or hurt—made me more homesick.

The air war continued for another three weeks. Intensive bombardment. Iraq had an army of 900,000 men spread across 63 divisions, 8 of them belonging to the elite Republican Guard, with a 300,000-strong occupational force inside Kuwait, and another 130,000 or so troops in southeastern Iraq. They had Soviet T-72 tanks, Sukhoi Su-24 and MiG-29 fighter jets, and of course SCUD missiles. They had Chinese Silkworms, French Exocets, and South African 155-mm artillery pieces. All in large numbers. AKs and RPGs up the ying-yang. We were talking about the fourth-largest standing army in the world behind China, the Soviet Union, and Vietnam. Back then, we ranked seventh, size-wise anyway. In military affairs, size isn't everything; but certain ratios do matter. As General Schwarzkopf would point out in his famous "Mother of All Press Conferences" at the tail end of the war: the Iraqis outnumbered us in artillery, tanks, and fighting troops. We needed to flip that into a roughly five-to-one fighting manpower advantage for our side before we ever went on the offense into Kuwait and engaged their frontline defenses—land mines, barbed wire, fire trenches. That's why the pounding from the sky.

Most of the frontline guys, the raggedy-ass conscripts that Saddam was letting go hungry, were worthless cannon fodder. They were already defecting and would surrender in droves—those who weren't already dead from our relentless bombing raids. Behind them was a tougher line of troops, battle hardened from eight years fighting in the marshes of the Aw Fao Peninsula in their almost decade-long war with Iran. These we needed to not just soften up, but to rock into submission. At the rear, in reserve (really so that they could retreat more easily) were the Republican Guard divisions, who were better paid, better trained, and better fed and had the best equipment and were more highly motivated. It was imperative that we spank them the hardest so that they couldn't come back to do it all over again.

By the cessation of hostilities, allied planes would fly over 100,000 sorties from land bases in Saudi Arabia and aircraft carriers in the Persian Gulf and Red Sea, dropping over 88,000 tons of ordnance in just six weeks, while losing only 75 aircraft. We wiped out Saddam's air defenses; pulverized his key command-and-control bunkers and communication facilities; destroyed his SCUD missile launchers and weapons research facilities; pounded his armor and artillery; and hit all bridges and supply lines to cut off his army inside Kuwait so that when we moved in, we could kill it.

The press called it "the Nintendo War," because of all the high-tech razzle-dazzle and laser-guided munitions. I called it the "SOF War"—like *soft* without the *t*—as in: Special Operations Forces, because at this point, my people were the only ones with boots on the ground actively engaging the enemy: lazing targets for the fast-air to take out, conducting search-and-rescue, unleashing the Resistance; giving the Iraqis all kinds of hell.

The operational tempo was fierce. By the time the ground campaign kicked off, I had forty-three missions in play, and had taken command of the entire Kuwaiti Navy—which consisted of two beat-up missile boats and another that looked like a tug but had a couple of depth charges or something like that. I had Navy SEALs executing Operation Imminent Thunder, conducting raids along the Kuwaiti coasts as part of a massive deception ploy that played into Iraqi fears of a large-scale amphibious assault and made them think the second D-Day was about to come their way. We leaned into it so hard with our offshore presence that if need be, we could have launched a real-deal landing and taken Kuwait City; but otherwise, it was all just misdirection to keep the bulk of their forces coastal, leaving their right flank in western Kuwait completely exposed to the brunt of our attack. I had a Special Forces A-Team draw up plans to drop behind enemy lines and derail a military train carrying SCUD missiles in a mission plan reminiscent of a World War II thriller, though Schwarzkopf understandably ended up pulling the plug when intelligence showed that there might be civilians on board. Task Force Normandy wasn't my only contribution to the air war. I dropped thirteen Daisy Cutters—BLU-82s, bunker busters, fuel-air bombs—on enemy positions. Three alone on an Iraqi division on Failaka Island. We dropped them off the back of C-130s and gave them names like "Huey," "Dewey," and "Louie," or "Jake" and "Elwood" (the Blues Brothers), marking them with messages to Saddam, until that got old. All of them hit their targets with earth-shattering effect. A British SAS team conducting special reconnaissance behind the lines saw one go off a few miles from their position and jumped on their radio back to their own operational commander, Colonel Andrew Massey, at their forward operating base in Al Jouf: *"Sir, the blokes have just nuked Kuwait!"*

KKMC
February 24

The main ground campaign, code-named Operation Desert Saber, kicked off with a massive tank offensive across the Saudi border into Kuwait and Iraq. It was indeed "the mother of all battles"—though not quite what Saddam had in mind when he predicted it as such—one of the most brilliant military campaigns in human history. Its near-flawless and rapid execution belying the grave danger and incredible fighting spirit of the allied forces. The press would call it "the

100 Hours War," because that was all it took for the American-led coalition to roll right over the "impenetrable tank barrier" of barbed wire and minefields and fire pits that the Iraqi dictator guaranteed "no one would ever get through" and expel his forces from Kuwait, busting them right in the chops.

The biggest and most audacious of Schwarzkopf's moves came from what he called his "Hail Mary" play: not because it was born of desperation, but because of the way it sent the main hammer of our attack forces—mostly American, British, and French—all the way out to the western fringes of the Iraqi border like a trio of wide receivers getting ready to sprint to the end zone. With them went thousands of tons of supplies—sixty days worth of food, water, munitions—in preparation for a "worst-case" bogged-down slugfest that never happened. All of this movement occurred in the dead of night under the strictest operational security, and only after our bombardment campaign had blinded Saddam, knocking out his reconnaissance and surveillance capabilities, so that he had no idea what we were doing. Once in place, and once the air war had succeeded in softening his frontline forces into jelly and knocking out their escape routes, the ground forces began their attack.

At 0400 Saudi time, February 24, the 1st and 2nd Marine Divisions, accompanied by the US Army "Tiger Brigade" of the 2nd Armored Division, stabbed into southern Kuwait and began engaging Iraqi frontline defenses in conjunction with two Saudi task forces along their eastern flank. Their mission was twofold: to charge into Kuwait in pursuit of the tiny emirate's liberation, and to keep the Iraqi forces fixed along the eastern coast as our western hammer went into action, also at 0400, as the French 6th Light Armored Division, reinforced by my old outfit, the 325th Infantry, 82nd Airborne, thrust into Iraq itself along the westernmost edge of the battle space to seize Al Salman air base. The French would then set up a vital screen to protect our western flank as the Screaming Eagles of the 101st Airborne launched their historic three hundred-chopper air assault; set up a forward operating base deep inside Iraq; and from there went to town with their Apaches on any and all Iraqi forces in the Tigris and Euphrates River valleys, less than 150 miles from Baghdad. I had Special Forces operators working even deeper behind the lines, running road-watches and calling in air strikes on anything moving that shouldn't have been moving. Back east, we sent in the Egyptian and other Arab forces on the Marines' left flank to continue the deception that the offensive into Kuwait was the main event, "a headlong assault," as the Bear put it, when really it was just a teaser, but one that kept Saddam's forces bogged down and stuck in an extraordinarily vulnerable position without them realizing it. It was then that the midwestern thrust played out, with the VII Corps and various British and American armored and infantry divisions launching into Iraq, and General Barry McCaffrey's 24th Mech Infantry throwing its famous "Left Hook" into the enemy's rear that smashed Saddam right in the jaw as the hammer slammed down to crush his forces.

I worked with Captain Fahd and General Jaber to coordinate the activities of the Saudi and Kuwaiti forces spearheading the drive alongside US troops. As Desert Saber unfolded, the operators from the 5th Special Forces Group that I'd months ago embedded as "advisors" with the pan-Arab portion of the campaign—many of them NCOs who'd been operating under the rank of "Captain" to command the necessary respect with the foreign forces under their "command"—went to work coordinating their battlefield movements with the allied coalition while calling down air strikes to help obliterate any threat that came their way as they breached Saddam's "invincible" barrier. With victory beginning to brighten what had remained since last August a very dark horizon, my thoughts drifted back to a stifling hot day six months ago in the middle of the Saudi desert, the hot gusts howling over the sculpted dunes that besieged us with desolation, as General Jaber addressed what remained of his officer corps.

I would never forget his words, and the stir of the wind over the sand, and the glistening tears on the faces of his brave fellow countrymen before him: "The first blood to be spilt liberating our homeland must be Kuwaiti. And the first Kuwaiti blood to be shed must be that of you officers."

24

LIBERATION DAY

Kuwait City
February 26, 1991

The Black Hawk landed us at Kuwait International Airport.

The US Marines had just secured it after heavy fighting, as the pan-Arab corps, led by the Kuwaitis and with my Special Forces advisors accompanying them, were the first to kick the door into Kuwait City as they liberated the capital. With me was the young Sheik Fahd al-Ahmad al-Sabah, whose father, also Fahd, had died defending the Seif Palace during the Iraqi invasion. The younger Fahd had escaped on the last aircraft out of Kuwait, but he'd promised to be on the first one back in—which turned out to be my Black Hawk. It was the middle of the day, but a shroud of darkness had spread through the sky from the almost seven hundred oil fires that Saddam had lit off as the occupation collapsed. The sheik greeted old friends who were trapped inside the city running the Resistance. It was an emotional, tear-filled reunion.

But there was still work to be done.

The Iraqis were in full retreat, coalition aircraft mercilessly pounding them into oblivion along the notorious "Highway of Death." It wasn't enough to simply drive Saddam out of Kuwait; we had to destroy his war machine so that he could never come back.

It was only the night before that I had reviewed my end of the game plan, securing Kuwait City, with General Schwarzkopf. He was counting on my operators—mainly the embedded advisors from 5th Group—to make sure there was no retaliation from the Kuwaitis against any Iraqi prisoners for atrocities committed during the occupation. No war crimes from our side.

Secretary of Defense, and future Vice President, Dick Cheney had made as much clear to me when I briefed him on the special ops side of things during his visit with General Powell a couple of weeks back. It was a tall order. I had over three thousand Kuwaiti Resistance fighters under my charge, many of whom had lost neighbors, friends, family to brutal and horrific war crimes under the occupation. Saddam had made his bones as a cheap, two-bit bandit, a street thug, and common criminal. He proved it by kidnapping over three thousand of their countrymen and taking them back to Basra and Baghdad and who knows where to use as bargaining chips. Many would never return. I thought of the girl who called herself "Zahra" and all the brave young Kuwaiti men and women like her who'd sacrificed their lives to draw a line in the sand against tyranny. It only made sense that their brothers and sisters would want some payback.

I tapped General Jaber to help keep things cool. Jaber was in the process of taking over as the military governor and had already declared martial law to maintain order as the Iraqis beat it out of town, and we kept the pressure on to make sure they were gone for good. As his official American advisor, I told him that the world was watching. Any goodwill or sympathy the Kuwaitis had banked since the invasion would go straight out the window the minute anyone caught wind of any atrocities—beatings, torture, revenge killings, anything like that. I asked him to speak to his soldiers and make sure they took no retaliatory action against any Iraqi prisoners. Jaber agreed. He understood more than anyone what was at stake—for both Kuwait and the coalition.

General Schwarzkopf was confident my people would keep everyone and everything on point; during our meeting, he'd complimented them for the superb job that they had done so far as both advisors and operators: "They're good men, and they've got a good, aggressive commander," he said. "Now, about the embassies. . . ."

French, British, and American.

I had put together a plan to retake them using special ops teams from each nation—French commandos; British Special Boat Service (SBS), their version of the Navy SEALs; a strike team from the 3rd Special Forces Group under the command of Lieutenant Colonel "Blank" Frank Toney, a hard-charger who sometimes got a little ahead of himself and had to be kept in line. The Bear wanted us to strike in tandem—"simultaneous reoccupation," he called it. "No mad dashes. No one-upmanship."

"Yes, sir."

That wasn't all.

General Schwarzkopf said, "I know you probably want to get in on the action, but when your guys retake our embassy tomorrow, I am counting on you to be a commander, not a point man."

I laughed. "Not to worry, sir. I have three Purple Hearts already, and I don't need another one."

On the tarmac at Kuwait Airport, I got word that some of the Air Force chopper pilots assigned to transport my strike team were reluctant to fly due to poor viz from the oil smoke. It was like Desert One all over again: the devil wind that shook up a couple of the Marine pilots that night—killed the whole mission. I should have used the Night Stalkers, but they were working other assignments, and these guys knew better anyway. I had my RTO get their commanding officer on the horn. "You better get your asses in the air," I shouted down the line. Done.

Somehow we managed to hit all three embassies at the same time. I didn't kick the door down myself; Blank Frank had already done that with a breaching charge which was probably a little over the top, but oh well. I came in with the rest of the team as we cleared the embassy. True to my word, I hadn't been the point man. I could hear the explosions going off blocks away down embassy row. Of the three diplomatic residences, the British one had the most elegant front door, and the SBS had just finished blowing it off its hinges when an Indian valet appeared with the key. Months later, I would meet with the British ambassador who was still looking to track down the person responsible—someone had told him it was me. "No, Mr. Ambassador, I am afraid your own boys did that."

I had already clashed with our own ambassador, Edward "Skip" Gnehm, in the midst of the liberation. Gnehm wasn't in-country yet when I set up shop, established my HQ, inside the embassy, sleeping on the floor instead of in the "Emir's Suite" at the luxury hotel next door. The ambassador and I had already crossed paths way back in August when we flew together to Taif to meet the Kuwaiti royals holing up at the Sheraton, including Minister of the Interior Sheik Salem al-Sabah; Minister of Defense Sheik Nawaf al-Sabah, and Crown Prince (and later emir) Sheik Saad al-Sabah. Gnehm had seemed all right then, a career diplomat already with a pretty distinguished career—hell, we had even enjoyed a nice dinner together in Taif—but military commanders and diplomats don't always mix well. The State Department could be gun shy around gunslingers. They felt our diplomatic skills were lacking. Never mind that diplomacy was exactly what my people and I had been conducting—and doing a damn good job at it—as special ops advisors to everyone from the Arab grunts on the ground, to the political leadership in their palaces and hotel suites. (After the war, I would accompany General Schwarzkopf to Cairo to meet with then-President Hosni Mubarak to thank him for Egypt's support during the war—even though the Egyptian forces had proven slower than silly putty rolling uphill getting their butts in gear on Desert Saber. As I sat in the Presidential Palace sharing tea with one of the most powerful men in the Arab world and listening to him rank on King Hussein of Jordan for supporting Saddam instead of the coalition, I couldn't help but drift back to Major Earl Witcher, the two of us sitting on that log or whatever it was we used as a bench at LZ Cat, somewhere on the Cambodian border—*a long way from Pocahontas.* . . . Amen.)

In all fairness to Ambassador Gnehm, he had an enormous weight on his shoulders, and one could forgive him being a bit *tense* (to say the least), with SecState Baker and the president of the United States watching his every move. The pressure cooker of politics.

But I had a job to do. Things came to a boil when he requested a C-130 with an escort of helicopter gunships to fly him back into Kuwait City, out of Saudi. I knew that was a no-go, and when I informed General Schwarzkopf of the request, he blew up and unleashed an impressively poetic string of profanity that made me wonder if he'd been a drill instructor in a past life. I had avoided being the subject of the Bear's wrath on all but one occasion when he threw his glasses against the wall over a minor misunderstanding. (Another time, he'd picked me up and thrown me out of the war rooms back in Riyadh, but that was for fun.) In the end, the ambassador had to make do with a single Black Hawk that flew him to the embassy grounds, where I saw to his security. Someone took a photo of me escorting him off the chopper that later made it into *Time* or *Newsweek*, or one of those magazines. Both of us raised the American flag over the building, and then I turned the embassy back over to him. It was a good moment, soon to be overshadowed by the meeting we later had in the ambassador's office, during which he made clear that none of the Kuwaiti Resistance fighters were to be decorated for their actions during the occupation or war. When I asked why, Gnehm explained that certain folks at Foggy Bottom were concerned it might embolden them to overthrow the Sabahs as well. That sounded like a bunch of Ivy League debating-society bullshit to me. The Sabahs were the ones who controlled the Resistance, and it wasn't as if these were fundamentalist jihadis like that "Arab-Afghan" billionaire's kid who'd gotten all colicky when the Saudis refused his offer of veteran Arab mujahideen foreign fighters to take on Saddam and instead invited US forces to defend the land of Mecca and Medina. Osama bin Laden was nowhere near a household name yet—but he would be soon enough.

This wasn't that.

I decorated the Kuwaitis anyway.

Then Gnehm kicked my men out of the embassy, arguing that it was illegal for them to run military ops there, but then invited me to stay.

"Thank you, Mr. Ambassador," I told him, "but I will stay with my men."

As I settled into my new digs, I got an unexpected call from "Barry," the CIA station chief in Riyadh. "Be careful using the STU-III," he said, referring to the NSA-designed telephone system that the US government relied on for secure communications. "Stick to military comms."

"What gives?"

"We got word a hostile player was tapping into you while you were at the embassy."

"Iraqis?"

"No," Barry said. "KGB."

"What?"

I was stunned. The Soviets?

"Yeah, they got transcripts. That's all I can tell you. Take it easy."

The line clicked off.

Wow. Crazy. KGB.

Then I wondered how the hell the CIA knew they had transcripts. Unless they were working their own wiretap. Or had a mole telling them so. . . .

One could only hope.

The brutality of the seven-month occupation revealed itself to be worse than anyone had imagined—beyond even the detailed intel reports we'd been receiving throughout Desert Shield and Desert Storm. I escorted General Schwarzkopf on a tour of the gruesome makeshift torture chambers at the main soccer stadium where, like so many vile despotic regimes, the Iraqis had inflicted unspeakable horrors on thousands of innocent Kuwaitis. There were hacksaws, hammers, power tools, a sharpened spoon that someone said had been used to pluck out eyeballs. Schwarkopf was livid in his disgust. If anything, the barbarity of it all only served to reaffirm his belief in the righteousness of our campaign to kick Saddam's ass out of Kuwait and pound his forces to make sure this never happened again. I took several photos to document the abuses, but I needn't have done so: the images from that day would stay imprinted on my mind and visit my nightmares for the rest of my life. A chilling reminder of the difference between those who prosecute war to oppress, and those who fight to liberate.

Less than a week later, General Schwarzkopf met with his vanquished Iraqi counterparts to sign an unconditional cease-fire. Eleven days after that, March 14, Sheik Jaber al-Ahmad al-Jaber al-Sabah, the thirteenth emir of Kuwait, would return to his homeland and resume his throne. I was the first to greet him on the ground at Kuwait International Airport, shake his hand, and welcome him back to his country. Who said gunslingers can't be diplomats?

New York City
June 10, 1991

The crowd was five million.

That was how many people had turned out to celebrate our victory and drop over ten thousand tons of ticker tape on the soldiers, sailors, airmen, and Marines who'd secured it. This was the ultimate weapon, the one we eventually lost in the morass of Vietnam: the support of the American people. I was marching near the front of the parade with my special ops team. Judith and the girls were there, cheering us on. You would have thought we just came back from World War II. The roar of the crowd down Manhattan's famed "Canyon of Heroes" was deafening. We'd just marched in the National Victory Parade in DC a couple of days earlier, with stealth bombers flying overhead, but no one did a party like New York.

Along the parade route stood several Vietnam veterans, wearing their old uniforms. As we prepared to march, my Deputy J-2, Mike Williams, who'd done a superb job working with the CIA to glean intel off the Kuwaiti Resistance, had approached one of them.

"You guys never got a parade, did you?"

"No," the veteran replied.

"Well, this one's for you."

EPILOGUE

Route Irish

Baghdad, Iraq
2005

After the Gulf War parade, I thought a lot about that victory—vindication, redemption, rebirth.

The country was alive again. For a while.

I thought of the loss, too, standing once again before the Vietnam Veterans Memorial.

I thought of Don Schroeder and Chris Cowen and John Stirpe. And all the names that would be engraved on other walls a long time coming but never too late. The few who perished in a desert storm. I thought of 5th Special Forces Group battalion commander Lieutenant Colonel Jerry Thompson, an old friend and a great soldier, who was in a Black Hawk running a mission when one of our own F-16s mistook it for an Iraqi chopper and shot it down, killing all on board. I thought of a dying NVA captain, fixing me with his far-off gaze as his hand sought harbor in my own.

I remembered that the price of war was always paid in the currency of blood. And loss.

I thought of Daily O, with his glass-shined jump-boots and easy movie-star grin.

"Contact left! Range one hundred! Suppressive fire!"

I emerged from the vehicle and took cover behind its Kevlar-lined door, raising my M4 assault rifle to pop off several bursts. IEDs had just exploded ahead of the convoy, taking out one of our vehicles. People were hurt. Maybe dead. Contractors. Like me. All ex-Delta. My people. My company. This was Route Irish. The most dangerous road in Iraq.

Forty years ago, I was a gung-ho NCO hearing my first crack of rifle fire.

Now here: different time, different place, different enemy. Different fingers on the trigger. But the same AKs, the same bullets cracking past my ear.

The same warfare.

Over a decade as "retired" military after thirty-five years in.

What the hell am I still doing this shit for?

I fired my weapon, charging ahead of my men.

Into the fight.

INDEX

Note: The photo insert images are indexed as p1, p2 etc.